Talk
Dirty
To
Me

ALSO BY SALLIE TISDALE

Stepping Westward
Lot's Wife
Harvest Moon
The Sorcerer's Apprentice

DOUBLEDAY

New York
London
Toronto
Sydney
Auckland

TALK DIRTY TO ME

AN INTIMATE PHILOSOPHY OF SEX

SALLIE TISDALE

PUBLISHED   BY   DOUBLEDAY
A DIVISION OF BANTAM DOUBLEDAY DELL PUBLISHING GROUP, INC.
1540 BROADWAY, NEW YORK, NEW YORK 10036

DOUBLEDAY AND THE PORTRAYAL OF AN ANCHOR WITH A DOLPHIN
ARE TRADEMARKS OF DOUBLEDAY, A DIVISION OF
BANTAM DOUBLEDAY DELL PUBLISHING GROUP, INC.

BOOK DESIGN BY JENNIFER ANN DADDIO

LIBRARY OF CONGRESS CATALOGING-IN-PUBLICATION DATA

TISDALE, SALLIE.
    TALK DIRTY TO ME : AN INTIMATE PHILOSOPHY OF SEX / SALLIE TISDALE.
    — 1ST ED.
        P.   CM.
    1. SEX CUSTOMS—UNITED STATES.   2. SEXUAL ETHICS—UNITED STATES.
3. PORNOGRAPHY—SOCIAL ASPECTS—UNITED STATES.   4. SEXUALITY IN
POPULAR CULTURE—UNITED STATES.   I. TITLE.
HQ18.U5T57   1994
306.7'0973—DC20   94-10304
                                                               CIP

ISBN 0-385-46854-7
OCTOBER 1994
FIRST EDITION
1   3   5   7   9   10   8   6   4   2

To the nasty girls who are leading the way:
Susie Sexpert, Carol Queen, Mistress Marlayna,
Laura the Girl Sloth, Lily Braindrop,
Lisa LaBia, and the rest

ACKNOWLEDGMENTS

I cannot name all the people who spoke with me, sent me stories and articles, and made confessions to me in the course of writing this book. Most of them are glad I can't, I'm sure. You know who you are; I appreciate everything you shared.

Steve Tyler, Karen Karbo, Megan McMorran, Barry Johnson, Larry Cusack, and Larry Downard read this manuscript in draft form and gave support when it was most needed; they were good friends to have during a long winter. I want to thank Jeanne and Don for long conversations, lots of help, and many interesting nights; and Brian, for great letters and comradeship.

I also owe thanks to the unflappable staff of the British Library, and to Linda Gibson, Niki Adams, Veronica Vera, Priscilla Alexander, Leanne Katz, Ann Harroun, and Tim Waterman. Thanks for enthusiastic support to David Gernert and Amy Williams. Kim Witherspoon is my agent extraordinaire; I'm glad she's on my side. And Bob, so many thanks.

This book was spanked into shape by Channa Taub, *editor dominatrix*.

I was influenced to my own surprise, and in surprising ways, by the written work of Norman O. Brown and William Irwin Thompson. I have also relied over the years on a large body of work created by several feminist scholars, including Carole Vance, Ellen Willis, Ann Snitow, Lisa Duggan, Paula Webster, and Kate Ellis. Both as a writer and a neurotic, I appreciate the depth of humor and clarity of thought in new writing by Leslie Feinberg, Trish Thomas, Cris Gutierrez, Sunah Cherwin, Lani Kaahumanu, and many others. I feel grateful in several ways to the staff of Good Vibrations, a resource beyond measure.

I am especially grateful to *Harper's* for publishing an early essay by the same name in which I explored many of these ideas, for giving me room in which to find this voice, and for continuing to be the most reliably intelligent magazine in the country.

Lastly, I give thanks to Kyogen Carlson for his steady, guiding light.

—April, 1994

"and we rose up like wheat,
acre after acre of gold
and we harvested,
we harvested."

—Anne Sexton

I

Desire

1

We talk about sex all the time, we moderns. We *see* sex all the time—raw, explicit images everywhere we look. There is "sex" in the media and "sex" in our culture; we argue over "sex education" and discuss our "sexual disorders." But "sex" always seemed less concrete than this to me, more disobedient. Sex troubled me—troubled me in proportion to how much I tried over the years to separate sex from the rest of my life, to manage and define it, to speak of sex as something that began, ended, lived separately from *me*. Sex demanded my close attention even when I would have preferred to attend to almost anything else.

Devilish reminders crop up all the time. The planet itself is laden with sex, marbled with my physical and psychic responses to its parts, made out of my relationship with its skin. How we are rooted to the earth through our bodies determines how we see other bodies, and ultimately the earth itself. This seems obvious, and yet we don't call this sex. To do so makes sex awfully big, but big is exactly what sex is. Freud was never more right than when he called the human animal "polymorphously perverse." To the unschooled body there are no good or bad sexual objects, no right or wrong responses. (Even the schooled body gets confused.) Sexual acts are one of the primary means by which we can act out our inarticulated inner lives.

The Latin root for pudenda, our genitals, means "to be ashamed." We are twisted between this and the body's blessed pleasures, living among a proliferation of sexual images even as we live in shame. The sex that is presented to us in everyday culture feels strange to me; its images are fragments, lifeless, removed from normal experience. Real sex, the sex in our cells and in the space between our neurons, leaks out and gets into things and stains our vision and colors our lives. This is what we can't see. This is what we never say.

The question is transparent: Why are we so unhappy about our own sexual acts and the acts of others?

There is a school of thought—two schools, in fact—

that holds sex to be simply dangerous. The cosmic school, which includes a fair amount of our religious instruction, sees sex as a natural force that must be allowed to exist only within certain absolute bounds. A related philosophy holds that sex as we know it is politically and socially unpalatable. This is most publicly presented by the conservative feminist dictum that in a sexist culture, sex hurts women and no woman lives a sexually free life until the culture itself is uprooted. These beliefs have seeds of truth in them, as does the idea—less a belief than a feeling—that sex is too intimate for public discourse. A different standard is applied to sex this way, a standard that removes it from any context but its most immediate one.

Each of us finds sexual censure in our individual lives, of one kind or another. As for myself, I've been struck (shamed) by highhandedness—the faintly damning gentility of the auteurs. Sex in this view lacks *aesthetic;* it's seen as a rather low pursuit—fun, but not exactly Ivy League. Sex invokes a kind of hindbrain howling in most people now and then, and because of this—in spite of this, perhaps—the auteur says humans should rise above their baser natures. People must seek the refined and the complex and intellectual in the world, should create, beautify, compose. Presumably art would be considered a more complex, symbolic, and layered act. But good sex is a symphony of experiences infinitely complicated with meaning, rich and unpredictable, as capable of disturbing and illuminating the individual as any formal work of art, as memorable, as fleeting. The real point being made is that sex is low because it's universal. After all, any chimp can fling paint.

Virtually all serious conversation about sex is sooner or later dismissed as trivial—as being too *small*. In the grand scheme of things sex is nothing beside the more publicly applauded accomplishments. Sex is the ultimate ephemera, a phantom. But our culturewide aversion makes sex more, not less, real. Refusing to look at an illusion gives an illusion body and strength, gives it power. If you want to make a mirage go away, walk toward it. If you turn and run, the lake gets bigger and the palm trees more inviting every time you look back. Sex is, truly, *not important*—that is, something we can cease worrying about—only to the extent that we look at sex and see it for what it really is, and nothing more.

Sex is as important, in much the same way and to about the same degree, as what we eat and how we sleep. Sex is important because it is central to being human, because it intersects everything else, because it is the physical realm's metaphor for the chaos and texture of our spiritual and psychological lives. Sex is a kind of intuitive art in itself, an art made largely by the human body on levels our frontal cortex can only partly imagine. Sex, in the end, doesn't matter as much as how we treat each other—how much respect and care we accord each other, ourselves, our place, and whatever we call God. What fascinates me most about sex is how many ways we—and I—have used the fear of sex to justify disrespect, castigation, condemnation, and destruction of all these things, including God.

Sex changes the way we see ourselves, breaking and remaking the boundaries of the body and of relationships. It's a door that swings only one way, preventing return. Sex turns us literally inside out, molds and subverts fundamental assumptions. Sex has a unique ability in the human realm to both brutalize and comfort the individual. Turning away from sex means turning away from ourselves, turning away others; fear of sex *means* fear of others. Without crossing through the country of sex, there's a lot of other territory we can't begin to traverse.

But then again. The first time I had sex—with forethought and contraception and careful planning—all I could say was, "Is that all?" My poor partner, years older than me but still naive about anatomy, could only nod. Was that really what all the fuss was about? I wondered. Was *that* what my parents did, what happened in the movies when the lights went out, was that momentary shiver the Sturm und Drang of eons? I felt a little . . . disappointed.

I grew up, in the late sixties and early seventies, into the kind of young feminist who believed in the agenda of equality without having read much of the theory. I learned the lingo, talked the talk, walked the walk a little bit. But my secret sexual fantasies seemed to wiggle free of my politics no matter what, seemed to expand and sometimes explode into my manifestly unfeminist consciousness. Part of the feminist agenda, I believed, was raising my own and other people's consciousnesses to the point where images of heterosexual oppression and traditional roles simply disappeared. Therefore, my sexual fantasies would be reeducated along with my relationships and language. But even reading feminist theory didn't help that. Parts of my consciousness refused to rise, staying far below the sanitized plain of social politics.

I didn't even know the words for some of what happened in my sexual fantasies, but I was sure of one thing. Liberated women, women who had thrown off the yoke of heterosexism, didn't even *think* about what I wanted to do. I wasn't ashamed of being preoccupied with sex— everyone I knew was preoccupied with sex, one way or the other. And though I was plenty confused by the messy etiquette of the early 1970s, and spent time wondering just how much shifting of partners I should do, that was more a source of embarrassed bumbling than conscious shame. The Amazon and Earth Mother images of 1970s-era feminism did me a world of good, in fact. I felt it was okay to have sex, to be sexual—as long I was sexual in a wholesome, Earth Mother kind of way. I felt a little work-ethic guilt at times, since I'd absorbed the solid lower-middle-class belief that whatever was fun didn't count as work, and sex, for all its drama, was sometimes quite a lot of fun. But I was also ashamed, simply ashamed of my own unasked-for appetites and shockingly incorrect fantasies, which would not be still, and which seemed to violate the hygienic dogma of sexual equality and Amazon health.

Sex is so often examined within marriage and relationship, one could almost imagine that's the only place sex exists. I want to deliberately examine sex outside the structure of long-term relationships because the psychic experience of sex doesn't stop at the edge of the relationship even if the physical acts of sex do. In other words, even if I am monogamous for life, my sexuality is promiscuous—roving and polyfidelitous and amoral. If we pretend our sexual feelings always occur (or only rightly can occur) inside the bounds of a commitment, we are lying to ourselves. Even within these bounds, sex takes many forms. In a way, it's unfortunate that we use this one three-letter word to refer to the incredible range of erotic behavior of which people are capable. Just for myself, I would say the best sex I've had and the worst sex I've had don't belong in the same box at all, can't be discussed with the same vocabulary, described in the same language. It's not quite fair to talk about sex in any general way at all.

Love can coexist with, and join, everything I'm talking about. I've learned more about sex through the tunnels of love than otherwise, by far. Sexual passion greatly complicates but also greatly expands the already labyrinthine complications of love itself. With sexual love can come moments of overpowering fulfillment, an almost devastating, a frightening, satiety. But even in a long-term romance there is a world of difference between the desire for the *lover's* body and the desire for the lover's *body,* and for now, this last is what concerns me.

Most sex research is touched by a slight whiff of erotophobia, written dryly and pedantically, tainted by what Kenneth Tynan once called the "whiff of evasiveness." When literary critics do deign to discuss sex, they pinch their prose up into tight knots, lest anyone think they were aroused by their subject. Unlike, say, particle physics or eighteenth-century landscape styles, the erotic as a study causes its students to repress and contain their enthusiasm. They must be careful not to wax *too* pleased. A surprising amount of intellectual material on sex discusses the subject as though it were a form of garbage, interesting in an anthropological way for all it says about the culture that makes it, but unpalatable nonetheless.

Over the years I've read a lot of the research and I've read theory and I've read plenty of mannerly and overblown literary prose on the subject, but what I really longed for all along was material that addressed the real experience of sex. My own study has never been an intellectual exercise even when I wanted it to be, even when I knew exactly why so many scholars write as though they have never had a sexual thought. Sex has always been, and remains, intensely emotional and socially powerful for me. Studying it was part of my reconciliation with a large and demanding aspect of my life. The most important part of that reconciliation is understanding just how individualistic sex is. I see how much pain people can feel around the subject of sex, how injured and afraid of sex a lot of people are—how injured I am in certain ways. I can see why people sometimes want so much to avoid the topic, why other people seem unable to avoid it. Either way, sex counts.

This book, even when it's about other people's fantasies and other people's myths, is largely about me. It has to be. These are my concerns, my interests, my own little fetishes, as it were. This behavior that is so much a part of our community and personal relations is very much a behavior of the single, lone self. All I've read of sex in history, in anthropology, in religion, in other people's lives, I've read more for my own reassurance, to assuage my own guilt and clear up my confusion than for anything else. And I've been reassured.

In February 1992 I published an essay in *Harper's* about my interest in pornography. It was the first time I'd written transparently about sex and its complicated, layered meanings. Pornography is a hall of mirrors, a central symbol of the societywide confusion over sex. By its existence, porn defines us as sexual animals; its only function is to arouse our primal sexual response. The urge (which I certainly felt) to discuss pornography in solely cerebral or political terms seemed, in the end, to be useless as well as silly. Pornography is designed to bypass the brain as much as possible. I was interested in the discomfort pornography brings up, both for others and for myself; no matter what else I could say about it, I had to admit that I found a lot of pornography exciting. It got me, down deep, and I could think of no better unifying metaphor for the impact of sex on my life. Sex has eternal charm for the body—a perpetual, organic hold. Porn is sex off the leash.

I received a lot of letters in response to that essay—a few dozen canceled subscriptions, a lot of thoughtful letters from women and men who had struggled to understand their own interest in pornography, a few huzzahs, a few mash notes, a few bare confessions. One woman wrote to say I should not be allowed to have children, failing to explain where her own children had come from. It's difficult for any of us to talk honestly and seriously about sex, and it may be especially hard for men to *listen* to anyone, male or female, talk about sex. One man wrote offering to cut his penis off and mail it to me. A radio interviewer in Canada asked me to describe what I was wearing, and then, please, to "talk dirty" to him.

Several letter writers who identified themselves as conservative feminists relied more on epithet than analysis; their insults were graphic and vile. I was struck by their rage, their venom, which was so much greater than the reservations I had expressed in the essay about the conservative feminist position on pornography. Their rage, in fact, was considerably greater and more personally expressed than that of the subscription-cancelers. That group was interesting largely because they equated my frank discussion of pornography with pornography itself. (Censorship, legal and otherwise, makes it impossible not only to talk about the censored object, but about censorship.) There was clearly something much deeper than a political disagreement going on.

Sometimes I'm shocked at what shocks, the cultural relativism at work. The sculptures of Pompeii shocked the Europe of the 1700s, Kinsey shocked Americans in the 1940s, and Shakespeare shocks us now. Our oldest stories validate desire. I sometimes wish that those who rail about morality and normality would read a little anthropology and a bit of Homer. Myths and folklore are full of blunt, amused, and salacious stories, full of castration and masturbation and incest, necrophilia and zoophilia, the mysterious power of the vagina and the clitoris. Many cultures have practiced freer and more open sex lives than our own.

Reading history makes it clear that the gradually increasing tolerance toward most sexual behaviors has come from the repeated inability of every culture to control them. Masturbation, adultery, homosexuality, and prostitution are not common—they are universal. One senses entire eras shrugging resignedly in the face of these sexual "crimes," committed not just by one's leaders, royalty, and priests, but by one's neighbors and oneself.

Babies are sexual, celibate people are sexual, all of us are sexual—and most of us do it right out there in front of God and at least one other person. I'm amazed how often conversations about sex mince around that particu-

lar fact. Everyone does it, and everyone knows that everyone does it, I know you do it and you know I do it.
American society is adolescent; there is no other word
for our restlessness and preachy finger-shaking. We live
in a world filled with a continual proliferation of sexual
images outside context. Still we find it almost unbearable
to talk openly about sex—with our friends, our lovers,
our parents and children, least of all to each other as
makers of our culture. The result is cultural puberty:
lewd, leering, intensely curious and ashamed and prudish all at once. Americans have lost their minds over sex;
sex is like a stick in the American eye—people can't see
past it.

I was flipping around the television channels late one
night, and for the first time saw a condom being demonstrated on this most proletarian of media. I had happened across a Spanish-language program. A handsome,
middle-aged woman sat comfortably in front of a large
audience of attentive young women. She was talking in a
rapid, maternal, lecturer's voice of which I could catch
only a few words here and there. All the while she
spoke, glancing quickly up and down at the audience,
making small jokes, she was very slowly rolling a lubricated, shiny condom down over a long, wide, green cucumber. She held the reservoir tip out, explaining its
purpose, slid the condom down a little way, talking all
the while, until it suddenly slipped into place. She made
another little joke, cool, relaxed, and I felt intensely jealous. I couldn't follow the speedy Spanish well enough to

get the jokes, but my jealousy was deeper than that. I envied her matter-of-fact ease. I am bombarded by insinuation and entendre, by seductive skin and promises. I am bombarded by recrimination for my sexuality, reprimanded, as are we all, all our lives. We seduce and reprimand each other. We can't make up our minds.

To pretend one has no sex life (no sexual desires, or no difficulty in controlling them) is strange. Moreover, the pretense leads quite directly to neurosis, just as our universal cultural denial of death has led to neurotic and excessive efforts to conquer death. To deny that part of the human condition is sexual desire is like denying we were each born; the denial has about it the sense of something bizarre and incongruous, because it goes directly against almost everyone's daily experience. Sexual denial is dysfunctional in the deepest, most psychological sense of the word. Who is crazy, me or you? Because there is no fit between my quotidian and lifelong erotic feelings and your repeated declarations that those feelings and ideas do not exist (or are *wrong,* wrong in nature, twisted). Only slightly less disturbing than your declaration that my feelings are wrong is your declaration that you have no similar experience, that what seems constant and obvious to me is strange to *you.* Even in 1994 there is almost no place and time where this is easy to discuss. The 1990s, in fact, may be one of the hardest times in history to talk lucidly about sex at all.

I have, perhaps, three absolutes about sexual expression. The first, the most obvious and infinitely arguable one, is that we should avoid harming each other whenever possible. Second is my belief in the importance of self-determination—the right of every mature individual to make decisions for herself, for himself. Last is my unquenchable belief (in spite of sometimes quaking neuroses and plenty of evidence to the contrary) in the final goodness of humans—of human life, the human journey, and the human body.

I recently spent time with a friend who had weathered a particularly painful divorce, and his new girlfriend, the first lover he'd had in the two years since his separation. I watched the cheer and animation that flooded his face, his body, his conversation, replacing the lethargy and depression he'd been under for so long. I saw her small, satisfied smiles. They were enjoying a lot of good sex, and by good sex I mean the kind that comes when your mind is moving in the same direction and with the same hope as your body. We often forget the amazing recuperative powers and life-affirming magic of sexual pleasure. Sex can help us to like ourselves and find a generosity of spirit, open ourselves to the world and simply be *alive*. We forget that sacred, respectful sex may not look like heterosexual monogamy, and we forget that human beings are sexual every moment of their lives.

I've always been entranced by the communal homes of certain Native American tribes, by the traditions of the Inuit, the Lakota, the Tillamooks. I imagine many people bedding down together, their odors mingling, their bodies entwined in sleep; I imagine a life where two people I know might make love beside me as I drift into sleep, hearing vaguely the distant, whispered sounds of pleasure and excitement politely muted, a tiny laugh, a moan of satisfaction. I imagine the accidental, fond caress of a hand stroking my back while I dream. Who would I be, there? Who might I become? But such scenes seem very far away. Here I am, in the patriarchal, materialistic, sex-drenched, sex-phobic West—and who have I become, here?

Sexual behavior and appetite is additive; it expands, enlarges, until everything is sexual. When I talk about sex, though I may not be able to escape erotic and arousing and embarrassing images, I'm talking about nothing more than the sensation of being alive—the myriad scattered and quotidian aspects of life. It's far too much for any one of us to comprehend. I suspect the inability to enter and know another's desires is the source of much bewilderment and rage around sexual issues. I have a number of friends and acquaintances these days with what might be called uncommon or alternative sexual lifestyles. But I probably always have had friends like these. That's one of the things about sex; you can't tell just by looking. I struggle to come to terms with my own desires, and then I look around and see the wildly varying desires of others, desires I may not understand, desires that might frighten me, disgust or confuse or, shockingly, arouse me without warning. And those other desires, those that are not mine, sometimes seem wrong to me just because they *aren't* mine.

By letting go of judgments I hold against myself and my desires, I let go of judgments about the desires and acts of others. I come to see sexual desire as a bell curve onto which each of us falls, with little choice about where we land. The magazine *Frighten the Horses,* which calls itself a "document of the sexual revolution," received a letter complaining about images of sadomasochism. She didn't understand S/M, the letter-writer said. The images made her uncomfortable. The editor, Cris Gutierrez, replied: "Here's the most important thing for you to understand: *you don't need to understand.*" I may in fact be, as I've been called, a perverted old cow. But so might we all.

Our experience of sex not only can be, but most likely will be, internally as well as externally contradictory. When I talk about sex, and most particularly when I talk about myself, I am struggling to be as honest as I can be. But I'm haunted by the fact that nothing I can say will be complete. I find myself saying different things to different people, at different times, and often what I say sounds forced, inadequate, insincere. Sex is a game, a weapon, a toy, a joy, a trance, an enlightenment, a loss, a hope. I contradict myself, because nothing I say can ever be enough. It's all true, though—just about everything is true, especially the contradictions.

2

One of the most pervasive modern American fears is that of the ordinary human body. We suffer an almost complete physical dysphoria, a cultural illness of physical inadequacy and shame. Fear of *the breast* and *the penis,* which everyone either has or has seen, haunts people, as though these items are deformities. Even though the loss of a breast or penis is considered a tragedy, the healthy breast and penis are condemned. They are treated like wounds that represent terrible acts.

The book *Where's Waldo?* has been banned in many

places because of one tiny profile of part of a woman's breast. Marianne Williamson's book *A Woman's Worth* was turned down by a major distributor because the cover showed a partial profile of the side of a woman's breast. (The penis is just never seen at all; even male buttocks are big news.) The very possibilities intrinsic to a word, "breast," the implication of pleasure, are despised. For the most frightened among us—and I count those most angry about such benign sexual images as part of that group—it isn't sexual behavior that is feared so much as the simple fact that sex exists. That sex might be evoked. Some small image—a breast, a cigar, a blooming flower, a glimpse of shoulder or knee—reminds us of sex, and must also be removed from sight.

The deepest fear and the greatest censure of the body concerns children. A desperate effort is made to protect childhood innocence by sparing children the sight of nude bodies as long as possible. The irony is that such efforts destroy their real innocence—the simple belief children have that their bodies are lovely gifts. It takes very little—only a few disapproving looks, a few wagged fingers and hurriedly closed books—to convince a child that there is in fact something wrong with the ordinary human body. Someone asks me if I don't think we're living in a time of wildly promiscuous sexuality and I remember the recent local uproar over a middle-school art class looking at a slide of Michelangelo's *David.*

Childhood is a dream we are doomed to awaken from, and we awake into a world of loss, disappointment, and change—and acceptance of loss, of disappointment, and change, joy in change, joy in being awake. Infantile sexuality is a waking dream that exists only as long as the fullness of life is held at bay. The fantasy of oneness dissolves into a world of compartments, borders, rules; oneness is reworked into metaphor and symbol. First children, very young children, wake into their separateness from other people and the nourishing warmth of other bodies. Then they find their own bodies and wake into the consciousness of private pleasure. (Adults believe children are sexless and at the same time vigilantly patrol for signs of masturbation.) There is a wonderful and awful moment for each of us when we practice masturbation as a conscious act—when we know what to do and why we want to do it, and make plans. Though I'd been chastised for my unconscious masturbation when quite young, it was not a sin until I planned and carried it out consciously. And ever afterward, masturbation has been accompanied by a strange, potent mix of emotions: desire, guilt, excitement, shame, fantasy, and, especially, the fear of getting caught. The fear of letting anyone else know I know.

When I was eight and nine, I played Barbie in the bedroom with my best friend, Janet. We lay on my bed together with our naked dolls, and wrapped their rigid plastic limbs around each other as well as we could manage, banging them together in our best guess at intercourse—which, vague as the notion was, was all we knew of sex. The reason children sometimes seem innocent of sex is that they have yet to consider sex as something outside themselves and their continual sensual experience of the world. What fascinates children is the way adults flounder to conceal their own attempts to control and define sexuality. A friend of mine, a man in his forties, admits that he sometimes likes to see women shorn of pubic hair. "The first nude pictures of women I ever saw were some books my father had rather carelessly hidden, and they showed women with mysterious gray clouds or simply bare skin in that region." When Janet and I were tired of dolls, we wrapped our arms around each other and tried the same thing, mumbling words we'd only half heard and didn't understand, wondering what the fuss was all about.

We learn virtually every skill by watching others do them, through lessons formal and informal, through a thousand observations and a million practice attempts. Everything but sex. When children begin to test their sexuality, they are told to stop and no further information is given. We grow up with only the vaguest and most unrealistic ideas of what people do and don't do, what other people think and dream about. We would never teach a child to call a car a "wheeled motor vehicle," but we tell a toddler to call his penis a million things but "penis" and never name the clitoris anything at all. And the motions themselves of sex are often treated as though they were imaginary; the child who asks a specific question is evaded, misdirected, or at best answered with inscrutable metaphor. When the child first says "fuck" he is punished.

I couldn't get my mother to explain where babies came from until I was ten, and confronted her with a Kotex ad and a demand for an explanation. She wanted to refuse then, too, but this time I wouldn't budge. She told me, finally, that to make a baby the man had to put his penis in the woman's vagina. Since all I knew of penises were fleeting, accidental glimpses of my brother and father, I spent the next year trying to figure out how that limp, fleshy thing got in there at all; I wondered if there was some kind of tool, a crochet hook, perhaps, with which to tuck it in. My ignorance was flagrantly sexual; the less I knew, the more I thought about it.

I read "Spider-Man" and Jules Verne and all the Conan novels, but never the romances or women's magazines my mother consumed—though if I'd known just how steamy some of my mother's romances were, I might have given them a try. I was more concerned with Davids and a Goliath or two, until childhood came to an end with what seems in hindsight a startling abruptness. Around the earthquake of puberty, America wraps a "cosmic silence," in the words of Matthew Fox. Americans mature with a complete lack of ritual, acknowledgment, or celebration. Our genitals are heavy machinery, race cars, explosives, but no one gets a license to operate them. We enter puberty ignorant, and alone.

Most people would agree you can pay someone to rub your back, but would then add you shouldn't pay the same person to rub your penis. Two women can kiss on the cheek, but not on the mouth. A man can hold a woman's hand, but not put his hand on her breast—because in each of the latter cases, something we call *sex* has begun, a boundary has been crossed, a new definition is in place. Define *sex*. Define its beginnings, its limits, its end, the differences between one pleasant touch and another, between something delicious and proper and something delicious and bad.

Greta Christina, in a very funny essay called "Are We Having Sex Now or What?" addresses this question of boundaries. "It wasn't just that the territory I labeled *sex* was expanding. The line itself had swollen, dilated, been transformed into a vast gray region. It had become less like a border and more like a demilitarized zone." Is sex whatever feels like sex at the time? she asks her reader. Is it any mutually pursued sexual pleasure? Is it penetration? "Maybe if *both* of you (or all of you) think of it as sex, then it's sex whether you're having fun or not." This last, Christina decides, is "too messy" to work. "Can you have a situation where one person is having sex and the other isn't?" What about behavior clearly erotic but not, as you might say, "wet," like play that involves bondage and spanking but no genital contact, kissing, or other traditionally accepted signs of sex? (Is a masochist with a hymen still a virgin?) Christina recalls working in a peep show. A man in one of the booths began masturbating as he watched her; she came up to his Plexiglas window and masturbated, too. "After he left I thought to myself: Did we just have sex?" And she has no answer. Neither do I.

When I was in the eighth grade a new girl came to my small-town school where hardly any new kids ever came. The whispers came the way whispers do; this new girl was something else. My mother was a teacher at the school, and so I had a certain privilege; I could usually get a hall pass simply by telling my own teacher I had to tell my mother something. So I finagled a pass and slipped through the empty halls to the office to get a look. All of thirteen, she lounged in a hard-backed chair with an insouciance I had never seen except on television —dressed all in black, her long limbs thrown about the principal's office like discarded clothes, her black eyes framed in black kohl. She was unmistakably, unbearably, sexual; I knew it without knowing the word. She was a *slut,* I whispered to my friends when I returned. We passed around notes. What a wonderful word I thought that was, a lethal insult, a sign of urban sophistication and danger, of having crossed a line. Slut. The girl who obviously knew what I couldn't get anyone to tell me. I admired her greatly, pretending dislike. Crowds parted when she passed, leaving a rustle of whispers in her wake. She must have been terribly lonely, but she disdained us all, and in six months she was gone without having taught me a thing.

Then my brother shared his stolen *Playboy*s with me. The pneumatic figurines seemed magnificent and unreal; they signified something foreign and only haphazardly interesting—interesting mainly because it was forbidden, adult, disallowed. *Playboy,* I knew, created a lot of fuss. But the women seemed to have nothing at all to do with me or my future. I couldn't imagine being a woman, only myself. I got a little older, and began to find scenes of sex and lasciviousness in books, sex which had probably been there all along. I had desperate crushes, lingering fantasies that faded into a Vaseline blur when my limited pool of information was used up. Before long I was lying in the dark, listening to "Black Magic Woman" and kissing my pillow, dreaming hotter and more painful dreams. And then came real kisses, and dark, rough fumblings, triumphant fingers inside my panties at last, a rut when all the rules disappeared, when I learned the true meaning of *impulsive.* All before I quite knew what sex was, exactly.

By no means is Adam and Eve, Eden and the Fall, the myth I want. But it's certainly the myth I have. You don't have to be a Christian or a Jew or a Muslim to be influenced deeply by this story. You need only to have been raised somewhere in the Christian or the Jewish or

the Muslim world, for the myth is inescapable, its per-
mutations fantastic and legion. As far back as my memory goes, I've seen Adam's shrinking terror and Eve's
guilty, sidelong glance as God chased them out of paradise.

Briefly put, the story goes something like this: Adam
was created by God—or maybe the gods. He was immortal, of huge size, had great wisdom, and was inde-
scribably beautiful. He was he and she together, her-
maphroditic, made in God's image as the great
androgyne and progenitor of a new race. God split the
male from the female, the first *adam* became Adam and
Eve, each halved, diminished. And when they fell, they
fell hard. People disagreed three thousand years ago,
when Genesis in its several forms was written, and they
disagree now about what exactly Adam and Eve lost in
the Fall: their virginity, their innocence, their divinity.
Both were reduced in size and made mortal, made to
decay and die, made shamed of themselves as they were,
naked. Eve took her punishment literally in the shorts:
pregnancy and the pain of childbirth, menstruation, eternal submission to the male in every sphere. But there's
more to the story than the Sistine Chapel ceiling, and lots
more than I learned from little felt-board scenes in Lu-
theran Sunday school in 1961.

Robert Graves and Raphael Patai tackle Adam and
Eve in their book *Hebrew Myths: The Book of Genesis,* a
compilation of Christian, Sumerian, Jewish, Kabbalistic,
Babylonian, mythic, and historical sources, compared

and compiled into a wholistic telling of Genesis. This is ur-Genesis, Genesis complete—as complete as possible.

After God made Adam and the beasts, write Graves and Patai, Adam was "already like a twenty-year-old man"—and we know what *they're* like. He kept trying to copulate with the animals. So God made Lilith. "Adam and Lilith never found peace together; for when he wished to lie with her, she took offence at the recumbent posture he demanded. 'Why must I lie beneath you?' she asked. 'I also was made from dust, and am therefore your equal.' Because Adam tried to compel her obedience by force, Lilith, in a rage, uttered the magic name of God, rose into the air and left him. Adam complained to God: 'I have been deserted by my help-meet.'" Funny how familiar all this sounds.

God sent angels to fetch her. But Lilith had already found a crowd of "lascivious demons" with which to copulate and was busy having baby demons. Not only did she not want to return, she pointed out shamelessly that she wasn't really wife material anymore. Lilith eventually became the queen of demons in Jewish literature, a seductress, succubus, and stealer of babies. She is mother, whore, creator, terror, and sometimes comfort. But she is never wife.

"God tried again, and let him watch while he built up a woman's anatomy: using bones, tissues, muscles, blood and glandular secretions, then covering the whole with skin and adding tufts of hair in places. The sight caused Adam such disgust that . . . he felt an invincible repugnance." This woman, sometimes called First Eve, disappeared, no one knows where. Second Eve was made much more hygienically from Adam's rib, or maybe his now-missing tail. God worked while Adam slept, to spare him the sight. Out of Adam came his femininity, and he was halved and mated all at once.

When Eve met the sinewy, penile snake and first tasted the forbidden apple, writes Milton in *Paradise Lost,* "Earth felt the wound." She herself felt euphoria, felt for the first time the little death of orgasm. Adam loved her enough that he chose to eat and die with her rather than live forever alone. And yet he calls her "adventrous Eve," the first of the long line of adventuresses who will ruin men down the ages. "The myth of the Fall licenses man to blame woman for all his ills," writes Graves and Patai. Certainly Milton saw it that way. After Adam eats, they see each other with new eyes, sexual eyes—eyes of "Fire"—and they make love, thus sealing the guilt. Adam asks Eve to help him figure out how to clothe themselves. Already, she's sewing. Confronted by God, Eve blames Adam for not being man enough to have restrained her from sin. Adam in turn blames Eve, complaining to God, in essence, You said she was perfect, and look what she did! And God replies, what kind of man are you to listen to a woman?

In Adam and Eve is everything I have found and fought within myself. Out of their story has come the brutal belief that female sexuality is the enemy of male civilization, and out of it also comes the message of my

personal sexual shame, my shame in being a woman.
Women awaken and unleash male lust: the beastly, roaring, insatiable lust that is the enemy of empire-builders
everywhere, the ultimate distraction. I waken my own
desire and pay in kind. What was their sin—sexual
knowledge or simple disobedience? It doesn't matter,
really, because all our sexual expressions now have the
flavor of disobedience in them, have the scent of shame
hidden in them somewhere. Disobedience itself has a
kind of sexual frisson. (If we were free of sexual guilt, I
imagine celibacy would be a fetish, an expression of radical sexuality, as its original early Christian proponents
intended it to be.) Adam is rational, albeit easily swayed;
it is Eve who is sly, passionate, untrustworthy, who se-
duces Adam with a lick and a promise. So, of course,
when Eve arrived, our goddesses had to go. She had to
become Adam's daughter instead of "the mother of all
living," she had to be taken out of Adam, when everyone
knows all people come out of Eve. In the moment of the
world's most devastating act she is made to seem a capri-
cious and peevish child. She is always, merely, eternally,
a woman. Adam is always, apologetically, eternally, the
man.

A few hundred years after Christ, Augustine wrote that
the natural world, fecund and uncontrollable, was a
symptom of human disease. He felt the spontaneous nature of desire proved its wickedness, because no rational

man would allow such a thing if he could prevent it. That's what Augustine, and others, wanted people to overcome, the spontaneous *fact* of desire more than how desire was acted on. God punished Adam with lust, and all people from then on were being punished by parts of their bodies refusing to obey their will. The erection is the body's betrayer, a Judas, and man the goat. Augustine called for celibacy and self-denial and in almost the same breath called tyranny the normal condition of the uncontrollable human race.

Augustine's own sexual history appears to have been one of furtive frustrations, and reading his later work is like reading the frenzied exhortations of the Puritans and Calvinists, of the Inquisitors, of madmen. He had influence, enormous influence; along with Genesis, the writings of Augustine have shaped most of the Christian view of sex that permeated the culture in which I was born. Sex after Augustine became something unfortunate, best not discussed. Sex was liable to lead one further and further away from God, into the world's corruption. Since early Christian times, monks have castrated and even killed themselves to avoid the temptation of sex, seeing suicide as a surer route to heaven than desire. Sex was a test, a sin, and a terrible sorrow.

(Of course, a grand tradition of the secret, twisted sex lives of priests and nuns also exists in many religions. An old Chinese joke tells of a Buddhist monk who has been in a monastery for many years, when he is taken to a brothel for the first time. Afterward, he says, "These people are strange. From the front they are like the nuns, and from the back they are like the acolytes.")

What we might call "alternative sexuality"—that is, everything forbidden, from homosexual behavior to masturbation—is punished because it is nonreproductive. In a number of religious systems, sex is a good largely insofar as it makes more believers. In a more philosophical vein, Freud said society must forbid sexual practices that are merely fun in order to reward procreative sexuality. Even Freud admitted lifelong heterosexual monogamy may not be the most gratifying sexual expression for everyone. Until fairly recently, for a woman to have contraceptively protected sex was tantamount to proclaiming herself a prostitute. By the mid-1800s female sexual pleasure wasn't only invisible, it was a perversion in itself, a twisting of the natural order of things. So much so that for a wife to enjoy sex with her husband degraded her husband. Such a marriage was considered, by some religious authorities, "homosexual." Most prosaically, nonreproductive sex (like the very concept of contraception) has been historically condemned by economics; inheritance and lines of succession were essential to traditional bases of power and the rise of the market economy.

The punishments involved can be severe; male homosexuality was a death-penalty crime in England as late as 1867 and any number of unorthodox sexual lifestyles can still cause you to lose your job, apartment, the custody of your children, and get you beaten and killed.

Homophobia, which gets a lot of press these days, never exists in a vacuum, though we speak of it as if it did. The fear of gay people, just another quirk, like the fear of open spaces or the fear of rats. Homophobia is part of a larger view of sex and what sex is for. Anyone opposed to same-gender sex is unlikely to be a friend to hetero-sexual sadomasochism or cross-dressing or foot fetishes or anything else outside the conventional stereotype of monogamous heterosexuality. (Not that real monoga-mous heterosexual relations are necessarily conventional. But an amazing number of people who know better like to perpetuate the idea that this convention exists.)

People who see gayness as a perversion sometimes seem to swell with an inexplicable rage, offering twisted and inchoate notions based in an anxiety hard to explain by circumstance. And when the barrier of belief against one alternative sexual practice falls, so do the barriers against others, like dominos. Who, after all, doesn't feel at least a little bit queer about sex sometimes?

The first time I had sex, so to speak, I was disappointed. But part of the problem was my definition. I considered myself a virgin at sixteen in spite of years of fumbling around with Janet, with Henry, my first teenage boy-friend, and a number of other people. As much as I had been given a sex education, it had been about intercourse and was phrased in somewhat confusing terms. The fact that I, as the girl, was responsible for "how far" the boys

I knew would go had been made clear. I was not very virginal by the time I decided I was in love with and would "give myself" to Keith, who was several years older than I. By the time Keith, with great gentleness and concern, put his penis in my vagina, I was prepared for fireworks. I was most certainly expecting to feel different when it was over, and I expected my parents and teachers and friends all to know immediately what had happened simply by looking at me. Now I can see I'd lost my virginity—and *lost* is not the right word at all, because I never went looking for it again—years before that, when someone or other had touched me in a way so pleasurable, I couldn't wait to be touched that way again. Sex begins, for each of us, when we feel as though we'd gone through a door and won't be going back. Don't want to go back. That's when the scales fall and the veil lifts. And I bet my mother noticed something then.

"Casual sex can be a good way of getting to know people," wrote Dennis Altman way back in 1971. I was a fourteen-year-old virgin then, and Altman was writing an important manifesto of gay rights. But he was right then, and he's right now, and if you read that quote again, you'll see there's not a whole lot to argue about in it. He is merely stating one of the facts of human emotion. When we strip away the veneer of religion, from which stems most, if not all, of our prohibitions about casual sex, when you see sex as *just sex,* it makes perfect sense. Two (or more) people who like each other and want to get to know each other better engage in mutually satisfying behavior leading to a greater intimacy. This certainly sounds moral enough, but the idea is widely detested in the West. We can't strip away that veneer of religious morality entirely in the first place, even if we were sure it would be a good idea to do so. Most important, sex is rarely just sex, and the cultural agendas we bring to every sexual meeting make getting to know each other difficult in the best of circumstances.

There seems to be almost no way in which male and female sexual behavior are treated the same. The difference between a promiscuous woman and a man-about-town is a gulf the size of human history, a cosmos of belief. The same behavior, the exact same acts and words, exhibited by a man has a wholly different meaning when exhibited by a woman. I know this isn't exactly news, but it keeps on surprising me; even in the latter half of my thirties I keep finding those waggling fingers and averted looks. I do it to myself, judge myself for a moment of aggression, desire, or fantasy that somehow or other I learned to call masculine—and learned specifically to allow in men and not in myself. Sexual acting-out by women in even minor ways is still a great surprise to a lot of people and capable of rousing strong emotions. We all know that cars, beer, and deodorant are sold to men with the promises of seductive women. But how many advertisements have I seen in the last year that tried to sell something to young, feminist-informed women with copy like "You can be smart *and* sexy!"? What a shocking idea, I think, shaking it off, and then

Esquire, that emblem of the adolescent male zeitgeist, puts out a whole issue on young, feminist-informed women under the tag of "Do Me Feminism." Do who? Maybe *I* will do *you.* And maybe I won't, and either way I'm a bit of a slut.

I became sexually active in the 1970s, a period of casual sexual partners, before AIDS and after the pill. It was a unique time, but not necessarily a fun one. I fell in love with boys and with girls, with men and with women, but generally I slept with men, because sleeping with men was what I knew how to do; it was easy, there were endless opportunities. The etiquette of sexual relations was strange and unknowable. Sometimes it seemed impolite to ask a lover his or her last name. More than once I found myself in bed with either a stranger or a friend, and felt an equal embarrassment.

It's an odd feeling, to run into someone at a party or reunion, to know I've had sex with this person and to know it's as though it never happened—because sex that doesn't engage our selves in some way is not really sex at all. There was this touch, that stroke, this exchange of bodily fluids, but no sex. Just bodies. There are also people whose paths I've crossed, people who I barely touched in the lightest of casual ways, who nevertheless *feel* to me as though they'd been my lovers—because between us, however brief, occurred a dance of some kind that couldn't be denied. Often enough, the sex in a sexual relationship has, over time, come to be not only the least important, but the least interesting part of an erotic and genuine experience. And now and then it's been the only thing.

Someone asked me not long ago if I had an "old woman" role model. Betty Dodson, I replied. In 1974, Dodson, now in her sixties, wrote a book called *Liberating Masturbation,* and with it women started looking at and touching their genitals in a whole new way. Certainly I did. I was seventeen that year, living in a college dorm and volunteering in a women's health clinic. We decorated the waiting room with big posters of the flower-vulva paintings Dodson made. I learned to do pelvic exams on other women, learned the beauty and variety of women's genitalia, held up a lot of mirrors for a lot of other young women so they could, for the first time, see their cervixes. But it took Dodson's book, her cheerful, unashamed paean to getting off in the privacy of your own room, to get me to look at my own. I couldn't stop applying the double standard that made me bless the sexual acts done by other people and live with horrible doubts about my own.

In this headiest period of determined tolerance, 1978, I was not quite twenty-one and several months pregnant. The social work office where I was employed held a seminar on sexuality, the point being, I recall, to help us support clients in a variety of sexual choices. Two things happened that weekend that I'll never forget. We spent a lot of time watching documentary-style videos of explicit sex, and then discussing the implications—look, a paraplegic having sex. Look, two women, how nice. In one

an old couple made love with admirable endurance and
fervor, on a bed in a sunny bedroom, on the floor, on a
table. This was all well and good, until the end, when
they were done and their conversation made it obvious
they'd met only for the purpose of making the film.
"We'll have to get together again sometime," the woman
said at the end of the film. The social workers' initial
approval of these cheerfully coupling elders suddenly
turned to noisy distaste, even disgust, at this revelation.
Sexual relations among the old was fine and good—as
long as certain expectations were met.

We were given a homework assignment on the first
day, to make a collage that expressed our own sexuality.
I took the assignment seriously and spent several hours
on it. The next morning I saw that my colleagues, male
and female both, had all made romantic visions of can-
dlelight and sunsets. Then I presented my own, a vision
of masked men and women, naked torsos, skin everywhere, darkness, heat. The 1970s fueled a new kind of
sexual ignorance. By then I was not so naive about sex
and what people did, but I was terribly naive about what
sex meant and how people really felt about it. I didn't
expect or quite understand the ringing silence with
which my collage was met.

Sometimes sex has slipped away from me, disappeared
in the confusion of my work or child-rearing or melan-
choly. And sometimes sex feels like a headlong tumble

taking everything with it, as though everything were changing all at once. Once I was really willing to look, these last few years, the world exploded with sex. I know women who find a conservative feminist polemic against intercourse so lushly written they masturbate to it, I know drag queens with rings in their penises, dykes with dildos in their pants, men who were women and women who were men. The edges are falling apart, angels and sinners are trading places. There is new etiquette, new vocabulary, new genders. I live in a world obsessed both with incest and fashion models who look like children; where there are marches against erotica and for the death penalty, where you can buy bikinis and makeup for little girls but not breastfeed in public; I live in a world sculpted to make room for missiles and skyscrapers and nuclear submarines, hot humming phalluses cutting through the dark waters of the deep.

3

"We all pretend to be more of a man or a woman than we secretly suspect we are," writes my friend Laura Miller. Thus, emblems: the tidy little acts of straightening a skirt and freshening makeup, shooting shirt cuffs, ruffling hair. Tiny details, unconscious habits, little trills of pretense and belonging. See me, they say, I am— whatever I hope I am. We cultivate those things which set us aside from the other, the opposite gender, squarely among our own.

Over the last year, and with considerable surprise, I've come to realize I can't define *woman*. I can't tell you why

I'm sure I *am* a woman, why others think I am, why my personal and internal experience seems to fit what culture tells me a woman's experience should be. I am a woman because I look and act like the social convention called "woman." But not wholly, or always. What I once thought a permanent and objective state seems to me more and more like a vapor, a fantasia, a wisp.

I cherish femaleness and the company of other women simply because, well, they're women. I don't know what I mean when I say that men won't "get something" I'm trying to explain, but I mean it, anyway. There are many feelings and ideas I would discuss only with another woman. Most of all, I crave the ease of women's company, the inexplicable psychic repose their presence allows. I don't have to know what they are, what I am, or what men are, to know the difference in how it feels to be with a woman or with a man.

The markers of gender are neither objective nor permanent. Certain characteristics that are thought feminine, like my hair, skin texture, and posture are readily mutable, easy enough to disguise. My dress, my voice, and my mannerisms are even easier to camouflage or, conversely, imitate. A good cross-dresser has me pegged, doing what I do unconsciously with care and attention. I am less feminine than a lot of men, and I swear I don't know how they do it, how it works. But for all that I'm less feminine in many ways than certain men are or could be, I'm infinitely more womanly, and it's a rare cross-dresser that can't be caught by a careful observer;

that thing the observer catches, that clue, is as hard to
define as any of these other terms.

We are made biologically male or female by chromosome 23, and everyone starts out as a girl. A fetal gonad
with two X chromosomes stays just as it is, barring disas-
ter, and the fetus develops female. A fetal gonad with an
X and a Y chromosome, though, transmutes and becomes a testis; the testis eventually begins to release androgens, and the androgens convert the genitalia to male
form. Most of the time, anyway; there are a number of
what are technically called sexual intergrades, rare in the
general population, endlessly instructive.

In fact, pseudohermaphrodites, with distinct characteristics of both sexes, are not terribly rare. (What is
called true hermaphroditism, or intersex, is very rare;
true hermaphrodites don't simply have physical signs of
both men and women. They have unique sexual glands,
gonads mixed from male and female material, and their
genitalia are an honest merging, an amorphous phase
between the genders.) It doesn't matter much which of
the myriad possible gene mutations or enzyme defects is
responsible—not unless it's you caught up in such a bad
biological pun. There are hermaphrodites with male
genitalia, but ovaries instead of testicles. Others have
female genitalia, but testes instead of ovaries; they appear
to be girls, only to become boys at puberty, to the enormous chagrin of all concerned. There are people with an
ovary on one side and a testis on the other, and sometimes both the ovary and the testis work at the same

time, a kind of salmagundi of stimulation, fraught with bewilderment for the poor body pulled hither and thither by hormones fighting for the right to meld the flesh.

What else makes me female? I can lose my breasts, my vagina, even my delectably female clitoris through surgery or disease. I would grieve, but I don't think my womanliness depends on these anatomical markers. I can dilute and transmute these same markers with male hormones. Will I still be a woman? This is getting closer to real change, because the hormones affect much that isn't objective as well as what is: mental states, emotions, desires. Gradually male hormones would erode the structure of femaleness, my female skeleton, and I would be transformed into something new, the same way steroid users, castrati, and transsexuals are transformed.

So I'm a woman, and I hope to stay that way. I like almost everything about womanhood. And I'm raising a daughter, and though I don't know who she'll turn out to be, I'm obliged to attempt a sometimes ticklish transition of knowledge. I can hardly define womanhood for myself, but I must teach it to her. After raising two sons, my relationship to her feels ontologically easy, a fetal unfolding into the self, at one and the same time that it feels difficult and important. (At least with my boys, I knew what I thought men *should* be. One of the ways I teach my daughter to be female is to talk to her about what it seems to mean to be male.) I give womanhood to

my daughter by showing her how I am a woman—and I
don't always know how to be one, and occasionally wonder how well I'm doing. I used to think I was beyond
caring what gender my children were, that I'd treat
them each the same, be as close to one as to the other. I
was kidding myself. I may not necessarily be closer to
my daughter just because she's a girl, but there is between us a particular comfort. What would change between us if she turned out to be that rare thing, that
"apparent" girl who becomes a boy? Or decides, as a
woman, to become a man? Would she still be—herself?

We are all, or almost all, either male or female, more
or less masculine or feminine, more or less heterosexual
or homosexual. But of course nothing of the sort is true;
sex makes mincemeat of rigid definitions. Binary biological systems are based in reproduction and the exchange
of genetic material, which works well enough for
orchids, raccoons, and black widow spiders. But the binary system breaks down utterly on the rocks of human
desire. Everything from homosexuality to a rubber fetish
to masturbation deny reproduction as the penultimate
sexual motive. Funny how most biologists squirm when
confronted with pleasure. It has no utility, they say, no
determining importance; therefore all these sexual aber-
rations must somehow be explained by physical or psychological malfunctions. Some of us might argue that
pleasure *is* utility, that human pleasure is part of evolution in the first place. It's certainly a potent manipulator

of behavior, and behavior influences nature, so why can't the pursuit of pleasure ultimately affect the evolution of the race? The human organism has had tens of thousands of years to play around in. Maybe romance is just another of DNA's little tricks, but that still doesn't explain masturbation.

In Plato's *Symposium,* Aristophanes ironically describes our original state. There were once three sexes, he says: man, woman, and the Androgyne, male and female both. All were round and doubled, each with four hands, four feet, and two faces, and they were very strong—partly because their unusual shape enabled them to practice a wide variety of sexual acts. When these people attacked the gods, Zeus decided to humble them by cutting them in two, which made them ugly and ungainly, unbalanced. Zeus also turned their genitals to the front so they could reproduce, so they could be at least momentarily satisfied, "each desiring his other half." Some men desire women and vice versa, some men desire men and some women desire women. It doesn't matter. In every case, says Aristophanes, this painful, eternal search is *love:* "so ancient is the desire of one another which is implanted in us, reuniting our original nature, making one of two, and healing the state of man."

These days, we tend to think of androgynous as a

synonym for sexless. The label is usually punitive, in spite of the fact that androgynous men and women are capable of stirring strange feelings of arousal in most people. The historical image of the hermaphrodite is of vibrant, almost burning sexuality, a person who has transcendent powers. Twentieth-century Americans, oh-so-postmodern, are still busily throwing off the cloak of gender segregation pressed on us these last few hundred years, and we move toward blending slowly and suspiciously. Most cultures hate the androgyne. Real hermaphrodites have historically been treated as monsters or criminals, unnatural corruptions. Man and woman, and most important, the cultural myths of men and women, are about filling and completing each other; the androgyne is already filled up. Androgyny in contemporary western culture, writes Jamake Highwater, is "an abomination so great that for centuries it could not even be discussed by decent people." And Highwater isn't referring just to the physical or biological state; he means the very idea of blending gender roles. For a time the idea that gender roles *could* change was obscene.

But this is mostly idle talk. For all I can wonder what makes me a woman, the culture at large isn't interested in metaphysics or myth. I would be offended if I were mistaken for a man; most men would be offended if they were mistaken for women. As far as the culture at large is concerned, I'm a woman because I have a vagina. If my vagina were removed, I would remain a woman because I had *had* a vagina and because I don't have anything else.

This morning I made a small purchase at a neighborhood store. The clerk watched me slip the bills she'd handed me into my thick wallet and then laboriously stuff the wallet into my small handbag, where it barely fits.

"How do you get by with such a small purse?" she asked wonderingly, a little wistfully. She was about my age, in her mid-thirties, with crisply permed blond hair and careful makeup. I told her I'd worked years to have a purse so light and lean, and then we talked for a while about all the things without which we can't seem to get by, for which we must carry everywhere a bag of some size hung awkwardly off our shoulders. She listed a few: makeup, hairbrush, hair spray, perfume, hand lotion, barrettes. I wanted to tell her I'd given up my larger purse because I've never been very good at these feminine skills, that my purses seemed to fill with books and receipts instead, just as my fingernails tend to chip and my hair hangs loose. But what I really felt was defensive. She said my purse was *small*. And while I may practice a casual pride about my freedom from the rituals of sexual relations in the 1990s, what I often feel is a niggling concern—and I reach in my purse and wonder why the hell I can never remember to carry a comb.

There's a lot to be said for gender roles. Mainly, they allow us to meet strangers on solid ground. One treats men one way, women another, period. Gender roles give us prescribed behaviors, the safety of the familiar, of knowing what to expect. Gender roles seem to make things easier, but we've all felt them at least as much as a source of pain, false expectations, thin hopes, disillusionment, and loss. Gender roles tell us we must fit a few categories and must choose, must pick one gender with which to be sexual, one gender in which to be professional, to be parental, to be everything.

Leaving your gender role in any way gets you punished. The transsexual is in league with the effeminate man as well as the sexually aggressive woman, the politically powerful woman, the sexually or socially retiring man. Jacques Lacan traced much anguish to every child's break from his or her mother, every person's discovery of the unattainably separate Other. This break, said Lacan, was true castration, this loss was real phallus envy, and we all, male and female, suffer it. The real tragedy of adult life is finding out that one's objects of desire, one's own whole self, can only be longed for and never truly possessed. Distinct gender roles are a panacea to our lonesomeness. Inadequate, all; neurotic, all. At least we can know the limits by which we dress, talk, and behave.

Friedrich Nietzsche, of all people, felt enormously confident in declaring that the female penchant for femininity was part of her "instinct for the *secondary* role." I say "of all people" because Nietzsche famously hated women; his biography is a study in the destructive potential of gender roles. His father died when he was very young and he was raised in a pious household of women. He was of delicate health, feared the sight of blood, longed to be a soldier or hero but found it impossible to tolerate military life. His greatest love was for a man, Richard Wagner, but even that romantic friendship broke up dramatically. Nietzsche probably had syphillis, perhaps went insane from it, likely died from it. Before he died, he wrote at length about women, saying that "woman" must accept not only her castrated status, but her actual castration. Only by submitting to her emptiness was a woman free to "dress up," "fill up" her emptiness in other, insignificant ways. A masculinized woman was a great offense to Nietzsche, a total fake; she used masculinity as adornment. In the exact same way analysts dismiss the gay aesthetic of decoration and exaggeration as a sign of the gay man's unnatural character. He is neat and natty because he is incomplete. He is emasculated and so he seeks the phallus of other men, and tries to fill his own lack with finery.

I go into this detail because it still counts, these punishments are still real. They are maddening, outrageous, self-referential. Of course anyone as injured by gender expectations as Nietzsche is the last person to make pronouncements on the subject, but historically these are usually the people making the pronouncements and writing our laws. These ideals of gender inform fashion on a constant basis, form the fundament of advertising and public relations and celebrity, and influence everything from my choice of hairstyle to my embarrassment at saying a "dirty" word in front of my grandmother.

What Nietzsche considered natural, Joan Riviere came to see as a necessary deceit for survival—for every woman's survival. Riviere was a Freudian analyst who suffered a great deal from the expectations of gender heaped upon her by society and her fellow analysts. She addressed one aspect in her essay "Womanliness as a Masquerade," written in 1929. "I shall attempt to show that women who wish for masculinity may put on a mask of womanliness to avert anxiety and the retribution feared from men," wrote Riviere. She was particularly addressing the case of women who display intellectualism, who pursue careers, who literally compete with men, including their fathers—and who also deliberately display womanly pursuits such as motherhood, homemaking, heterosexual flirtations. "Womanliness therefore could be assumed and worn as a mask, both to hide the possession of masculinity and to avert the reprisals expected if she was found to possess it." Womanliness itself, Riviere continued, her prose a model of quiet clarity, couldn't be divided into "real" and "pretend"; there was no difference between femininity consciously displayed and femininity unconsciously lived, because "whether radical or superficial, they are the same thing." To be perceived as a woman by society was to pretend, period. Femininity is deceit, deceit is femininity, anatomical women who don't display the "masquerade" fail to be women. In society's eyes, only masculinity is whole, complete in itself. "Woman" was that which made a man feel like a man, by being less than male.

Augustine spent a lot of time trying to figure out what the point of woman was. Why did God want to make someone different from man? He noted that if she was meant as a helper, she should have been a man for strength. And if she was meant as a friend, she should have been a man for comfort. So why was she there? Psychoanalysis had at its bedrock this same semi-secret belief—that no one would *want* to be a woman, given a choice. A "healthy" female identity, which was of course heterosexual, had to be about what the analysts called *lack*—giving up, giving in, submitting, being filled. (Therefore, disguise and pretense—you have to fill up with something, only part of which is men.) Transsexualism "experts" persist in disbelieving in the female-to-male transsexual not because no one would want to be a man, but because everyone must want to be one. The butch woman sows seeds of discontent wherever she goes; she disturbs merely by being. The tide of her passage pulls at the seams of power. About the butch woman the Greeks had nothing to say. No man has ever had much to say about her, but the fear of her propels convention.

Freud wisely thought sexual identity was unstable,

unreliable. One was always having to reinvent oneself as
man or woman, always having to cling to the markers of
gender, because otherwise they would slip away. It is one
of Freud's wisest and most enduring wisdoms, I think,
whether he understood the implications another century
would give it or not. Freud presumed that noting the
slipperiness of gender and sex would encourage society
to shore up and strengthen the artificial roles we have.
Instead, a century later, gender roles seem an ill-defined
mess, and each generation more marked by the clash
between gender bending and gay bashing. We are prov-
ing Freud's theory of gender confusion more true every
passing day.

The polarity of male and female has never been ignored. Not only have men and women rarely worn the
same kinds of clothes, they have rarely been trained to
move or sit or eat the same way, speak the same way,
about the same things. It was presumed (by men, who
largely created the social conventions) that the hopes,
desires, talents, and the nature of women's souls were
different from those of men. There have been periods
when men wore wigs and women didn't, when men
wore corsets and women didn't, but the point has always
been the *difference* itself, not its form. The masquerade
of womanliness persists. Every man trying to pass as a
woman knows this, and so does every woman who
doesn't wear the mask.

Inasmuch as male and female exist as separate forms,
they are parallel, perhaps complementary, separate and

entwined within every individual and every relationship. Some mornings looking feminine seems like a lot of work because I don't feel feminine at the time, and I don't care, and not caring is a sign of not feeling feminine. Other times I wake with an urge to cultivate the disguise, put on lipstick and lingerie. It might be because I'm feeling a little doubtful about myself; then again, it might be because I'm more confident than usual, enjoying the game. My own comfort level with feminine disguise is fairly low, and my best results aren't particularly vivid in the larger scheme of things. Sometimes I put on lipstick and feel like a clown. Straight men who like to cross-dress and pass as real women are fond of calling themselves "girls," and they are almost as afraid of being mistaken for lesbians as they are of being read as cross-dressing men. Both are failures of the feminine disguise. Fashion is psychoanalysis in action.

In Aristophanes' story of love, when Zeus divided the Androgynes, the halved people formed into pairs. Those who had been a combination of male and female became lovers of the opposite sex. ("Adulterers are generally of this breed," writes Aristophanes.) "The women who are a section of the woman do not care for men, but have female attachments . . . they who are a section of the male follow the male . . . they hang about men and embrace them, and they are themselves the best of boys and youths, because they have the most manly nature

. . . they are valiant and manly, and have a manly countenance, and they embrace that which is like them. And these when they grow up become our statesmen."

The bisexual Greeks worshiped beauty in all forms. They also practiced abortion, manufactured dildos, and tolerated the occasional transvestite and child prostitute. The highest form of beauty to a Greek man was male. Women lived separate lives, outside the cultural fervor of the male community. In that marvel of double-think that has characterized so much of sexism, women were deliberately excluded from the life of the mind and then denigrated for their lack of intellectual achievement. Because of this, Greek men (who, after all, have written virtually all we know of Greek history) considered women incomplete, not wholly formed, and thus not perfect in their beauty. So what was left to worship but men, and among men, what is more perfectly beautiful than a boy on the cusp of maturity? They were the opposite of an androgynous society; Greek thought celebrated, elevated, the difference between the genders.

From the Greeks through Augustine and Nietzsche to now, the world has turned upside down. For centuries, men who love men have been vilified as less than wholly male, as girlish, in the worst sense of the word—the Third Sex, incomplete, "inverts." A man who loves men, who loves semen and the erection, would seem to be intensely male. All men love these things, don't they? The phallic is universally admired by men; the homoeroticism in so many of our institutions, from the social club to the football field, is largely a result of male insecurity, the urge to buoy up one's male identity. The straight man uses them to validate his straightness. The gay man enjoys them because they're male. Can I go so far as to say this insecurity is a male trait? Why not? Men have been making such pronouncements about women, gay and otherwise, for a long time now.

Jamake Highwater makes the case that whether or not a society is particularly homosexual or heterosexual is beside the point. Modern America and ancient Greece are similar cultures because both devalue the feminine. The Greeks had open homoeroticism and open contempt for women. We have disguised homoeroticism and only thinly disguised contempt for women.

Many gay men *are* effeminate—meaning they display traits we in this culture consider feminine, subtle and not so subtle hints in posture, voice, gesture. I suspect Aristophanes and his Platonian-era pals, sitting around in robes discussing love and sipping wine, may have seemed effeminate in much the same way. The problem arises in connotation—in our narrow ideas of what constitutes not feminine and masculine, but appropriately male and female. It's the belief that the male should be unbalanced, should be *only* male, that has given the queen a bad name.

"When I was in high school I didn't know any gay people at all. I thought I just acted normally," says Brian, a short and unassuming man with curly red hair and a red beard. "I was in an acting class, and one of the impromptu assignments was that we each had to imitate somebody in the class, and this one guy, who was a really nice guy, got up and imitated me. And he was so *queeny*! I'd known I was gay for a long time, but I thought I was hiding it so well. It got a big laugh and I thought, Good. I'm proud of myself. And I came out right after that."

"Last year I went to Oklahoma with my mother for a family reunion. As soon as we got there my grand-mother asked me to take my earring off. I love my grandmother, so I did it for her. But I was so *threatened* by these people. I butched it up so *much*! I thought, we're only going to be here for two days, I can butch it. I thought they were going to take a hose and squirt me down. But it didn't work. I couldn't fool them. Anyway, when I was a child, people would speak of me as a sissy boy before I even knew I was gay."

"Before I knew I was gay." Lots of people say some-thing along these lines: My mother knew, others knew, before I did. What exactly is seen to tell the tale? I went to an assembly at my daughter's school today. Each of the primary grades had prepared a song, and marched upon the stage above the parents in neat, well-groomed rows. As I waited for my daughter's class to sing I was scanning the fresh and nervous faces of the third-grade children, when I saw a child who struck me instantly as gay. I simply had the thought, "That child is gay," be-fore I was aware of it, without any conscious consider-ation. I looked again and saw I couldn't tell if this child, who could not be older than nine, was a girl or a boy. A girl who dressed and stood as a boy? A boy with a particularly loose and feminine bearing? He, she, stood out, was different, because of that ambiguity.

Even by kindergarten the nuances of our sex roles are deeply embedded. It's odd not to be able to tell a child's gender at an early age, even many years before puberty, even though at that age the bodies of boys and girls are very much alike and both might dress in T-shirts and sneakers and jeans. We might tell by hairstyle, but as much or more by posture, where the hands are kept, how the head is held, a smile, the angle at which the foot rests. (These are exactly the nuances that betray the careless adult cross-dresser, the nuances transsexuals must learn and unlearn in order to pass. Compared to posture and inflection, makeup and hair are easy.) This ambiguous child seemed gay to me because the nuances were blended. Longish, soft hair—and an upright, balanced bearing. Hands in the pockets, and a shy smile. The direct gaze—and the quiet voice. Here was a child who seemed to have within himself, within herself, the opposite of him or her, and very likely without the slightest conscious knowledge. That *blending* is the essence of gay and bisexual presentation, and that presentation is almost completely a texture of the individual rather than anything put on. What it is, is *not-straight*. All blending softens the rigid contours of the straight.

And how much am I just projecting my own clichés? William is in his late twenties, is thin, slightly built, bookish. He is smaller than his wife, Rebecca, a striking blonde with bright red lipstick who tells me she is mistaken for a lesbian from time to time. "I've always felt myself to be really feminine," William says. "I enjoy being around women a lot more than men. And I've always, as long as I can remember, had to deal with people talking to me about being feminine. 'Are you gay? Are you not really one of the *guys?*' My mother was convinced I was gay—absolutely convinced. My best friend *is* gay, and she was sure we were lovers, and we were going to be living together, and she was ready to have him as her son-in-law. I had to say, 'Sorry, Mom, no. I'm straight.' That's why I love living in San Francisco. I grew up in Colorado with cowboys, real butch guys, and here I look so *straight*! When I first moved out here I went to lots of gay bars, and I'd never felt so masculine and so butch in my life."

What makes us men and women? A little chromosome, a spurt of chemical here and there, an idea, a hope, a holy terror. All of this begs the question, which I am reluctantly getting to, after all. You can look at bodies, at male bodies and female bodies, and see how different they are—and how much the same, how tiny and irrelevant are the things that separate us. Our bodies are combinations of extensions and folds and little more, and we can see sex as the mere slipping of one body part into and through and over another. Even a simple kiss can be devastatingly intimate viewed that way, and intercourse numbingly mundane. Why do the folds and extensions matter so? Why has so much of human history been a history of sex—of uterine envy and castration fear and homicidal jealousy, taboos and sacrifice and obsessive symphonies of passion? So much so that the poor infant in the cradle needs a set of nicely defined folds and extensions right from the start. The shape of its little hairless crotch means ever so much.

And still I don't know what a woman is, or a man. Gender isn't genitals, hormones, or chromosomes; attraction and desire isn't based simply on the shape of things. I find myself thinking again and again that I can't even know what sex is, let alone what it means to me, until I know what I am, what a woman is, what that means. But I can't know, and I think that's just one of the little lies I tell myself about sex. In a vital way gender has nothing to do with sex and sex has nothing to do with gender. Sex is far, far more than the fitting of genitals and hormones together, and gender is what it is without sex at all. Identity isn't a wholly fixed thing. If we can call into question all the forms and signs of gender, then perhaps there is no such thing as gender. Gender is *all* illusion. We create this gestalt that makes gender possible; we *make each other* men and women.

I'm sitting outside a coffee shop, watching: There goes ponytail, crew cut, miniskirt, black-belted raincoat, linen suit, like names or stories; there goes gold chain, knit vest, T-shirt, all names, all stories. Presentation and its etheric body, *presentation,* is always with us. Everywhere I turn the world drips with message and meaning, hidden agendas and outspoken purpose, rules and hopes and massive uncertainty. There is such fun in it, and such fear. We are all dressed up with no place to go.

4

"What attracts you?" I ask a man. "I'm attracted to women," he says. And already we're through the looking glass—because what does this mean? He means to tell me he is not attracted to men. He may be telling me he is attracted specifically to me. He is putting himself in a particular pool, allying himself with all other men who are "attracted to women." (But not to women who are "attracted to women.") But what does he really mean? He's not attracted to *all* women, is he? He's not even attracted to all of the women who fit a particular age or body type. He means, I think, that what we might call his "primary erotic object" will be a woman, but beyond that—what? Like all of us, he may find himself surprised by desire someday, find himself without warning attracted to someone who doesn't fit any of his notions of attractive, who may not look anything like any woman who has ever attracted him before, who may, in fact, not even be a woman. And then what does he say when I ask?

The heterosexual dynamic is about difference. This is in the plainest sense of things, bearing in mind that very little in the way of sexual attraction is compliant or even conscious. Sexual relationships are part and parcel of a larger aesthetic, a weltanschauung of community, and sexual attractions may not have anything to do with, may in fact be at war with, one's emotional ties and preferences. Both men and women are generally more comfortable and communicative with their own gender. We are meant to believe (and it certainly feels this way to anyone caught up in it, as I have been at times) that in spite of this, men and women can't leave each other alone, that life is about this bittersweet dance, the very difficulty is part of its joy. Explanations from the cosmos won't be forthcoming. Sometimes heterosexual relations seem potent, almost thrilling in their potential: opposites combining like acid and base, two warring pieces made into one. They contain the fantasy of dualism, the blending of opposites, clash and resolution: male and female, dark and light, hot and cold, soft and hard. When they work, they feel like a code deciphered.

I have at various times in my life felt seduced as much by the idea of heterosexual relations as by the experience of them. I want to surrender to heterosexuality's potential, to all the gasping satisfaction in my mother's romances, the large and small thrills of counterpoint. I gaze at classical European paintings, with their fine, pale women's faces, their soft, longing bodies, the angular, upright men; I imagine their constraints and their unspoken desire, the stays of whalebone and social restraint. And the images shiver with erotic charge, with the intense and immense separation between the genders, the stir of intimacy a single touch from the other can bring. Sometimes it doesn't matter that I know those gasping satisfactions are more fiction than reality, and that few male-female relationships really bridge the separation. Sometimes I am attracted to a man because of his sense of humor or intellect or charm; now and then, to my surprise, I am attracted to a man because he is so *male*.

Then I watch women with men and men with women—I see myself interacting with a man, and all the little skips and the failed hopes, and I think: What's the point? Men—and I mean *all* men here, I mean men— sometimes seem so different from me that any shade of eroticism disappears. They are shaped differently, their textures and aromas are different, their voices and thought patterns and vocabulary, all the colors, sounds, smells, and tastes are different, their very heads are different. I recognize nothing. Opposites don't always attract. Opposite also means alien, without common ground. This sensation is not attraction and it isn't aversion, either, but disconnectedness, as though "men" and "women" were two species that could never breed, could not conceive of breeding. They are bears, and I'm a tiger; men want one world, I want another.

I have at various times in my life been seduced by homosexuality, by the very idea of it, to the same degree and with a similar sexual charge. I want its *possibilities,* its infinite variations on a theme. Women I recognize; they are the familiar, the known, different patterns cut from one fabric. One and one combined into more than two, additive rather than diminutive. The fantasy of homosexuality isn't about being completed; it's about being *increased.* And this is as much fiction as reality, too.

Homosexual institutions are natural and universal, intense same-sex friendships the norm rather than the exception. We form all our small communities, and many of our bigger ones, largely by gender and the stereotypical myths of gender. (Witness the homoerotic, homophobic, American military.) We celebrate sameness in the fraternity, the sorority, the football team, the bridge club, the shopping trip, the dance class. Every tribe of humanity makes its male and female divisions, myriads of them, and I don't particularly care if the motivation has often as not been male fear of female power, or if the original purpose of some of these divisions was to strip women of political control. I can acknowledge that—and acknowledge with it how fearful men really are, especially of being found out to be fearful —and still be glad for the institutions. Looked at through a long lens, nothing is more unnatural than the heterosexual nuclear family. No other social institution puts two fundamentally different people together with no net, no support, no one else to turn to for love and understanding. Marriage separates where the human animal naturally groups.

Perhaps all sex is dualistic at heart. And all dualisms are sexual. Perhaps the most interesting divisions and connections have nothing to do with gender. My attraction to any particular woman, if not to women, is also fundamentally about difference. I am talking not about specific attractions, but our fantasies of attraction, the stories we tell each other and ourselves about why one person pulls, another doesn't, why we get worked up over someone when it makes no sense, why we all spend so much time concerned over the anatomical details of whoever interests us at the time. The fantasies of sexual attraction probably take up as much time in our lives as the attractions themselves, and I'm not sure they ever die completely.

All relations spark with conflict from the movement toward *anyone* outside ourselves, since all others are inevitably apart from us, separate, ultimately unknowable. For all the ease in female friendships, my romantic and sexual attractions toward women have never felt safe or bland or controlled. They are just as risky and terrifying and pregnant with possibility as any involvement with men. Not because women necessarily are as terrifying as men—but because all my sexual attractions are. Much as I dream (and my body dreams) of sex without relation or affection, sex that is just sex, I can't do it. I don't know how, and I don't think I want to learn, if only because learning such a thing would require a complete renovation of personality. Only from a distance can I have the hope of sex without emotional risk and personal responsibility, without the incredible baggage of gender and social pressure and ingroup demands. But I can dream.

My friend Don is tall, sandy-haired, with a mobile and amusing face. He still looks a lot like he did the first time we met, a long time ago. One day when I was in seventh grade, the homeroom door opened and a great gangling boy walked in with the principal. Don, at twelve, was as tall as the adults, even stooping as he did then, and he had about him a brittle quality, a mortifying shyness that made him seem ready to stumble and break apart. He sat where he was told and didn't speak. We were drawing landscape murals on big squares of butcher paper with colored pencils. A few days after his arrival I was spying on Don, who fascinated me. He was not drawing an ocean or desert or pastoral meadow like the rest of us. He had in a few days made a world, a strange, parched, off-kilter scene. He'd drawn another *planet*. And what I felt was exultation. We would be friends; we both walked outside the center of things.

Within a few months we began to go steady, to call each other "boyfriend" and "girlfriend" because we didn't know how to be friends any other way. There were so many rules, and the way we failed to master them was one thing we had in common. Don and I took long walks, and sat after school in our friend Danny's garage, playing "I Am the Walrus" forward and backward, trying to decide if Paul was really dead. We wanted to figure things out. We wondered if the way we felt was the way it was supposed to be, and we wondered what we would become. There seemed to be so few choices.

When we were freshmen, Don moved. At fourteen we were still best friends, still walking slowly to and from each other's houses after school, still calling ourselves boyfriend and girlfriend because it was how to keep the questions away, even our own questions. His leaving wrenched something loose in me. Don and I wrote to each other every week, and after several months he wrote to tell me that he was gay. I'd been lost without him, and he was telling me he'd been lost all his life.

For years afterward we saw each other only rarely. We had different demons. Once he gave me a drawing of a water glass, titled *The Glass of a Pariah*. He went through what he called his "misogynistic period," when he struggled with feelings about his mother and sisters, when he could hardly speak to me. And then we were best friends, and then we hardly spoke again, and then we talked a lot, and lately, months of hurt silence went by before another patch-up. In certain ways our worlds could hardly be more unalike, and reconciliation means taking a lot of things on faith.

Years after he first told me he was gay, I came to realize what it meant to me. I saw that he hadn't just moved away. A part of him was truly lost to me forever, had never been mine to have. I was bereft all over again when I understood that, years after he'd gone. When Don talks to me about "appreciating his own sex," he means gender and genitalia both, and he means himself, and he doesn't mean me. There is an element of masturbation in every relationship, a way no one else gets in. We are all in search of balance, an evening out of things, and whether we seek in our lover the "other" that is missing or the "self" that we recognize, it is our *selves* with which we are stuck.

Alfred Kinsey was a zoologist who specialized in the gall wasp until he became interested in human sexual behavior. In spite of many criticisms of his methods and cultural biases, his name has become synonymous with statistical sex research for a good reason. Most Americans have some sense of what he did—which was simply to talk to several thousand people and compile complex data on their sexual histories and desires. Kinsey's results aren't the whole truth. What is? But they are a part of it. When Kinsey published, he was censured and attacked for it, and the attacks continue.

The book *Kinsey, Sex and Fraud: The Indoctrination of a People,* published in 1990, is one recent example. The book, written by Judith Reisman and Edward Eichel with a cover quote by Pat Buchanan, is a frenzied and personal broadside against Kinsey and all of his work, some forty years after the fact. Reisman and Eichel claim Kinsey's real agenda was "obliterating the existing heterosexual norm" in order to create "a society in which children would be instructed in both early peer sex and 'cross-generational' sex" and heterosexuals would be encouraged to "have homosexual experiences." Reisman and Eichel are furious that "school children"—that most innocent of populations—are being taught that gays are "normal." Kinsey, they claim, was a "heterophobe"—a condition often "evidenced by gay activists, radical feminists and pedophiles."

What Alfred Kinsey really said to anger the right wing—besides the fact that "school children" had sexual feelings and fantasies—was this: Of the "total outlet" of orgasm for men, 24 percent was masturbatory, 69.4 percent was heterosexual, and 6.3 percent was homosexual.

Kinsey understood the myth many men tell themselves about gay sex: that the aggressive male is essentially heterosexual and only passive homosexual sex is truly homosexual. ("Even clinicians have allowed themselves to be diverted by such pretensions," he wrote in 1948.) His studies "make it apparent that the heterosexuality or homosexuality of many individuals is not an all-or-none proposition." He believed exclusivity of response was, in fact, unusual; that many people shift from one focus to another over time, and that about half the male population was bisexual to some extent.

Kinsey developed a scale for sexual orientation ranging from 0 to 6. A person scoring 0 on this scale has no erotic physical contact or, more important, "psychic responses" to their own sex; all "socio-sexual contacts and responses" are toward the opposite sex. A person scoring 1 has had "incidental homosexual contacts," either physical or psychic or both, and perhaps only at one period of time. And so on. A Kinsey 6 has never had any attraction, physical or psychic, to the opposite sex, and the rare 3 is "midway." Kinsey 3's "accept and enjoy both types of contacts" and have "no strong preferences" for one over the other. One in eight men will be more homosexual than heterosexual as adults, he concluded, and four percent exclusively homosexual for life. Only half of adult men are exclusively heterosexual, and many of these had homosexual experiences as adolescents.

Kinsey wisely realized that circumstances—social, religious, and otherwise—had enormous influence on sexual behavior. (He did, however, claim his research on women was free of these biases.) He thought one's degree of response more telling than one's behavior, and pointed out that behavior and desire do not necessarily accord. On the Kinsey scale you can rate more homosexual, by virtue of desire, than someone who has had more actual homosexual experience. ". . . The reality is a continuum, with individuals . . . occupying . . . every gradation between each of the categories . . ." This was Kinsey's revolution, really remarkable for the time and disturbing to the ongoing convention of clear-cut sexual preference even now. Much of what he did right was to phrase his questions for the reality of people's lives.

In 1993, a lot of media attention was given to a summary of male sexual practices, the results of a survey of 3,321 American men aged twenty to thirty-nine. The survey reportedly showed that only one percent of men were "homosexual." What it really reported was that 1.1 percent of these men had been exclusively homosexual for the last ten years. Whether or not this small sampling, which didn't account for the fact that gay men tend to group in particular regions of the country, is accurate isn't particularly meaningful. The fact is, if the surveyors really wanted to know whether or not people identified themselves as gay, felt gay, or had gay feelings, they asked the wrong question altogether.

With women Kinsey placed even more emphasis on psychological reactions than experience, and he included category "X," for women who reported no erotic responses of any kind. (A very few men qualify as X.) Women who qualify as X, Kinsey thought, may just not recognize or know how to describe their erotic response. He found more 0's among women, fewer 1–6's. Whereas fifty percent of men had had at least one response to his own sex, only twenty-eight percent of women did—a figure that seems not at all borne out among the women I know, but then, those are the women I know.

If the continuum of sexual orientation is a blur, how do we know when we've reached a certain point? Why do we care? Do people who call themselves heterosexual truly have absolutely no erotic feelings toward anyone, ever, of the same sex? Do they have these feelings so rarely or with so little intensity that their heterosexual attractions will always predominate? Or is it just a whole lot simpler and socially coherent to call oneself heterosexual (or gay) rather than bisexual? Plenty of gay men and women dislike the idea of bisexual leanings, too. Seeing orientation as an infinitely subtle blending makes choosing any single point on the scale a trifle silly, though most of us do just that, choose 0 or 6 as an identity even if our desire doesn't always mesh—even when our behavior doesn't mesh. These are the comfort zones of the twentieth century.

The deviant culture of homosexuality has ways of making fun of the "normative" culture around it, by virtue of its normative characteristics. Then normality becomes strange and invites ridicule. To call a straight person a "vanilla het" is a double insult. But more disturbing still is to refuse the proferred labels of either. This is an inherently political challenge.

My friend Carol Queen identified herself as a lesbian

for more than ten years before she "came out" as a bisexual. She wisely acknowledges the fearsome meaning of bisexuality. If you identify straight, you have to deal with half the population as potential lovers; if you identify as gay, you have only to deal with perhaps ten percent. (And either way you can proceed to cut large portions off by virtue of age, race, and body shape.) But identify as bisexual, and suddenly you've got to deal with *everyone*. (You've also got to deal with the fact that you, your solid self, has the ability to slide across the map.) Carol likes to call both gays and straights "monosexuals," but she isn't particularly fond of any of the new terms being promoted by an increasingly visible bisexual movement—words like pansexual and omnisexual. (A magazine aimed at bisexuals calls itself *Anything That Moves.)* Carol still thinks "queer" is the best word for anyone who steps outside the heterosexual rules. To call yourself queer is to step boldly off the continuum altogether.

There are so many letters to choose from these days, I feel like I could give myself the equivalent of postgraduate degrees in sexual orientation—and sometimes that I have to in order to be a card-carrying member of an approved group. In the long run, all these labels feel a little dishonest to me, because none of them say enough. Saying I'm bisexual is nothing like saying I'm in the middle of Kinsey's scale, 0 through 6, a perfect 3. I'm a 2 one day and a 5 the next, a 1 with one person and a 6 with another. And an X, nonsexual, with many others.

I believe most people are bisexual to varying extents. This seems so obvious as to sound mundane. In a more perfect world, it would not be any easier to side with one's heterosexual instincts than any others. I believe we are all penetrable, we can all penetrate, we can all be top, bottom, masculine, feminine, up and down. I also think love and passion can transcend a great many physical things, from double mastectomies to amputations to the changes that come with illness and aging. When we describe what attracts us, we are usually thinking too narrowly, and forgetting where our loyalties in fact lie, who our lovers really are and what they look like and how little that matters.

The range should not be zero through six, but zero through six hundred, or six thousand. There are not only many sexualities, there are many homosexualities, many heterosexualities, more than 31 flavors. Perhaps there is one sexuality for each of us; five billion sexual orientations, five billion patterns of desire. I suspect most of us (myself included) are capable of loving more people of different types than we realize. It's scary to be open to so much love and passion, to be so ready, to be able to respond erotically to so many people even if I never act on it, because being able to respond means being able to care. Easier to narrow it down, draw lines.

I have a fantasy about a new kind of sexual revolution. I've watched the annual Gay Pride parades become Gay and Lesbian parades, and now, just this year, become Gay, Lesbian and Bisexual parades. Perhaps in a few

years we will have Gay, Lesbian, Bisexual, and Transgendered parades; and then a little further along will
come a time when we march together in the Gay, Lesbian, Bisexual, Transgendered, Heterosexual, and Celibate Pride parade, which becomes the Sexuality Pride
parade, which then disappears for good. Obsolete.

5

Most people believe the animal closest to humans is the chimpanzee. Although not uncontroversial, current theory focuses on the other primate in the genus *Pan,* called the bonobo. Bonobos look a lot like chimpanzees. Little is known about their life in the wild, but one thing they do in captivity is spend a lot of time standing up quite straight. When I first saw photographs of bonobos I was startled at their distinctly human stance, and then wondered if, perhaps, our stance is not distinctly bonobian.

Bonobos are almost continually sexual with each other. Desmond Morris, in *The Naked Ape,* claimed that continuous sexual receptivity was a necessary part of human relations, that only the power of sex could bind men to women. Only the need for an available and fertile partner could prevent men from fighting over food and territory and force them instead into protecting women and children from other males. It's a rather bleak vision. But bonobos and other nonhuman primates present a case for at least one aspect of Morris's belief—that sexual energy is very near the darkest emotions, and the act of sex is almost magical in its power to create alliances and heal upset. Bonobos are always going at each other one way or another, and the line between sex and aggression, peace and fighting, competition and co-operation, is blurred almost as much with them as with ourselves.

Relative to body size, human males have the second-largest genitals of all the primates. Bonobos have the largest. The female vaginal opening and clitoris of the bonobo are frontally placed, as with humans. And most of the time, bonobos have sex face to face, reports Frans de Waal, a primate scientist, in his book *Peacemaking Among Primates*. Bonobos also have sex in the rear-entry position, while lying beside each other, and even while hanging from ropes. They practice open-mouth kissing and have long-lasting eye contact during sex. There is regular sexual contact between adults and children. Virtually all bonobos masturbate routinely. There is a large amount of homosexuality, both male and female, including mock intercourse and mutual masturbation, fellatio, and group sex in many variations. When a couple is engaged in sex, other bonobos will often surround them, poking, teasing, and chiding the mating couple. The rate of sexual contacts climbs dramatically after a fight.

In one of de Waal's photo sequences of captive bonobos, one dominant male charges another. The second flees, only to crawl back a few moments later. The dominant male hugs him, both grinning nervously. The submissive male then lies flat on his back, his knees drawn up sharply, arms stretched over his head, while the winner rubs the loser's genitals. This is a routine bonobian event, repeated frequently throughout the day, but captured for us on film it becomes a peculiarly embarrassing display. Bonobos are more dramatically *in public* with their sexuality than cattle or squirrels or even dogs. Their sexual behavior can't be excused as the result of just rut and pheromones. Both males and females have orgasms, de Waal believes. "The official line of reasoning is that satisfaction is irrelevant for female primates . . . I believe that we should never place theory above observable facts. Female primates are equipped with a clitoris, an organ with only one known function."

Bonobos are so near to me and yet so different, but I believe absolutely in bonobian erotic pleasure, in the complexity of their response and desire. I think bonobos share, with humans, elephants, and cetaceans, a sexual consciousness—an ability to choose sex both for its immediate and its more lasting consequences. They make plain the twin faces of sex: tranquilizer and amphetamine. Sex as meditation, as a trance, melting the self away. Sex as a kick, a psychic cattle prod, solidifying the self and those around us. Bonobos lust.

Augustine believed the real punishment given to Adam and Eve wasn't nakedness or shame, but lust. The nakedness and the shame followed the libido, as it were; they were part and parcel to the God-given agony of sexual desire. Punishment it certainly can seem at times —and punishment it was for Augustine, who suffered miserably from recalcitrant desire. If sexuality is a body, then desire is its blood.

Born with predispositions, shaped by the environment, the sexual individual is a palimpsest with many sets of writing one atop the other. The things that contain enormous importance in moments of sexual contact —those *things* that we desire and can't explain—are the fruit of tiny moments, they are acts unbidden in childhood, dreams never remembered, bodies barely seen. A perfume, a sound, the shape of a leg, eventually becomes the arousing potential of hair or leather or shiny black shoes, the urge to feel the riding crop, to encircle a tiny waist or embrace large buttocks. An idea never spoken, a deed secretly done, becomes hunger—for lingerie or cotton rope, hunger to be entered or tickled, whispered to or beaten senseless or kissed for hours. Once given to us, these dreams can't be given back.

One of the good questions Alfred Kinsey asked in the 1940s had to do with the "non-sexual sources of erotic response" of preadolescent and adolescent boys. The list generated was long and instructive, and included sitting in class, punishment, accidents, fast elevators, sitting in church, fear of intruders, tests, getting home late, big fires, marching soldiers, band music, harsh words, losing one's balance, a long flight of stairs, the national anthem, money, dreams of giants and wild animals, and much, much more. Was there anything not on the list? Could there be? I wonder how much of a kick the boys got from thinking up things to tell the interviewer.

I had a professor many years ago, a strange man who taught me anatomy and physiology for a year. He was tall, slim, bald, and never seen without a lab coat on. He was famous throughout the small college for a number of reasons, but one was his seeming ability to memorize the names of every one of his hundreds of students the first day of class, and from that day on to never forget, even recognizing voices in the dark as he showed slides. He kept specimens in his office, including a row of about twenty preserved fetuses in jars, graduated by size and ending with a one-day-old infant. "Someone found it in the toilet at the Greyhound station," he told me when I asked.

Dr. W. never talked about himself. He was all business, seeming to have no other pleasures or desires than his students, his slides, his cadavers. One could not imagine him naked, or subject to any whim or impulse. (Believe me, we tried. He could not even be embarrassed.) He was the best teacher I have ever had in any subject, and I was one of several students who volunteered to assist him for that reason. Late in the year we studied that most undissectable and slippery thing, memory.

"Why," I asked in the office one day, "are some of our memories of childhood so vague and others so bright when they aren't any more or less important?" I had long ago learned to phrase my questions to him with care; we all talked that way around him.

For the first time I saw him take on a look of abstraction, a look, as it were, of *memory*. "Once when I was a small boy," he said, "I remember sitting in the back of the car, and looking up, and seeing a window high on a house. It was oval"—he sketched it in the air—"and I remember looking at it until we passed by, and I have never forgotten it. It's like I saw it yesterday." He paused, holding this sensation of seeing in its depth. For the first and only time I saw appetite in Dr. W. for that window, that boy. "I have no idea why some memories are bright," he added, and turned to the next task. But from these tiny moments our selves, erotic and otherwise, are born.

Our "primary erotic attachments," whatever they may be, *are* dissectable; they can be reduced surprisingly far. A man is attracted to women, he tells me. What do you find particularly attractive? I ask innocently. "I love long legs," he says. So the primary object has its own primary parts. Of the leg, it is perhaps most delectably the calf, the calf turned a certain way—but again, not all calves, on all legs, on all women. All desire is fetishistic. Fetishistic objects need to be touched again and again, as though to ensure us they haven't disappeared, are still there, still real. The fetish *is* what is abnormally focused. My own desires are compulsions that rise and fall, retreat, compel: The triangle of a man's shoulders, back, and hips, moving as he moves, gliding, turning. The delicate hollow at the base of a woman's neck, that pulsing depression, that gentle U of bone, the plain of soft skin below. And the fetish goes on, enlarging, clarifying. A falling corner of clothing, the slither of sheets. Acts are like this, too, so fraught with erotic potential, they take on the characteristics of objects: to *do* a certain thing, to slip a hand between the buttons on a lover's shirt. The act is infinitely variable, infinitely repeatable, the way an object is always new and always there.

Sexual desire is unwilled, but it has a literal life—any given desire is born, lives, evolves, ages, changes, dies. You enter, or *go into* a state of desire without warning, and you can exit it the same way—*come out* of desire all at once, surprised, suddenly cool, frustrated, bereft. The person who has the desire is not its tool but not exactly its master, either. Any one of us can try not to act on any of our impulses, and we often succeed, but the impulse lives on no matter what we choose, demanding, insistent, tedious. And some are far more irresistible than others. Lying in bed in a hotel, hearing the faint, rhythmic squeaking of the bed on the opposite side of the wall, you're bound to feel an impulse of some kind or other.

Looking at your own sexuality, you reach a point where you can abandon yourself to it—to the *fact* of your sexuality, whatever it is. At first, I wrote "you reach a point where you have to abandon yourself," but of course you don't *have to,* there is nothing inevitable about it. To do so is truly wanton, in the purest sense of the word: The wave climbs up until it collapses of its own weight, and you drown. Control is gone. You are willing to be wholly and truly seen; you have abandoned everything.

The broad plain of sexual desire rises unbidden, of its own separate, uncontrollable accord, and it surprises, disconcerts, and sometimes pleases the person in whom it rises. Roland Barthes caught himself scrutinizing his lover's body, and, fascinated with his own scrutiny, sought to know *"the cause of my desire . . .* I am like those children who take a clock apart in order to find out what time is." But such obsession is only partly about the other's body. It is more, and more importantly, about the *other,* the maddening, fascinating opacity of the other who can't be forgotten even for a moment.

The aroused state hurts and pleases at once, and the degree of painful frustration rises exactly in accord with the degree of deepening pleasure. When we are aroused, the ego wrestles the superego to the ground, and while they're fighting the mute and mindless id runs the show. Hormones, genetics, pheromones, who cares? I just want *that*—or this. I want it so much I can barely think of anything else, I want it here, now, any way I can.

Another's appetite can destroy us. Hunger makes us into food, a thing, something to be devoured, even if the hunger is for love. Too much desire makes desire's fulfillment impossible, because desire itself becomes the goal and the conclusion.

I had a lover years ago who seemed insatiable. It wasn't sex he couldn't get enough of, but nearness, and sex was the only way he thought that could happen. He kissed me as though he were willing to chew through my skin to get inside me, own me, to be not alone. When I left him I felt eaten up, and I hated it. At that time I was caught up in romantic ideals and thought I should want to be adored. But when he approached me with such single-mindedness, I couldn't breathe. With him, I wanted less desire, far less, not more.

I walked out, not long ago, at eight-thirty on a clear, fragrant spring morning. Gnats were stirring in the still sunshine and no one else was about. I was still sleepy, thinking only of the morning paper and a cup of tea as I walked down a path between apartments. Suddenly in the hush of the day I could hear the repeated moans of a woman through a curtained, half-open window. Her voice was breathy, catching in her throat, climbing higher in tone and louder in volume. I stood rooted to the path for a few seconds, saw the open window next to me with thin white curtains fluttering in the slight breeze, and then walked on, hearing how quickly she was racing toward her finish. I couldn't help but imagine her, what she looked like, what she was doing, whether she was one of the neighbors I nodded at when I picked up my mail. Her guttural, meaningless sounds infected me with desire like a virus caught from the air. I could barely walk a straight line to the sidewalk.

The way water ends thirst, and food ends hunger, sex ends arousal. For now, at least, because it will inevitably return. People I see every day without reaction will suddenly change, their appearance will have new meaning, their walk, smile, smell will signal me as surely as a baboon's buttocks signal her mate. Perhaps I have a crush, all at once; certainly this shift in awareness carries enormous weight. Perhaps I'm merely . . . *horny.*

Horny means a million things: It means wanting sweat, but also skin, to touch and be touched, *anywhere,* to suck and lick, be penetrated, to feel a finger slip between my shirt buttons, and then in between my breasts. Feeling horny is like being pregnant with desire, restless and premonitory, swollen. Predatory, as though I were hunting. I begin to act unseemly, I get reckless, attentive to every person with whom I have the most casual contact. The smallest of meetings shivers with imagined meaning. Alone in this state I get restless, and watch television, and every show seems laden with entendre, each character on the screen speaking directly to me.

"To submit to lust is to declare a panic, a state of body emergency," Susie Bright writes. She is trying to explain the illogical urge with which she left one lover for another, against what might be called better judgment. Desire can be a pure frenzy of neurotransmitters, like acid in the drinking water, voodoo, hypnosis, a curse. I know exactly what Susie means; I'm still embarrassed by a brief affair I had many years ago with someone whose company I couldn't stand but who nevertheless drew me sexually like a drug I had to have, a monkey on my back. Can judgment, rational thought, or foresight affect us, once panic has hold? And can anyone outside, looking in, fully appreciate the frenzy involved? That we *can* just control our sexual selves is one of those maddening pronouncements with which Americans are raised, a pronouncement often delivered with smarmy self-righteousness. Promiscuity is a mental illness; "sex addicts" seek treatment. (A gay male friend tells me that a men's sex addict group he attends is his best pickup spot.) One of the most widely censured of behaviors—passionate sex with total strangers—is perhaps the most common fantasy shared by men and women alike.

Sexual jealousy is almost as violent a state as sexual desire; both are composed mostly of misery, with flecks of rage and grief mixed in. Both are about possession of another, of *the* other. Both are obsessive, racking, poten-

tially lethal; they are Shiva alive in our groin, hard
enough to break lives, murder, wage war, destroy em-
pires.

In his book *Smut,* Murray Davis talks about the slippage
involved in arousal, the way we just wake up already in
it. "Erotic reality is entered so gradually that the unwary
may find themselves entering it against their will . . .
as if by some gravitational force: the closer they get, the
stronger the pull, as though the very space around the
object of their desire were curved in an Einsteinian
way." There may be something to this sublimation
thing, after all; when I want sex, it tends to get in the
way of empire-building. And everything else. If I were a
baboon, I would wear a red and swollen flag on my ass
and stink of sex to all around me. Sometimes I swear I
can smell it on myself.

There are people still who think the so-called sexual
revolution of the 1960s was "caused" by the birth control
pill, that if we pass out condoms in high schools we will
somehow cause teenagers to have sex. This theory seems
to be based on the belief that we can control ourselves, be
it through hard work, prayer, or whole grains. But it is
really based on the belief that even in the best of times
we're barely in check. Humans are really raving beasts
held back only by the threat of social punishments like

disease or pregnancy or a scarlet *A*. That animal rut is not unnatural or perverse, but all *too* natural, always straining at the leash, waiting to overwhelm and destroy civilization ("the family") as soon as it's released from sublimation. "Family values" advocates and others who bemoan our society as degraded and apocalyptic, pointing out various ills like homosexuality and pornography as examples of what is destroying the fabric of our society, would be distressed to know how Freudian they are. They are evangelically Freudian: They believe human desire is enormously powerful and that the human animal has no natural urge to live in monogamous nuclear families. They believe giving teenagers condoms is tantamount to moral lawlessness precisely because sex *is* what teens really want to do. The only way to maintain social institutions is to ferret out and suppress all temptations not to be in social institutions. Freud predicted terrible things from the free release of the instincts, and so does Jesse Helms.

There is lust, and then there is *my* lust, which sometimes makes me pull up short and say, Hey! Wait a minute. I'm a *girl*. Nice girls don't. Within the realm of desire is female desire, which has always been treated differently and with a lot more contradiction than male desire. In old pornography, I find more interest in cunnilingus than fellatio, an obsession with the maidenhead, with plump and voluptuous women, lingerie, and a male desire for submission to the power of a woman's body. Reading historical pornography, I sometimes have to remind myself it's all been written by men—or so we are told.

If I imagine some of these old books written by anonymous country women, they take on a whole new meaning. So many of them take female lust as their driving force. *Forbidden Fruit,* published in 1898, creates a world of oral sex, spanking, orgies, and incest out of that monster, the lustful mother. A year earlier *School Life in Paris* was published, consisting of letters from seventeen-year-old Blanche to her cousin Ethel, describing the adventures of lesbian schoolgirls. They use strap-on dildos, named—in order of size—the Baby, the School-boy, the Captain, and the Giant. The girls even invent fake ejaculate. A short while later *Female Lust* was published. The plot is a roller coaster of lesbian wantonness, female ejaculation, and dildos. Old aunts fuck young maids, friends fuck friends and strangers, nuns spank schoolgirls and then fuck each other. A woman butt-fucks a boy of fifteen with her clitoris. All this and more in the first forty pages.

In the world of pornography, female lust has usually been constructed as a force of great power, and the consequences of unleashing it is a dominant theme. Erotica —and not coincidentally, much of religious thought on sex—has through the ages concerned itself either directly or indirectly with what women want, what women do, what women *are.* A Chinese monk once said,

"Females are demons. If there were no women, every man would be a Bodhisattva." Homosexuality among Tibetan monks was seen as a good thing because it helped the monks get over their desire for women.

One of the common themes of dirty jokes in China is that of the woman who is always aroused and ready for sex, who tries to hide behind a screen of decorum but can't. Whether jokes focus on the act of intercourse itself, or adultery, or the secret sex lives of priests and nuns, the theme is often that of a lack of control, indiscreet and wild sex behind the extremes of etiquette in Chinese society. The bride who can't get enough sex, who goes so far as to prevent her husband from having a concubine, might even disguise herself *as* his concubine, is the taboo source of humor here.

The Orientalist Howard Levy, who has made a study of erotic jokes, tells this one: "On the first night the groom embraced the bride and said, 'Because of the wedding your father was extremely bothered but finally we're here.' And having said this right away he did it once with her. 'Your mother too was extremely bothered but finally we're here.' And he did it with her a second time. 'Your elder brother didn't do a thing on our behalf but now we're here.' And he did it with her a third time. As soon as they finished, the bride spoke and said, 'My sister-in-law didn't say anything good about us either!' "

I know the belief that there is something unnatural about female desire is embedded in me no matter how much I fight it. Appetite in a woman is wanton by its very existence. Many sexual attitudes hinge on the belief that women either are not or somehow should not be as sexually aggressive, voracious, or emotionally disinterested during sex as men. "Women are more interested in relationships than in sex" is a cliché repeated in a thousand ways, ad infinitum. The real message is that women *should be* more interested in relationships than in sex. People will argue the truth of the assumption that women are not as sexually aggressive as men by nature by the fact that women *don't* in fact act as aggressively, despite the fact that there are a thousand and one culturally imposed reasons why they don't. They don't because they're not supposed to, because they're punished if they do, and that's proof they naturally should not. It's a merry-go-round of illogic.

Because they don't need to have erections for sex, because they in fact show no objectively visible signs of arousal necessarily, women are doubly suspect—supposed always to be reluctant when it comes to sex but perhaps always ready for it at a moment's notice. This is the weird, circular logic of misogyny, in which women are supposed to be the opposite of what they are suspected to truly be, and that suspicion fuels endless devious efforts at control. Clitoridectomies, oophorectomies, and sometimes complete hysterectomies were done in great numbers in the mid to late 1800s to cure female sexual appetite and various medical ills, including the rampaging epidemic of hysteria.

I don't think it's an accident that religious and moral

fundamentalism—of all kinds, in all religions—always has a core of misogynism. Religiously based antisex attitudes focus both on the evil power of female sexuality and the dread consequences to a pure woman soiled by sex. Likewise, religious and moral tolerance and celebration of sex as a life force, an expression of joy, love, and creation, tends to venerate women however it is constructed.

My mother, far more than I, was raised to fear the free release of sexual impulse. A World War II marriage manual has this to say about undue desire: "The most common sign is an increase in weight. . . . Many of the great women writers and designers are those who have learned to use their sexual emotions along lines of creative endeavor. This requires great will power and persistent training. . . . The woman who is constantly on the go, who is active mentally and physically, will have little time left for morbid thoughts."

As for men, the same author blames drugs and alcohol: "Narcotics, such as opium, mescaline, heroin and other dangerous drugs will arouse a man sexually far beyond his normal needs." He recommends sports, travel, and sedatives, and cautions against masturbation. "No autoerotic indulgence is entirely normal. It is best that they all be avoided. A more practical solution is for an oversexed man to marry an oversexed woman, but this is much easier said than done."

Prudery is essentially contempt. The prudish view is one of the human as permanently immature, of all people as children, or, more precisely, morons—malleable, easily led, unreliable. If it's not sex, then it will be alcohol or gambling or other temptations that will lead us astray from our proper course. The life we should lead is never seen as a temptation; the desire to do right, make a family, have a career, or serve others is never tempting enough to hold us in the face of other, more immediately satisfying pleasures. Sex and its expressions, like pornography, are drugs. One taste leads to the next; soft-core leads to hard. And think what hard-core leads to.

Watching my first adult movie, watching, for the first time, a man penetrate another woman, was like leaving my body all at once. I was outside my body, watching, because she on the screen above me *was* me; and then I was back in my body very much indeed. My lust was aroused as surely and uncontrollably by the sight of sex as hunger can be roused by the smell of food. I know how naive this sounds now, but I had never quite believed, until I saw it, that the sex in such films was *real,* that people fucked in front of cameras, eyes open. I found it a great shock because it told me how many different things sex could mean to other people than it had yet meant to me. Suddenly I *had* to see sex as both bigger and smaller than I had before. I didn't, contrary to certain predictions, then leave home and hearth for a life of degradation. I probably didn't even have sex that night; the experience was too confusing to be that simply solved. Desire isn't necessarily pleasant at all, and rarely pure.

Soft-core leads to hard, and sometimes hard-core leads to soft. Sometimes I feel a surfeit of desire, a topping out, a longing for release. I've felt more with dirty movies and books than arousal. A scene: A woman going down on a man, avidly sucking his cock, the man pulling away and shooting come across her face, the woman licking the come off her lips. When I first saw these images I felt a heady mix of disgust and excitement, and confusion at that mix. Porn mixed things up too much. The more I watched pornography, the more layers peeled off my experience of lust, one layer after the other, because I didn't always like my own response. When something dark and forbidden emerges, I resist it still. My body is sometimes provoked by what my mind reproves.

Desire doesn't always fog vision and confuse thoughts; there is in desire the power to see a new way; desire has a way of enrapturing and elevating the object of desire. We find desire in us for a person we love, no matter what our preconceptions about our preferences; an instantaneous love might rise from the bed in which we have sex. We love in the moment when we *see,* clearly, into another's heart, and that can happen all at once, as truly in a moment of sexual touch as in any other. In my more contented moments I think sexual desire can peel away the artificial constructs we place on each other. The ugliness layered on our bodies and hearts is transcended, overridden, by powerful arousal, until true beauty is revealed. By admitting our physical desire for another, we admit our humanity, and in that admission, open the possibility of psychological love.

"When I go to bed at night it is a kind of torture for me. I will not write on this page what fills my mind, the very madness of desire," James Joyce wrote to his beloved Nora. "I see you in a hundred poses, grotesque, shameful, virginal, languorous. . . . Be beautiful and happy and loving and provoking, full of memories, full of cravings, when we meet." A few months later he wrote of his deep love for her, his affection, but, he added, "side by side and inside this spiritual love I have for you there is also a wild beast-like craving for every inch of your body, for every secret and shameful part of it, for every odour and act of it. . . . It allows me to burst into tears of pity and love at some slight word, to tremble with love for you at the sounding of some chord or cadence of music." Joyce felt his terrible itch, and in it, the terrible strangeness of Nora. The next day he writes that he is "in a fever-fit of animal desire. . . . As you know, dearest, I never use obscene phrases in speaking. You have never heard me, have you, utter an unfit word before others. When men tell me in my presence here filthy or lecherous stories I hardly smile. Yet you seem to turn me into a beast. It was you yourself, you naughty shameless girl who first led the way . . . I love you, Nora, and it seems that this too is part of my love. Forgive me! forgive me!"

For his whole life Joyce was desperate with sexual urging, embarrassed and obsessed by it, bewildered by the addictive power of sin. (What I quote here from his letters are the tame parts.) The fear of sin is never far away. To desire is to live God's punishment; to be a woman and feel desire is to repeat Eve's disastrous act. There are times when a sad and empty feeling comes over me as I contemplate sex. I feel not so much that it is degrading or dangerous, but cheap. A sanctimonious voice whispers in my ear: *We must transcend ourselves.* We must cultivate the higher arts. Why am I not distracted, as I hurriedly cook dinner, by a strain from one of Mozart's operas instead of—what distracts me? But Mozart's operas are all about obsession and desire. Why is my mind not filled with the paintings of the masters? Naked women, velvet drapery, Leda and her swan—no help there. The classics—Homer, *Pride and Prejudice, Anna Karenina.* No help at all. I suspect even the purveyors of high-toned reprimands, the ones who claim more mature and refined interests, have been on their knees howling at the moon once or twice.

I get a lot of interesting stuff in the mail these days, underground miracles of desktop publishing. Some of these magazines are rough and homemade, others slick and witty; most are funny, creepy, smart, and bizarre, and I'm often struck by the sophisticated intelligence in their pages. They are filled with stories of fantasies and fetishes, overwhelming lust, hopeful secret journeys toward understanding. When I get that feeling, that blue-blood nonsense about higher callings, I pick up *Slippery When Wet* or *Taste of Latex* or *Tit Clamps* and feel better. My role models aren't so much people who are doing anything differently from me, but all the other people trying to figure this damned thing out, bravely walking through their own shame and nonsense.

Besides, as one friend points out with a laugh, "Some of the best sex I've ever had was cheap, tawdry, and meaningless." I can hear the chuckles of my role models now, tarty girls in black leather and nasty boys grabbing their crotches. If everything was coated with a seal of approval, some of the fun would go out of it. Let's get away with something. Degrade me, baby.

II

Arousal

6

I'm surprised still by my own conservatism, my own rather fussy aversions. Aversion suddenly appears, without warning. I've read a lot of explicit sexual material lately, fictional and otherwise. I am frequently aroused and sometimes disturbed. I am disturbed not so much by the acts others perform and dream of performing, but by the consuming intensity of their dreams. I want more safety in my own sexual response, more control over my own reactions. But any judgmental feeling I have about sex tends to be directed toward myself. My whispered words might be, "That's naughty," or "That's bad," but what I mean is "Pervert."

Murray Davis, in his book *Smut,* rather neatly delineates the limits of socially acceptable sex by defining its unacceptable forms. His list begins "Sex Through Distance" (as in voyeurism and porn), "Sex Through Pain and Provocation," "Sex With Things" (or people treated as things), "With Beasts or Gods" (or people treated as beasts or gods), "With Two Few and Too Many Others," "With Wrong Sense Receptors" (such as the mouth or anus), "Within Ingroups" (like families or people of the same gender), "With Outgroups" (like people too different in age, race, class, or religion), and ends with sex "Involving Subjugation and Domination." Looked at this way, it becomes a daunting task first to find an allowable sexual partner and second, to avoid doing the wrong thing—wanting the wrong thing, *thinking* the wrong thing ("Oh, master!").

Perversity, like obscenity, is a relative condition; we define it for ourselves. Joyce, in his Catholic confusion, certainly believed himself to be a pervert—a pervert because of what he desired, and because he couldn't stop trying to get it. He hated his desire's *drive* as much as its content. (And again and again, he blamed Nora for that drive.) The word *perversion* is so insidious and sly; it sounds rich and oily on the tongue. One likes saying it out loud. But it means only what we don't respond to ourselves; a perversion is whatever we can't enjoy.

Everyone, everywhere, considers something outside

the pale; phobias can be latent just like desires. Last year I was a guest on a radio talk show. The topic was pornography, but the agenda, it turned out, was titillation. I was not surprised; it's surprisingly difficult for otherwise hard-hitting interviewers to make sense about sex, to see beyond their own blinders, to even acknowledge their blinders.

"What about perversions?" he asked me in the middle of a discussion about the regulation of adult bookstores. "Isn't there something wrong with that?"

"What do you mean by 'perverted'?" I asked. "Define the term."

"Well," he said, and, "Well, you know."

"Tell me what *you* think is perverted—or, better yet, tell me what is *not* perverted. What's normal sex?"

And he said, "Well, I guess, a man and a woman having intercourse."

"Do you mean gay people are perverted?" I asked, and he cut to a commercial, and after the commercial he ended the interview. Because he is a liberal, after all, and he would never say he thought gays were perverted; I doubt if he knows he believes that at least a little. But the question betrayed him, the very notion of perversion betrays us. If he'd been willing, I would have asked him where he drew his other lines, his other boundaries. Was bondage all right? Was it all right with a silk handkerchief but not with chains? Was anal intercourse perverted? Was oral sex, leather play, dressing up?

To call a sexual behavior "abnormal" means to ignore

the fact that to its practitioner the act feels utterly, ineluctably *normal*—normative. Not only does it feel right for a gay man to kiss another man, it feels wrong for him to kiss a woman in the same way. "Normality is, of course, a very difficult concept to define, being usually considered the equivalent of statistically common and accepted acts in the society doing the defining," wrote Gershon Legman in his peculiar treatise on oral sex, *Oragenitalism.* "So understood, obviously neurotic and mentally diseased actions are regularly applauded as normal in cultures that are themselves abnormal or insane." And acts that might somewhere else seem ordinary are condemned as mentally diseased.

The first time I thought about sex in terms of perversities was when I read *Rubyfruit Jungle,* Rita Mae Brown's lesbian-coming-of-age novel. Brown's heroine, Molly Bolt, is in the big city at last and completely broke when she's offered $100 to throw grapefruits at a man who can't have orgasms any other way. "I picked up another one and carefully took aim. Squish! I got him square in the middle. He squealed with delight and got a hard-on. This isn't so bad. I like throwing things. By now I was into hitting Ronnie. I aimed for cock. Bull's-eye. He loved it." I was seventeen when I read *Rubyfruit Jungle,* and still bless Rita Mae Brown for that scene, which I've remembered many times over the years. I remember wondering at length about all its permutations. Why grapefruit, and not oranges, for instance? I took it to heart—Ronnie's happy squeals, most of all—

and my ideas about sex and what it could be grew a hundred-fold that day.

Perversity is not only relative to the culture, but, like obscenity, a condition in constant flux. Religiously and criminally persecuted perversions have at one time or another included all forms of homosexuality, incest, prostitution, adultery, fornication, oral sex, anal sex, and exhibitionism. A 1942 marriage manual lists as part of "the perverse component of the normal libido" voyeurism, cunnilingus, kleptomania, pyromania, and the use of fantasy. "Fortunately, in normal persons," the book informs us, "these perverse elements are so thoroughly repressed that they give no trouble."

Perverse sex acts are considered "crimes against nature," a characteristic not dependent on their being rare. Annie Sprinkle was arrested for sodomy (and "conspiracy to commit sodomy," a curious twist) because of a photograph of her making love with a female friend of hers who has an amputated foot. Afterward, she said, " 'Sodomy' in Rhode Island was an 'abominable, detestable act against nature.' Nature didn't mind at all." In fact, little has changed; some of the most common, even universal behaviors like oral and anal sex are still considered perverse by a lot of people and are still crimes in a number of states, prosecuted only when convenient. In Las Vegas in 1993, Nina Hartley and ten other porn actresses were arrested after a benefit show. (The ten cops involved first watched the entire three-and-a-half-hour show.) Hartley had given a comic lecture on how to make love to a woman while two other actresses "demonstrated" the joy of cunnilingus. They were charged under the Nevada "Infamous Crimes Against Nature" law, which prohibits same-gender sex even in private, even when nature doesn't mind. Perversions exist only when there are rules about acceptable erotic attachments.

We all have limits, and not always the ones we expect. What about behaviors most people haven't tried and many haven't even imagined? Frottage: the getting of sexual pleasure from rubbing your body against something. (That's a frotteur behind you in the elevator.) Acrotomophilia: depriving yourself of oxygen during sex to increase the power of an orgasm. What about a love of douches, a love of urine, a love for boots, a sexual desire for pregnant women? What about bestiality, of which there are myths, paintings, limericks, and anecdotes galore? The Navahos said Badger gave women desire by licking their genitals. And then there's Leda and the swan, a pretty picture. What about infantilism, the urge to wear diapers and be put to bed by Mama one more time? Hyphephilia, the love of hair, fur, furry things. Klismaphilia, the love of enemas. One person may fetishize rubber, another leather, and yet another may simply fetishize *costume,* the idea of dressing up any of a hundred ways. What about the secret things most of us do now and then, or wish we could do, but never speak about? Like algolagnia, otherwise painful sensations that turn into sexual pleasure, like the getting and giving of hickeys, scratches, love bites, and pinches. Like spanking, whipping, slapping. What about begging, please, talk dirty to me, dear?

The editor of *Leg Show* magazine says: "I'd say the most common interest is in a small, well formed, high arched, straight toed, soft, unblemished female foot with a certain amount of odor." Fetishism is infinite; by definition, there are no bounds, no places the experience of fetishism cannot (will not) go. The fetish can be anything, can mean anything. Fetishes are almost always harmless, not only in content but by nature. But they can cause tremendous anguish if they aren't the shared fetishes of culture, like the female breast. Now *that's* a fetish for you.

One need only read a column of personal ads to know sex comes in a lot of shapes and sizes. In my little provincial city weekly I've found ads searching for people with amputations, for slaves of both genders and all sizes, for fellow lovers of lingerie, for a "white girl with overlapping toes," for an albino. Sometimes I laugh, and then catch myself laughing. I never want to laugh at the desires of another; I'm sure a lot of people take what I consider trifling or silly to be terribly important, and vice versa. I'm told by women who do phone sex for a living that it's very common for men to fantasize about being anally penetrated during intercourse, an urge they can't confess to their lovers but have to tell *some*one. When you have an urge this strong, you will be restless until it's filled.

James Joyce sent money to Nora in his letters, with a

detailed description of the kind of underwear he wanted
her to buy: "I would like you to wear drawers with three
or four frills one over the other at the knees and up the
thighs and great crimson bows in them, I mean not
schoolgirls' drawers with a thin shabby lace border, tight
round the legs and so thin that the flesh shows between
them but women's (or if you prefer the word) ladies'
drawers with a full loose bottom and wide legs, all frills
and lace and ribbons, and heavy with perfume . . .
Goodbye, my darling whom I am trying to degrade and
deprave. How on God's earth can you possibly love a
thing like me?" It bothered him that she left her clean
laundry about so that others could see her underwear.
"O, I wish that you kept all those things *secret, secret,*
secret. I wish you had a great store of all kinds of under-
clothes, in all delicate shades, stored away in a great
perfumed press . . . Are you offended by my horrible
shameless writing, dear? I expect some of the filthy
things I wrote made you blush. Are you offended because I said I loved to look at the brown stain that comes
behind on your girlish white drawers? I suppose you
think me a filthy wretch. How will you answer those
letters? I hope and hope you *too* will write me letters
even madder and dirtier than mine to you."

What about encratism, the deliberate abstinence from
sex for a period of time in order to build up sexual
energy so strong it magnetically attracts others? What
about celibacy? A rare practice, if I've ever heard of one,

and often practiced not out of any spiritual goal but from a neurotically narrowed sexual identity. If all sexual desires were acceptable, would there be closet celibates, getting a thrill out of their deprivation? (Are there now?) The existence of what I might call the less commonly expressed sexual appetites is a double proof. That the intense sexual flavor of an act may not even include genitalia proves the textured complexity of our sexuality. At the same time, it proves what any thinking person knows: The acts of sex are about a lot more than the acts.

Murray Davis points out that our erotic arenas are sometimes manipulated or touched or used in ways that mimic sex but are not sex, such as during pelvic exams and prostate exams. Woe to the foot fetishist, to the man who loves a woman's neck or ear above all, to the woman easily excited by the rub of cloth against her thighs, because these people, like prudes, are surrounded by the bare revelation of sex all the time. Eroticism intrudes now and then upon the least imaginative among us, in small hints and little reminders. The fetishist and the prude have the same problem; sex is everywhere.

I was watching a short film called *Daddy and the Muscle Academy* with three other women, two of them gay and one straight. *Daddy* is a documentary of the art of a man known as Tom of Finland, who created an entire genre of superrealistic images of gay men. Tom's men are heroic, idealized, and enormously muscular; they have square heads, round buttocks, and exaggerated

genitalia. They are often attired in military uniforms or
biker leathers. Tom's art has inspired an adoring audience of men to dress in similar fashion; he was an influence on Robert Mapplethorpe, Herb Ritts, and Bruce
Weber.

In the film Tom talks about the outsized, mythic quality of his subjects as a way to expand behavior as well as
ideas, to tweak people. Much of the work is obviously
tongue-in-cheek (and in everything else, too). Its more-
of-everything quality, he insists, is aimed at men who
feel like failures, who have been criticized and abused
for their gayness. "I want to encourage them," he says,
with these proud images. I've heard criticism of Tom's
work before from people who felt he idealized Fascism.
But the images are essentially anarchic, something Tom
himself understands as a direct result of his boyhood
experiences in World War II. He draws images of authority, often terrifying authority—Nazis recur frequently—and then he makes these authoritarians sexual
and vulnerable by virtue of their sexuality. In the end the
authority figure is literally undressed and seduced. Fascism gets fucked—and likes it.

"Sick," said one of my female companions. "Boring,"
said another. "Disgusting." But how can any of us be
critical of an aesthetic or offended by a behavior we
cannot truly comprehend? Tom's world is not only outside our experience as women, but outside any possible
experience we could have.

———

National Geographic has always held a fascination for pubescents of both sexes. It certainly fascinated me, but not because of the occasional bare breast or man wearing nothing but a codpiece. The real eroticism of other cultures to this middle-class, small-town white girl was *decoration,* the exotic world of decoration almost wholly absent from my own world. Tattoos all over the body and on the face, the oddly pleasing geometry of scarring, the elongated earlobes and lips and nostrils, women who wear piles of heavy metal rings around their necks till their collarbones droop like pine boughs under snow.

Tattoos, scarification, and body piercing are normal among many people, perhaps among *most* people. To be untouched and clean-skinned is taboo, then. What and where the marks and holes end up is culturally determined, but getting them seems to be an unquestionably good idea to most societies. Piercing seems to be a way of learning the world doesn't end where your skin does, that *you* don't, that you extend outward and can join and be chained to, bound up with the world, bound to others sewn together in the same way. Americans have their own few and meager methods of binding and belonging. Instead of elaborate body painting, we have lipstick and eyeshadow. (Red lips like red vulva, eyes big and dark in arousal.) We have lingerie, neckties, tight jeans, high heels, anorexia and liposuction.

There are about twenty-three "traditional" sexual piercings. You can pierce through all or part of the penis, the frenum (that web between the foreskin and the penile head), the edge of the penis head, the foreskin itself, through the skin between the scrotum and anus, between the scrotum and penis. Women pierce their inner and outer labia, their clitoral hood, and even the clitoris itself if the clitoris is big enough to hold a ring or bar. Piercing often increases sexual pleasure. For a few people the piercing itself may carry an erotic thrill, but for most it's the finished piercing that counts. Both the pierced and their partners claim sex is better with genital piercings.

There is something strange and also serenely common about the whole idea of piercing. Is it any stranger to pierce your nipple than to lift iron weights until your body becomes a new shape altogether? Women in this culture get their breasts sliced open and have two pillows of saline inserted, men pay doctors to withdraw a little fat from their buttocks with a needle and inject it into their forehead wrinkles. Which incision is the oddest one?

Perversion. The normal. Confession. Release. I have five photos. Each shows two people making love on a couch in essentially the same position. In one a man is penetrating a woman, who lies below him; her legs are embracing him, and you can just see his penis as he enters her vagina. The second shows a man and a woman as well; in this one the man is lying down and the woman straddles him; you can just see his penis entering her vagina from below. The next shows two men, one on his back, his legs embracing the other, who lies upon him, and you can just see his penis as he enters the man's anus. The fourth picture shows two women, one lying and embracing the other with her legs; you can just see a dildo strapped around the waist of the woman on top, entering the vagina of the woman lying down. In the fifth picture, a man lies down with his legs around a woman; the woman, who leans over him tenderly, wears a dildo, and you can just see where the dildo enters his anus, as *she* penetrates *him*.

When I lay these five pictures side by side upon a table, two things above all strike me. (No, to be honest, three things—because first of all, they arouse me. That's the coloring of what follows.) My first thought is, What's all the excitement about? Almost every element in all five of these photos is the same. Almost nothing is different—only small details of composition, small blebs of flesh protruding here, receding there. Each shows tenderness; the viewer sees the gentle hand reaching for a cheek, the eyes half closed in pleasure, the tension and relaxation of careful movement. But usually the focus—and the fuss—is on what is different. We pay so much attention, seem to care so very much, which blebs protrude and recede, who is above and who below, which orifice is full and which empty.

This is my second thought, my secret thought. Of these five images, I could be in four. There is nothing to stop me, nothing at all but my own desire, my willingness to enter the image. To be the pervert of my own perverted self.

In San Francisco, near the Mission District, is a store called Good Vibrations, founded several years ago by Joani Blank and owned and run by women ever since. The store is spacious and well lit, with sheer white curtains hiding the windows. The big front room is painted a soothing light blue. There is a lot of space between the displays of sex toys, books, and movies so people can browse without feeling crowded. All the products, which are also available by mail order, are out on shelves, open to the touch. There is a popular "museum" of antique vibrators. The electrical toys are plugged in to outlets, and accompanied by descriptive brochures and explanatory signs. In the back, there's a discreet vibrator testing room with a locking door.

Vibrators are the only new sex toy in the world, the only thing that hasn't been around since the farthest veils of ancient history, but they are the easiest one to talk about, to discuss. There's something hygienic about a vibrator, since it can (unlike the anal beads or penis sleeves) have uses other than orgasm. Vibrators are mechanical, machines in a world of machines. And vibrators make female orgasm as quick, easy, reproducible, and simple as any male orgasm, ever. They are machines of revolution. The writer Susie Bright worked at Good Vibrations for a time; one thing she learned, she says now, is that having orgasms encourages the having of orgasms. The notion that women will become "addicted" to orgasms, especially the quick and easy ones offered by vibrators, offends her. "There's a tremendous fear of liking sex too much," she adds, noting that having difficulty coming has always been the number-one problem women brought to the clerks at Good Vibrations.

Several years ago I met some of the women who work at Good Vibrations. I had been testing the waters of my own anxiety about pornography and the kind of in-your-face sex stores women have traditionally avoided as much as possible. I had come to feel relatively comfortable with both. But I wondered how far that ease extended, what it felt like to live with other people's sex lives all the time. What it felt like not only to buy a vibrator, but to sell them.

Carol Queen is a petite woman with little black-rimmed eyeglasses. She wears red hot pants and high-necked black velvet dresses, like a hallucination of Alice in Wonderland all grown up. She is one of the full-time employees of Good Vibrations, and a sex educator. Carol told me: "One of the most important things we do here is role-model comfort about sex. We can hang out here, and feel comfortable in the room, and we wouldn't have to know a damned thing about silicone dildos. Just being here and saying, 'Come and look at the butt-plugs!' is enough. People can't *believe* someone just said that to them, as though you were saying, 'Hey, come look at the zucchinis!' " When I laughed, she added, "And then we tell people that if they don't know what size dildo they want, to go to Safeway and buy five zucchinis, and try them."

Carol offered to shadow me as I worked in the store for a day, trying out the other side. There was a new employee starting training that day, so I simply tagged along, at first just watching and listening, feeling nervous and ignorant. I didn't want to blush, not there.

When people came in, I tried to guess which part of the store they would go to, and I was always wrong. (Where people go first is sometimes a feint, like a fox making extra tracks to throw off the scent.) Many headed to the nearest shelf of books and stood there, shyly glancing around. Women seemed more willing to be approached by a clerk, and women were more sure of what they wanted, sometimes in considerable detail.

Laura Miller, who now works on the administrative side of the business, says of the customers: "There's the know-it-alls who come in with their friends to show off how much they know, and they can't stop giggling. But I remember explaining to one woman, who just sort of knew she had a clitoris, how it worked. She said, 'It's amazing that women ever have intercourse if it's not really what gives them an orgasm,' and I said, *'Yes!'* She was suddenly realizing that it's not about the pole in the hole, necessarily. I sold that woman a vibrator. She walked out the door and I thought, 'Her life has changed.' "

"When I hear all these stories about brutal men with their rapacious sexuality, I'm, like, 'Where are they?' I find that when I tell men where I work, they're terrified. I've been told that I make men feel inadequate, that I scare them away. If I don't tell men where I work, it's not because I'm afraid that they're going to grab at me. I'm afraid they're going to be afraid of *me*."

A big lunch-hour crowd milled around, all ages, all shapes, couples and singles, friends and lovers. A man in an Armani suit, a man in coveralls, a man with a ponytail and two inquisitive dogs. One bought leather handcuffs, the other inquired about the penis sleeve, the other bought a vibrator for his wife. Two young women bought books of erotic stories. A bookish college student spent forty-five minutes comparing lubricants. I sold a vibrating cock ring to a man in a three-piece suit. With Carol's expert help, I sold several expensive vibrators to men, ostensibly for their wives. A woman about my age hefted the dildos, weighing them in each hand. I spent a half hour with a balding man wearing glasses and a suit who wanted to know how to get started using butt plugs, and needed to compare sizes, materials, and costs.

A man in his forties spent nearly an hour quizzing two of us about vibrators, comparing them, listening to the long lecture Carol gave about the relative merits of battery-operated vibrators versus electrical ones, and coil-driven vibrators versus motor-driven. He asked about noise, and attachments, and finally I said, "Well, you know what she likes best," and he said to me, seriously, "Does any man really know what his wife likes?"

A short, middle-aged plump woman dressed all in black came in late in the afternoon and said her boyfriend wanted her to wear a butt plug during intercourse and she was game. She ended up buying anal beads, too, and telling one of the clerks a long story about the best places in Golden Gate Park to have sex.

"One thing I've noticed," Laura told me once, "is that I don't laugh at dirty jokes anymore. So much of the laugh in dirty jokes is just the fact that someone's talking about sex. People go into giggles when they hear that we sell butt plugs. I don't have any patience with it anymore. It's like making a joke about avocados! *No one* talks about avocados in polite company!"

"I do get tired of people's attitudes," says Carol. "People don't see nuances because this fog descends on them and they get sweaty palms. I've had the same conversation so many times, with friends who think I've gone to hell in a handbasket. I've talked about anything a person could do sexually, in public. What I get is, 'Oh, I couldn't imagine doing anything like that!' I really think that's at the bottom of a lot of people's sexual politics. 'Uh-uh, I couldn't do that,' and that means, 'You can't do it, either.'"

Sometimes it's precisely because we can imagine doing

that, doing what we're quite certain should not be done, should not be imagined, let alone permitted, that we hate the explicit representation of sex—of sexual desire, sexual fantasy, and as at Good Vibrations, sexual gratification. "You come in here on Saturday, there's tons of people, they're all talking and laughing and sometimes you see the more traditional dirty-bookstore client wander in, and usually they flee," says Laura. "People are here with their *kids.* But for every person who comes up to tell you they've found something to object to in the store, there's fifty who practically kiss your feet with gratitude."

I left feeling enormously cheered, and distressingly aroused, the last a feeling I expect would diminish quickly enough with time. Selling butt plugs, after all, isn't so much different from selling toasters or Chevrolets. People want a bargain, and a decent product they can depend upon, and they don't want to be patronized while buying it. A lot of my cheer is simply the reminder that there's nothing new under the sun. A nineteenth-century Scottish doctor complained that half the women in Scotland used dildos. A thousand years ago Buddhist nuns were exhorted not to use dildos—not even vegetable ones. And people are still complaining about them today.

I need this occasional reminder that we're all in it together, trying to solve this damned conundrum of desire and shame. I wanted to know how hard it would be for me to meet strangers head-on like this, to heft the dildos alongside an attractive woman and discuss silicone versus latex, to demonstrate the anal beads to a young couple using my fist—to do this in the bright light of day. And I found that after the first vibrating penis sleeve, the second one is easy. I watched Carol's easy, reassuring manner and, likewise, the ease of many customers who've long ago come to terms with their own appetites. And I felt that little thrill of evangelism, selling a man his wife's first vibrator. It made me a little restless, all this talk of body parts and the way people seemed in a hurry to get going, once they'd made up their minds.

7

Pornography, I'm told, has no *social value*. This is a very odd thing to say. What is meant, I think, is that porn doesn't serve the social conventions. But of course it has *value*—that is, meaning, distinction, significance. Simply as a well-established, multimillion-dollar business it has to be taken seriously. Pornography is an expression of that conservative icon, the free market: reviled but incredibly profitable, popular with a wide cross-section of the population, compelling in spite of enormous criticism. It wouldn't exist if it had no value. What that value might be is worth careful consideration.

Pornography, like prostitution, is a unifying metaphor for sex. Both these things fascinate and repel us at once, because they are bluntly about sex as sex and nothing more. Prostitutes and pornography remove sex from the arena of romance and love and directly address the libido. People tend to make both too much and too little out of both.

A good example of American confusion over pornography is the movie *Basic Instinct*. As filmed, *Basic Instinct* fit the Motion Picture Association of America's NC-17 rating—an adult movie made for adults with adult themes, not appropriate for kids under seventeen under any circumstances. The only other mainstream film with this rating at the same time was *Henry and June*.

Widely reported was the fact that the director of *Basic Instinct,* Paul Verhoeven, filmed different versions of potentially objectionable scenes. He knew (and probably hoped) that the MPAA would give the film an NR-17 rating, at which time he could make a fuss, reedit the film, and squeak by with an R rating and a lot of free publicity.

Obviously, many of the people who went to see *Basic Instinct* went because they'd heard about the fuss, about the explicit sex and violence at its core. No one seemed particularly ashamed about their motives, either, or unwilling to admit wanting to be aroused. A number of stories at the time of the film's release explained the technical nuances of this breed of film-making: how the nudity and ripping of clothes was handled, as well as the slamming of women up against walls during sex, the so-called "lesbian kissing," and, of course, the ice-pick-slashing-during-intercourse. All I wanted to know after seeing the film was why all these regular folks lining up to see this moronic and boring movie because they thought it would turn them on didn't just go get a dirty movie at the XXX store.

I don't just mean to say that more explicit and arousing (and in some cases, better produced) sex is available in the nearby adult store, though it is. There is something at work here, because adult sex films in the United States rarely have violent overtones and what force is used is almost always within the dramaturgy of bondage or sadomasochism. Adult sex films are full of little more than explicit consensual adult sex. The sex found in *Basic Instinct* not only isn't particularly arousing, it is one with mutilation and murder—the murder fuels the sex, the sex fuels the murder. This is true of virtually all action films, teenage slasher films, horror movies, war movies, martial arts movies. For all that people persist in assuming pornography is filled with violence, a quick trip to the adult store proves otherwise; images linking sex with violence are simply not readily available in adult stores. Somehow in our social thinking we've come to a point where people feel morally upright at the mall multiplex no matter what is playing, and immoral when they rent a soft-core romance for the privacy of their home.

Blockbuster Video won't stock NR-17 movies. Their aisles are filled with a lot of films I won't rent for myself and won't allow my teenagers to rent—cheap horror movies, ninja combat films, "super-action" movies filled with brutality, and bimbo-driven sex comedies like *Happy Gigolo.* Blockbuster also has a section of cheap and rough soft-core with titles like *Stripped to Kill* and *Night of the Wilding, Gator Bait* and *Bad Girls Dormitory* —films loaded with images of sexual violence and rape that would be laughed out of a XXX store. These movies are labeled with stickers that read "Youth restricted viewing—must be 17 or older." Not far away, both *Basic Instinct* and *Body of Evidence* are sticker-free. I watched a boy not older than fourteen rent *Basic Instinct* without a hitch.

Perhaps *Basic Instinct* reflects a time of promiscuous interest in sex, a pornographic culture. Many people, I'm sure, would use it to prove their belief that the corruption caused by the existence of pornography is infecting mainstream film. I say *Basic Instinct* reflects a prudish and censoring culture, much like the particularly intense pornography produced in Victorian England. The filmmakers and actors were willing to produce as explicit and titillating a film as possible. The censors with their oddball ideas of what is and isn't okay for children to see think the often tender sex of *Henry and June* is more objectionable than mutilation. *Basic Instinct* is a film about how confused and scared people are about sex.

Michael Douglas and Sharon Stone, the stars of *Basic Instinct,* have made it clear they can't stand each other. They simulated sex with each other, anyway—and de-

liberately fueled the "did they or didn't they" contro-
versy—because, after all, that's acting. If you rent a good
X-rated film, you can see unsimulated sex between people who might well *like* each other very much. This is
also acting. What exactly is the difference?

Now and then I visit my neighborhood adult store to
rent a movie or buy a magazine. This is nothing like
Good Vibrations, or the local version of Good Vibrations, with incense and crystals and cheerful houseplants.
This is a XXX adult dirty-books-and-video store. I am
often the only woman there, although more and more
lately I see other women, alone, with a man, with another woman. Some days there may be only a single
clerk and a few customers; at other times I see a dozen
men or more: heavyset workingmen, young men, busi-
nessmen. To enter takes a certain pluck, but less so all
the time. I pass the neon sign, silvered windows, and go
through a blank, reflecting door. I used to imagine eyes
on me then, and the eyes were my mother's eyes, and,
worse, my father's. They watched the little girl inside me
and chided her for a naughty girl. But this has disappeared, too.

I don't make eye contact. Neither do the men. I drift
from one section of the store to the other, going about
my business. I like this particular store because it is large
and well lit, and because the owner has made a point of
advertising to couples, gay people, and women without

pulling the XXX punch. They are his untapped target consumers, and he knows it. The male customers give me sidelong glances as I pass by, and then drop their eyes back to the box in their hands. Pornography, at its roots, is about watching; but no one here openly watches. This is a place of librarian silences. As I move from shelf to shelf, men sometimes gather at the fringes of where I stand. I think they would like to know which movies I will choose.

In the large front room with the clerks are glass counters filled with vibrators, promising unguents, candy bowls filled with condoms. On the wall behind the counter where you ask for help are giant dildos, rubber vaginas, rubber faces with slit eyes, all mouth. Here are the more mainstream films, with high production values and name stars. Here is the large and growing amateur section, a small section of straight Japanese movies, a section of gay male films.

It took many visits for me to relax in this place, and I didn't learn to relax simply by inuring myself to discomfort. Eventually I realized (and spending a little time at Good Vibrations helped) that this is just a store, with merchandise, some of which interests me, some of which does not. The clerks are just salesmen and the men only customers. I started to relax when I stopped caring about the nervousness of the other customers around me, stopped assuming and projecting—and stopped making more of things than was really there.

On one of my first solo visits, I didn't want the clerk

to glance at the titles of the movies I had requested by number. I tried to distract him with a question. I asked if any women still worked there. He was young, effeminate, with a wispy mustache and loose shoulder-length hair, and he apologized when he said no.

"Even though we're all guys right now, we try to be real sensitive," he said, pulling my requests off the shelf without a glance. "If anyone gives you a hard time, let us know. You let us know right away, and we'll take care of it." He handed me my choices in a white plastic bag.

"Have a nice day."

Some of my women friends have never seen or read pornography. That I don't find strange; traditional porn is a world of women that sometimes seems not to be about women at all. One thing that's wrong with porn in its current limitations is that there's no room for some people—no "fit."

Women who have seen little pornography often assume there is nothing in male-produced, male-oriented pornography to interest them; they further assume that the images in most films are primarily, obsessively, ones of rape. There is undoubtedly an iconography of porn. The main theme running through American pornography is an obsession with virility and lust, both male and female. To that end, traditional porn tends to show actors in quick, unhesitant arousal, free of doubts. It uses close-up film loops of intercourse over and over, to give the impression of male endurance. For the same effect, there are frequent scenes of male ejaculation—the come shot, the "money shot"—and lots of close-ups of ecstatic women's faces. In fact, cunnilingus and the clitoral orgasm is a stock event in a lot of porn; part of the American obsession with lust is the goal of satisfaction.

The boogey monsters and demons of porn are like boogey monsters everywhere—imaginary. There is no such thing as a "snuff" film. I know a number of people with experience in porn who have tried to find these mythical films, and failed. (There is a film titled *Snuff;* it was a parody.) Anyone who thought to film an actual act of violence (and where could they have gotten such an idea?) commits a crime unless the film is given up as evidence. "Kiddie porn" does exist, but not only is it illegal, it's not sold in stores anywhere, as the saying goes. I'm not sure how to find it; I've never seen it.

The images of pornography are many and varied; some are fragmented and idealized. Some are crude and unflattering. I like the dreamy psychedelic quality of certain scenes; I like the surprises in others, and most of all, I like the heat. Porn lets me have all the curiosity of the anthropologist and the frank hope of the voyeur. Our pornography is, for the most part, adolescent and dumb; it fits perfectly and profitably into our adolescent culture. Criticisms of pornography as a form—lack of character development, narrative, and plot, a numbing of imagination, and so on—are criticisms that can be extended to all bad expression. I can take a diatribe against porn and insert the word "television" or "Hollywood" or "damned liberalism" in place of the word "porn" and it still makes some loopy kind of sense. There are the surface criticisms, of production values and stagnant images, that can be extrapolated to all porn only if we assume that badly made pornography is the only possible kind. But the deeper criticisms extend as well—like the fact that pornography gives us a world of unreal power, false intimacy, lousy psychology, and crummy rhetoric. Television, Hollywood, liberals. All kinds of art and expression create illusions of power, numb the imagination, and fail at insightful analysis. Beer commercials do this. Congressional filibusters do this.

Porn is treated as being intrinsically different from other forms of expression because sex is treated as being intrinsically different from other acts. It's really the sex itself, not the form, that's being criticized; the fact of expressing sex explicitly is being criticized, not how well lit or complex or intelligent is the film in question.

There is a stereotype, the one occupied by the little old man in a raincoat, that teaches us pornography is a product for the lower classes. Criminalization of prostitution and various forms of social control on hard-core material have created ghettos of sexual hunger, ghettos apart from the ordinary daily lives of this country's middle class. But by all indications it is the middle class that uses pornography in the United States. In other times and places, hard-core material has been the exclusive luxury of upper-class men, and in fact was largely created by upper-class men for their own use. They, after all, could read and write, although not always with great clarity.

Porn evolves, but some parts of it never seem to change. Ancient India, Pompeii, sixteenth-century Japan, all had explicit and artistically sophisticated pornography. Europe has been less urbane over the centuries. One of the big books of 1683 was called *The Present State of Betty-Land* by "that great Mafter of HUMOUR, *Charles Cotton,* Efq." (I've seen the same book under other titles as well; "Betty-Land" is sometimes called "Merry-Land.") Betty-Land is a thinly disguised parody of the Queen's England, a kind of Land of Cockaigne, inhabited by people who "are vaſtly *ticklifh,* and ſo fond of it, that when they can get no-body to pleaſe them that way, they will *tickle themſelves."* For many pages the (presumably) titillated reader is regaled with mildly seditious and winking descriptions of Betty-Land's "Flowers" and "Soil" and "Prospects."

In 1899, in France, *The Memoirs of Dolly Morton* were published, purporting to be the story of one woman's effort to free the slaves in America before the Civil War. The introductory note states that *Dolly Morton* is only for "scholars and accredited bibliophiles." The publisher, in time-honored pornographer style, deplores any who would sell this book "with no other object" than "pandering to the erotic tastes of libertine and debauched men." Sample chapter titles: "A Rabelaisian banquet of nude demoiselles," "A shocking orgie," "Hot viands and bottom-spanking escapades," "The joyful craft of arse-wriggling."

In 1993 I rent a stylish film with expensive sets and a pulsing soundtrack. The beautiful actresses wear sunglasses in every scene, and the wordless scenes shift every few minutes. Now there are two women together; now two women and an adoring man, a tool of the spike-heeled women. A few scenes later there is only one woman, blond, with a luxuriant body. She reaches one hand slowly down between her legs and pulls a diamond necklace from between her vaginal lips, jewel by jewel. She slides it up her abdomen, across her breast, to her throat, and into her mouth. *Betty-Land* and *Dolly Morton* seem quaint and antiquated now. I wonder how this movie will look in two hundred and three hundred years.

Even when I'm not bashful in the act of purchase, I'm bashful watching. I can feel that way with friends, with my lover of many years, and I can feel that way alone. Suddenly I need to shift position, avert my eyes. Sex awakens my unconscious; pornography gives it a face. Bashful is not a bad feeling, either; I'm repeatedly reminded this way that sex holds, perpetually, a special place.

For years after Betty Dodson and Rita Mae Brown had gotten hold of me, after a decade of sexual experience, I struggled with a deep sexual shame. For a time I was most ashamed of the shame itself. Didn't I believe sex was good? What was wrong with me, that I resisted the depths of my feelings? Why was I able to cheerfully and publicly throw myself into all kinds of sensual pleasure, able to pretend to accept the validity of sexual pleasure, and still feel such shame? Like a lot of pretend libertines, I acted with an unconscious hypocrisy, picking and choosing my joys. I was in fact ashamed of all my urges, the small details within the larger act, the sudden sounds I made. I could hear that little voice from long ago: *Bad girl. Mustn't touch.*

I was propelled toward the overt—toward pornography. I needed information not about sex but about sexual parameters, the bounds of the normal. I needed permission. I needed blessing. These narratives are about the unspoken aspects of sex, all that we never discuss—porn *is* what we never discuss—so they give a kind of crude permission simply by their existence. They are fragmented and idealized, yes, and limited; they are psychically as well as physically masturbatory for the most part. But I'm less concerned with that effect than I am with the original source of the material—the sea of human hunger, the itchy cravings of sex in others, that tells me I'm not alone and not bad.

I first went to a "dirty" movie in my late twenties. The man I was living with took me to a theater on a back street. It was very cold and dark inside the movie house, so that the other patrons were only dim shadows, rustling nearby. The movie was grainy, half blurred, the sound muddy, the acting awful. At the same time, I felt as though I'd crossed a line: There was a world of sexual material to see, and I was very curious to see it. But years passed before I could imagine entering this world alone, not even for a quick foray into the screened-off section of the local video store, behind the sign reading OVER 18 ONLY. There was always men back there, and only men.

I've had a number of people tell me that people become addicted to pornography, to this dangerous substance like opium, which feels too good. There are people who become obsessed with certain images of pornography, of course, but I believe they have the images to begin with, are obsessed in the first place. They react to pornography (and TV movies-of-the-week and star athletes) because these things conveniently mirror their obsession, freeing them from the rigors of imagination. As for using pornography as a "blueprint" for violence, not only are such images hard to find, I think this belief supposes far more concentration on the part of impulsively violent people than reality should warrant. And how many murders have been inspired by religion?

I recently saw an adult movie, something of a send-up of other movies, called *Wild Goose Chase*. In the midst of mild arousal, I found a scene poignant with reference to the world of fantasy and solitude. The actor is Joey Silvera, a good-looking man with blond hair and startling dark eyes. In this film he plays a detective; the detective has a torrid scene with his secretary, who then walks out on him. He holds his head in his hands. "I don't need her," he mumbles. "I got women. I got my *own* women!" He stands and crosses to a file cabinet. "I got plenty of women!" He pulls out a drawer and dumps it upside down, spilling porn magazines in a pile on the floor. He crawls over them, stroking the paper cunts, the breasts, the pictured thighs, moaning, kissing the immobile faces.

Men, like women, are susceptible to a kind of oppression from sexually explicit material, the oppression of performance: Do I look like that? Do I perform like that? Does my lover feel that excited at my touch? Women I know say they feel uncomfortable watching their lover turn on to another woman's image, even as they turn on to the image of the man in the same film. In fact, this can be marvelously liberating as a shared fantasy, to be "with" that woman, "with" that man, to *be* another woman, another man. But these dreamed and edited visions of other people's sexuality, virtually the only sex done by other people any of us ever see, can leave us in our unedited lives lonely and confused. How to know, if we never talk? A greater freedom among us to tell the truth, about ourselves and our desires, would largely eliminate this.

Very little of the pornography available uses images of coercion, and those are the carefully contracted ones of bondage and S/M. (Sometimes I wonder if the narrowed focus of porn, coupled with the natural intensity of sex, simply doesn't leave much room for anything else.) The rest of our culture positively drips with violence. So it seems odd, and telling, once again, to presume that hard-to-find pornography is somehow more deeply influential than the news, advertising, and prime-time TV. But such is the fear of pornography, which is held out for censure as a special case, something apart, existing in another sphere. Lisa Palac, who founded the magazine *Future Sex* and has both done sexual performance and worked on pornographic films, sighed in a conversation with me the other day. It was a weary sigh. I'd been telling her about a feminist protest against an adult video store, a protest "against violence against women," the kind of protest Lisa herself has endured. "I don't care if the actors are really fucking or really coming. I don't care as long as I *believe* they're coming," she said. "Everyone knows that the people who are shot and killed in *Lethal Weapon* don't really die. They *know* what acting is. Why can't they believe pornography is acting, too?"

Many women enjoy adult films from the 1950s, 1960s, 1970s, once they see them. Other women enjoy—when they discover them—gay male films, which are often tender as well as powerfully erotic, and feature remarkably good-looking men. Laura Miller, who works at Good Vibrations, has hosted video nights for women who have never seen pornography. She shows clips from some of the new, more romantic, female-produced films, and then clips from older hard-core films with more traditional themes. "The difficult part for women is that they haven't had the opportunity to even see what's available," she says. The surprise is how many of the women prefer the old hard-core films. "It's so politically incorrect. I'm glad when they're willing to admit that it really turns them on, but they also say, 'It really disturbs me, but this works, and the other one didn't.' "

That every culture has its own sexual mores is a given. That every country has its own pornography is not: In our ethnocentricity we tend to assume that with minor variations what is erotic to us will be erotic to another. But the sexual material of a culture reflects that culture's concerns. In America, the adolescent rut—eternal erection and ready orgasm. In England, book after book about spanking, sex across class lines, and a detailed interest in underwear; in Germany, leather-clad blondes whipping swarthy men; in Italy, an interest in feminized men; in Japan, a preoccupation with icons of innocence (schoolgirls, nurses, brides), soiled innocence (widows), and maternal nurturing. In Japanese pornography active female pleasure is considered a turnoff. I've never seen an American film that didn't feature it.

Looking at what disturbs us is not at all the same as inuring ourselves to it or apologizing for it. It's simply *looking,* the first step to understanding and change. All of psychoanalysis hinges on this. (But therapists resist the idea that one might want to look at sexual images outside the context of therapy—that is, for fun.) There are examples of pornography, films and stories both, that genuinely scare me. They are no more bizarre or extreme than books or movies that may simply excite or interest me, but the details affect me in certain specific ways. The content touches me, just there, and I'm scared, for no reason I can explain. It may be nothing more than sound, a snap or murmur. And I want to keep watching those films, reading those books; when I engage in my own fears, I learn about them. I may someday master a few. When I happen upon such scenes, I try to look directly. Seeing what I don't like can be as therapeutic as seeing what I do.

The other night I was watching a film called *Images of Desire:* a naked woman, blindfolded, strapped to a chair by her ankles and wrists, expressionless, seen through bars. There is a thwack-thwack sound, and she's being circled slowly by two men, one blond-Nordic type, one swarthy-Arab type, dressed in dark leather uniforms, playing with police batons. The setup, the subsequent action, the woman's steady, expressionless silence, the soft, seductive commands of the men—I *like* that fantasy. But I didn't like this, and it took me a while to identify the two problems—the uniforms and the way they hit the batons into their hands. For someone else, that *is* the juice; for me, the opposite, and the "why" there is one thing I want to understand. The uniforms bothered me, something smacking too much of the real, of authority I have an honest reason to fear. (Again, for many people, that's precisely the thrill.) But the batons were worse. Something so much more viscerally frightening than a neat little whip or riding crop. Such an intriguing difference, for my own libido, between the oh-so-charming threat of a hiding and the possibility of being *beaten*. All unsaid, undone, the baton never touches the woman. The baton meant hitting to me, and I don't like hitting. And again, this is what it meant to me. It could mean something else to you, and it could mean the same thing and cause the opposite reaction.

I think it's important to point out—because so many criticisms of pornography miss this point—that many women are turned on by this kind of film, and many men would enjoy it only if the roles were reversed, and the person tied to the chair was a man. That's what I mean when I say that pornography is a story we tell about ourselves—and maybe the only, or most revealing, way to tell certain secrets that are not necessarily sexual at all.

I was a kid who loved libraries, a free place in which to roam, to be left alone, to think and imagine without the constraints of the classroom or other people's demands. My mother, who was a schoolteacher, believed firmly and loudly in letting me check anything I wanted out of the library, anything I could figure out how to find, and so for the most part I didn't read the kind of juvenile books recommended in school. Then one day, when I was about thirteen, I found and tried to check out *The Joy of Sex*. The librarian called my mother at home. And I can only imagine her struggle, while I waited by the library desk. In the end she agreed, and it was only much later that I realized she probably decided it was easier for her to take this semipublic stand against censorship than it was for her to talk to me about sex, and that my discovery was a kind of relief for her. For me, this was just another confirmation in a lifelong affair with the very idea of libraries—the delving into, the search for, the small discoveries, mysteries, learning secrets in dark places, among hidden things.

That most stalwart of institutions, the British Library, keeps one of the world's largest and perhaps rarest collections of pornography. The British Library is still housed within the daunting gray building of the British Museum, off the front lobby echoing with the noise of milling school groups and tourist groups and wandering travelers. You must have a Reader's Pass to enter the library, and to get a Reader's Pass you must fill out an application explaining how the material you want to read in the British Library is not readily available anywhere else. With the pornography, kept in a collection charmingly known as the Private Case, that's fairly easy; a lot of this material is virtually impossible to find anywhere else, and certainly impossible to find in one place.

There are such "private" cases in many libraries, variously labeled. The erotic books in the Bibliothèque Nationale in Paris were labeled "l'Enfer"—Hell books. The New York Public Library catalogues erotic material with five stars instead of classification numbers, making it virtually impossible to find a specific book if you don't know what you're looking for in the first place. Patrick

Kearney, the author of the only bibliography of the Private Case, remembers trying to study a couple of erotic books at the Library of Congress in the 1960s. "Both of these I was allowed to examine freely, but was forbidden to make even the slightest note, and so was constrained to sit memorizing their rather complex title pages and a few relevant passages, for all the world like an Elizabethan theater pirate . . ."

The reading rooms of the British Library are scenes of marvelous anachronism, and it's hard to imagine a more interesting place to read a dirty book. There are horseshoes and rows of leather-covered tables, standing lamps, and wooden podiums, with studious, silent people reading and writing—only with pencils, as pens are forbidden here. There are tall white columns and books locked in glass cases and circles of soft yellow light falling at every reader's place.

I take my pile of old, dusty books to my seat, pick the largest one, and set it on the podium, and open to an eight by eleven drawing of a man with an enormous erection. I close it and open *Cythera's Hymnal, or, Flakes from the Foreskin,* bawdy and scatological verse published in Oxford in 1870; most of them seem to be fart jokes. Then I skim through *Amok,* by Hank Janson, a pulp novel from 1954 once ordered destroyed, and get caught up in the heated story of a condemned man's prison escape and brutal adventures, during one of which "two bodies pulsed in unison, pulsed and burned with a fierce, savage intensity."

The British Library is obliged by law to keep a copy of almost everything published in the United Kingdom. In addition to that voluminous intake, the library frequently receives bequests and donations from private libraries. The Private Case was conceived as a place to store under lock and key work that, by virtue of its obscene nature, was deemed inappropriate for the general collection. Note the word "obscene" as opposed to sexual. Works of particular violence and brutality, such as those of Aleister Crowley, have also been relegated to the Private Case, which is housed in a locked steel cage out of sight. Until 1981, when Patrick J. Kearney finished his several years of research and published one, the Private Case didn't even have a bibliography. Kearney found its neglect to be fantastic in scope, many of the books in dusty, half-forgotten, unsorted piles.

A lot of P.C. books, as they're called, are frail and rare. I was put in mind of the concern of librarians everywhere over erotic material, that one's duty as a librarian is not really to protect the reader from the book, but the book from the reader; too many *Playboy*s stolen or ripped apart, too many copies of *My Secret Life* glued shut by surprise emissions. Every day, when I asked the librarians for my requests of the day before, they rummaged in the request files until I pointed them to a separate little box, since even the P.C. request slips are segregated. They would then take a set of keys and unlock the books from a special storage cupboard. Thus I was handed *Flesh in the Ring, The Lascivious Abbot, The*

Platonic Blow, by poker-faced librarians, until they all finally realized I was one of those P.C. readers they get now and then, and I was never going to request anything else.

It's hard to know which criteria have granted P.C. status to one book and not another; no one at the British Library admits to any kind of objective system. *Sex with Your Hamster* and Madonna's *Sex* are in the general catalogue; bawdy songs from the seventeenth century and *The Strange History of Joshua Josephson,* a cartoon biography of Jesus Christ, are in the Private Case. A lot of the P.C. material is in French, Latin, and German. Among the 2,143 books in the P.C. there are many unique and lovely works almost any bibliophile would desire. There are rare first editions of erotic classics like *Fanny Hill* and *The Story of O,* and private editions of the same with engravings by the preoccupied publishers, such ephemera as pseudonymous poetry by Swinburne (praising flagellation) and by Auden (explicit paeons to homosexual passion), works by de Maupassant, Apollinaire, and Voltaire, and a coffee-table-size abridgment of *Lysistrata* with drawings by Aubrey Beardsley. And there is material capable of stimulating intense arousal, I can attest; it stole upon me now and then without warning where I sat quietly, pencil in hand, crossing and uncrossing my legs and coughing politely.

The Private Case began at a time when the material included was not only unacceptable, but in many cases illegal. A number of books were probably saved from extinction altogether by the Private Case. *The Rainbow* by D. H. Lawrence was judged obscene and publicly burned in 1915; librarians chose not to mention they had a copy. Lesser works like *Here Lies John Penis* by Potocki, and the works of Eric Arthur Wildman, who was convicted of publishing obscenity in the 1950s, were also ordered burned but kept safely under wraps. The English are great book-burners; prosecuted at various times was *The Well of Loneliness, Ulysses,* and *Fanny Hill* —oddly enough, not prosecuted for obscenity until the 1960s—and *Last Exit to Brooklyn* by Hubert Selby, this last also kept under wraps in the Private Case until recently. In such cases there are often protests against censorship and attempts to define pornography, based on claims that these "artistic" works didn't qualify—always with real porn the poor, demented stepchild.

Until the 1960s a request to see P.C. material meant an interview, the purpose of which was first to daunt the casual reader, and second, to vet the solemn and academic purpose of everyone else. One still must explain why one wants a Reader's Pass in the first place, how these books will be used. But now anyone with a Reader's Pass can have P.C. books without question—if they know of the Case, if they can find the bibliography, if they can convince clerks who, I found, aren't always sure the Case exists.

A gradual, quiet "desegregation" of P.C. books began in the 1960s—works by Havelock Ellis, Henry Miller, Emile Zola, and D. H. Lawrence, scientific treatises and bibliographies all once kept in the Private Case are now in the general collection. One day I asked a library clerk if, in fact, the P.C. material wasn't being quietly returned to the general catalogue. She answered with a resounding no. "Some of this material, you know," she said confidingly, "is very hard-core." That same day I requested one of the newest books in the collection, *Wet Dreams,* a 1973 account of a somewhat orgiastic sex film festival held in Amsterdam, supposedly attended by various luminaries like Betty Dodson, Germaine Greer, Al Goldstein, and Anthony Haden-Guest. I leafed through the diary accounts, poems, and stories and came across naked photos of not one, but two writers I know. There is nothing like a library.

England, like the United States, is generally contradictory about sex. After several hours poring over Victorian flagellation erotica, I stopped at a small pharmacy near Russell Square. There was the *Daily Sport,* with its ads for sex phone lines ("I like something done to my backside. I'm touching my toes right now") and for videos, sex dolls, and vibrators, and, surprisingly, for an inflatable sheep. But England is also a monarchy. Paul Cross, a longtime British Librarian, writes that the Private Case is not the only collection of hidden books in the British Library. There is also a collection labelled S.S., or Suppressed Safe. S.S. books are subversive, to "the throne, of religion, or of propriety." They are considered the worst books of all, worse than *Flesh in the Ring* and *My Secret Life.* "Because of legal implications"

they are omitted from the general catalogue and, unlike
the library's pornography, "under no circumstances are
they made available to readers."

Conservative feminists such as the lawyer Catharine
MacKinnon, Andrea Dworkin, and Dorchen Leidholdt
believe that violence, even murder, is the end point of all
pornography—and that pornography is the natural
product of a sexually violent culture. (For all its crude-
ness, there's a lot of ironic humor in pornography and
virtually none in conservative feminism.) Leidholdt has
written that within the "governing sexual system"
women have "no meaningful choice, real agency, or genuine pleasure." If I believe that, there is very little I can
do; I am stuck with what we have, for life.

Certainly a lot of violent material has sexual overtones; the mistake is assuming that anything with sex in
it is primarily about sex. Sex is so much a part of our
media culture, and ourselves, that it would be surprising
not to see sexual overtones in any emotionally intense
work. It is hard to separate sex out of the complex texture of our lives. But my point is that such weaving of
sex and pain, death and desire, in art and media takes
place outside the limited world of porn. It takes place in
the mainstream culture rather than on the edge.

Susan Sontag, exhaustively trying to prove that certain
works of pornography qualify as "literature," notes the
form's "singleness of intention" as a point against it. A

narrow focus seems less important to any work's merit than the narrowness of its effect. I am interested in literature, pornographic and otherwise, by my responses to any given piece. My responses to pornography are often layered and complex and multiple. Some explicitly sexual images are almost Jungian, repetitive and exaggerated, filled with mythic potency and symbolic acts. A lot of porn is junk.

Much is cheesy or mechanical. Some films disturb me by the unhappiness I sense, as though the people I see wished only to be somewhere else. I wish for more craft. I tire of browsing stacks of boxes titled *Fucking Brunettes* and *Monumental Knockers*. I am sometimes overwhelmed by how entrenched the iconography of porn is, what a huge and immobile rock this is for women to move. I don't dislike all these repetitive images so much as I dislike the limited menu. Sex is infinitely variable, and porn should be, too.

The only way porn will expand is by women entering its walls and pressing outward, to make more space. I know I break a rule when I enter the adult store, whether my entrance is simply startling or genuinely unwelcome. Only once has anything happened to remind me of this, and it happened the first time I went to the adult store alone. I had dressed in baggy jeans and a pullover sweater, and tied my long hair up in a bun. After a while I was approached by a fat man with a pale, damp face and thinning hair.

"Excuse me," he said. "I'm not trying to come on to

you or anything, but I can't help noticing you're, you know, female."

I could only nod.

"And I wonder," he continued, almost breathless, "if you like this stuff"—and he pointed at a nearby picture of a blond woman in red lingerie. "You see, my girl-friend, she broke up with me, and I'd bought her all this stuff—you know, sex clothes—and she didn't like it." He paused. "I mean, it's out in the back of my truck right now. If you just want to come outside, you can have it." I turned away without a word.

His approach bothered me, because I know he wouldn't, couldn't approach me in a grocery store or even a bar. But I'm not necessarily safer in a grocery store or bar, or my own home. Traditional pornography does degrade the male vision of women in this way. When I stand among the shelves there, I am standing in a maze of female images, shelf after shelf of them, hun-dreds of naked women smiling or with their eyes closed and mouths open or gasping. I am just one more image in a broken mirror. I don't, however, want a world in which there are *no* images of sexually hungry and will-ing women. That's precisely one reason I went to por-nography in the first place. I just don't want this image to be the only one around, any more than I want images of women as victims, mothers, or virgins to exclusively fill our eyes. And I know that if more women simply walked into this store, this world, that particular man's vision of women would begin to change—because he would be looking at real women as well as these reflections. He would have to change, he would have no choice.

Porn uses people as objects. Well, yes, it does. So much does. Can we choose to be objects in certain situations and not in others? And aren't there lots of situations in which men allow themselves to be objects—objects of profit, harm, exploitation? I wonder at this when I watch professional football. The feminist writer Ann Snitow thinks one of the biggest mistakes about conservative feminist theories of pornography is the belief "that in a feminist world we will never objectify anyone, never take the part for the whole, never abandon ourselves to mindlessness or the intensities of feeling that link sex with childhood, death, the terrors and pleasures of the oceanic. Using people as extensions of one's own hungry will is hardly an activity restrained within the boundaries of pornography."

One long-held western standard of obscenity and justification of censorship was to repress anything that might put a "blush on the cheek" of the archetypal innocent. A blush meant knowledge, self-knowledge, and in hearty Old Testament style, self-knowledge was thought to lead directly to corruption. (Catharine MacKinnon and Andrea Dworkin seem not to realize how old-fashioned their ideas are.) Part of the assumption is that the archetypal Man is already corrupt, and archetypal porn is that which will inflame him, shatter the thin veneer of his civility. But seen in the larger context of history, when we include the ancient Greeks and the Ottoman Empire and the Egyptians and the Chinese and all the aboriginal cultures of which we have record, this standard is, of course, silly; in those cultures, a blushing cheek was valued. This American urge to protect the young is one with the urge to protect Woman, which has as much to do with real women as it does with tuna casserole.

I find the erotic culture of Japan, torn between its own rich history, its highly stressed society, and westernization, to be a kind of case study for definitions of obscenity and innocence. "Japan has never been too preoccupied with realism," writes Nicholas Bornoff in his study of the matter, *Pink Samurai*. But it's that quality of unfettered fantasy that makes Japanese pornography so illuminating.

The typical text of much Japanese pornography (and a lot has essentially no plot at all) is that a woman is always either a victim of male sexuality or of herself; in the words of the anthropologist Ian Buruma, she is "a compulsive man-eating ogress consumed by her sexual savagery." Typical "victims" are the innocents—schoolgirls, nurses, young brides. They are raped, often with objects, and then fall in love with their rapists, victims of their own treacherous appetites. Often their husbands are inadequate, impotent, ignorant of their sexual needs; the rape awakens, enlivens them to themselves. The female body is essentially degraded, naturally so; sooner or later, nature will out. Perhaps the rapist will tearfully apologize, perhaps not; if he does, the woman becomes his comforter, a maternal figure, the lavishly adored mother-whore. Buruma sees modern Japanese culture as divided and contradictory, torn between sensuality and guilt, artificiality and naturalness, and further rended by the physical crowding and the veneration of both conformity and anonymity. Japan, after all, has created a unique theater of transvestism out of a culture of sharply divided gender roles.

I could point at this running plot as a good example of how dangerous pornography really is, because these images will, undoubtedly, encourage male violence against women and increase oppression of women in all spheres. Won't they? (Does the fact that Japanese women are freer to make choices for themselves than ever before count here?) Or I can consider how very much Japanese pornography has changed since the Ukiyo-e school of a few centuries ago, when gorgeous drawings of loving sex were common. I can place these images in a context, noting that erotic violence is a part of Japanese history, that Japan has always had a culture full of real sex and sham violence as well as real violence and fantasized sex. I can see these brutal films as evidence less of male terrorizing of women than as evidence of male terror. Violence by men against women is universal and very old. This acknowledgment, of how men fear women and especially women's sexuality, is new. In Japan, as culture changes, art changes; the rape fantasy is less prevalent, the female dominatrix, once unheard of, is increasingly visible. And the rape fantasy is as much a fantasy of the cuckold as of rape, a very old source of irony and humor in Japan.

The idea of not tolerating images of brutality in porn sounds terrific at first. But it falls apart as soon as we enter the real world. A lot of women get turned on by images that some other women might consider brutal. I can't imagine whom I could trust to define the term. But brutality takes a lot of forms, and many of them invade us in the most mundane ways. Consider this commercial: a woman's pale, slender hand, her fingernails painted bloodred, is rubbing, rubbing with a white cloth. Her strokes are languid, loving. She is cleaning the base of a white toilet, and as she strokes she talks about the problems of "living with men," of how difficult it is to "keep the bathroom clean" when men and boys are so phallically present. She has debased herself as far as she can go, and wants us to be pleased. *That* offends me, that is the image of women that sparks me to take my daughter aside for a little conversation about the history of sexism. How could the face of a woman in orgasm be more depraved than this?

Men—always the Man who is the standard-bearer for what is obscene and forbidden. The man I fear whether I mean to or not, in elevators and parking lots and on the street, is the man who acts on impulse, whose desires are twisted in this crazy culture, who has lost himself in its maze. But all influences considered, I don't think *Big*

Knockers is more dangerous to me than our nutty gun lobby, not by a long way. When I haven't the temerity to go through one of these veiled doors, it's because I haven't the temerity to go anywhere; I am afraid of the men inside in a generic, unspoken way, afraid of Them, everywhere. I can even hope that the warmth of sexual release, however brief, gentles men a little.

I want, hope, that images of such things as cunnilingus, the female orgasm, and mutually tender homosexuality will open men's minds, give them ideas, teach an expanded sense of normality. But I don't want the images of female desire to be misinterpreted. This is the same argument we are currently having about violence on television. Is it worse today, or somehow better, than the pop western cartoon violence I saw as a child, the bloodless and undisturbing death of bad guys? I can't believe, firmly don't believe, that having *no* images of sex would be better than the imperfect images we have now, and I can hardly imagine what a police state would be required to make such a thing come about.

Certain ethnic and cultural periods have forbidden or severely restricted image-making itself. Statues of Jesus have at times been forbidden because of the fear that children might actually think the statue was God. Many people who claim to think sex acceptable resist its representation. The reason given is frequently the discomfort caused by the fact that a representation is never complete, especially in such a complex subject. It must, one thinks, restrict imagination. But how can showing *no* representations lead to a more complete understanding than partial ones? If completeness is the goal, more, better, and more diverse images would seem to be one way to get there.

A number of optimists (or pessimists, depending on your point of view) like to think that pornography would disappear in a more perfect society—that it represents something artificial between us, a repression we all share and from which we might someday be freed. Certainly the pornography of a sexually relaxed culture would look very different from what we have now and be marketed and consumed in different ways. Such a society requires a much higher degree of personal responsibility than the one in which we now live. On the other hand, I imagine that if our culture becomes more sex-fearing and sex-obsessed than it is already, the unreconstructed pornography of today will become more widespread and more widely consumed than ever, and responsibility for expressing one's wishes become ever less valued a skill.

Cutting off images of female sexuality goes beyond the question of censorship—it goes into the heart of the lives of women, whose sexuality is invisible in so many ways. But the imperfections of the sexual images we have are sometimes great. Inevitably I return to the same position: Porn needs to change, improve, and it's women who will do that improving, and not by ignoring it. Kate

Ellis points out that the image of women as victims of men is an image of a static culture—a culture that *can't* change. And that is precisely the image conservative suppression of pornography promotes, whether it comes from feminism or the Christian Right. Women must be *rescued,* not respected.

I see feminism as empowering women as a group, a diverse community bound by their femaleness, not dividing us into good and bad, enlightened and deluded women. Censors are always concerned with how men *act* and how women are portrayed. Women cannot make free sexual choices in the censor's world; they are too oppressed to know that only oppression could lead them to sell sex. And I, watching, am either too oppressed to know the harm that my watching has done to my sisters, or—or else I have become the Man. And it is the Man in me who watches. By insisting that no woman could honestly like porn or sex work, that all such women are puppets, feminists against pornography have made women into objects. Women can *never* be the agents of sex to them.

My negative reactions to pornography are like my reactions to many things in my world—to fast food and the people who sell it, to cheap trinkets, poorly made toys, and multimillion-dollar children's films filled with sadistic violence. With porn, there are days when I experience a kind of ennui, a *nausea* from all that grunting labor, the rankness of the flesh. Sex smothers me sometimes. But I can feel saturated and weary about many things in my life. That reaction is as much a product of who I am as of what I am seeing.

Improving pornography for me doesn't mean refining the hard-core images into a blurry soft focus. Those movies—and there are plenty of them, romantic as can be—are too hygienic for me. They're not *dirty* enough. Any amateur psychologist could have a field day explaining why I prefer low-brow, hard-core porn to feminine erotica. I've spent enough time trying to explain things to myself: why I prefer *this* to *that*. I don't want anyone else to try. Pornography has to be politically incorrect. If it's not outside acceptable conventions of family and culture, it's not porn.

Feminists against pornography (as distinct from other antipornography camps) hold the opposite view—that our entire culture is pornographic. To them, pornography *is* convention, and all our sexual constructions are obscene; sexual materials are necessarily oppressive, limited by the constraints of the culture. Under this construct, I'm a damaged woman, a heretic. Catharine MacKinnon calls women like me "Uncle Toms"; according to Andrea Dworkin and John Stoltenberg, anticensorship feminists are no better than pimps.

There is so much wrong with traditional pornography. It just plain disgusts me sometimes, with its juvenile assumptions, boring repetition, lack of depth. But as much as what is wrong with porn, I see what is right: In porn, sex is separated magically from reproduction, marriage, and the heterosexual couple, all of which most feminists would agree have been oppressive to women. In porn, people have many and many different kinds of orgasms, and intercourse is only a part of sex, sometimes a small part. That alone, sex which doesn't focus on intercourse, is a very important image. Sex in porn is had by people of varying ages and appearances. Porn treats taboos openly and often humorously, emphasizes foreplay and a broad view of what is erotic. If you don't think this is true, you haven't seen much porn; these, as much as the come shot, are its icons. And getting rid of the come shot is easy—until more movies are made without it, that's what the fast-forward button is for.

Women like Catharine MacKinnon and Andrea Dworkin have allied themselves with a political camp that is also against reproductive choice, gay rights, and gender equality. Dworkin's lurid antisex prose reads like arty dime-store pulp to me. She looks down on me and shakes her finger: *Bad girl. Mustn't touch.* I've heard those words too many times before.

The male viewer of porn, like a prostitute's john, is a metaphysical presence. Is the act of viewing fundamentally exploitive behavior? It's an interesting notion, presupposing as it does a rigid boundary in which almost identical acts have diametrically opposed meanings; their meaning, in fact, depends as much on the volition and intent of the participant as it does on the object in question.

If we believe that sex (or porn) is "undignified" or

"degrading," we have to question what the definition of "dignity" is that we're using. We have to check out our semantics in order to reach agreement. "Degradation" by one act implies "purity" by another, or by not acting, so we not only have to define the acts involved, but "purity" and "degradation." This is remarkably hard to do.

"It's difficult to be an enemy of pornography without also disapproving of masturbation," wrote Kenneth Tynan. "In order to condemn the cause, it is logically necessary to deplore the effect." The condemning types usually find that fairly easy, though. Masturbation is undoubtedly the single most common sexual behavior in the world, but porn is frequently condemned for its "masturbatory" effect. Not only does condemning masturbation mean condemning all who masturbate, but I think the initial assumption is wrong. Pornography's single-minded intent is not masturbation, but arousal, which can be felt and acted upon in all kinds of ways, by people alone, in couples, in groups, and at later times, called upon like any memory. Also, perhaps more important, no matter what its purpose, pornography actually has many results: It validates desire, of course, but it also uproots traditional female roles of passivity, creates emotional confusion, stimulates introspection, and presents a world without the nuclear family.

No matter how much we talk about pornography as a "problem" or a "plague," or argue cause-and-effect relationships, to talk about pornography means having to talk about the millions of people who like to watch it, read it, think about it. If we talk about pornography with disdain, we have to talk about these millions of people with the same disdain, limiting them to the level of chess pieces in the propaganda game. If I may borrow a metaphor, people who want to eliminate pornography view the users of it with the same lack of feeling with which they accuse the users of viewing women. Also, and this is often forgotten, it's not possible to know how pornography affects people, any more than we can know how voting by mail, fast food, or moving to a subdivision affects people. We can't know such things about others, except in limited and suspiciously inadequate ways. All cultural analyses, including this one I'm making now, are little more than guesswork.

New pornography is quickly changing the course of the argument as well as making the semantic gymnastics that much more complicated. Lesbians are making films for lesbians. In fact, some of the most intelligent and thoughtful voices defending the liberating and even revolutionary possibilities of pornography are those of lesbian and bisexual women. There have always been "lesbian" films made by men for men, peopled by women groomed to fit a traditional and limited idea of what men find attractive, doing to each other what men imagine women want done. There are frequently fake lesbian scenes in heterosexual pornography, too, inevitably dete-

riorating into a three-way scene with a man who steps in
to finish the job as only a man can do. New films made
by lesbians, like *Suburban Dykes* and *Safe Is Desire,* are
wholly different in conception and shape because their
makers have wholly different points of view. These are
films born from a point of view traditional pornography
didn't even know existed, films that simply could not
have been made twenty years ago, because the women
who are making them had little or no access to film
production then. They are more than an updating of
pornography; they are a new form altogether. I wonder
if *Suburban Dykes* would be even ambiguously arousing
to men, or if it would instead engender the kind of
prickling anxiety in a heterosexual man that *Big Knockers* can engender in a lot of women—the kind of anxiety
that destroys arousal.

A whole genre of film involves dominant and aggressive women using and exploiting men. These films have
always been around, of course; the dominatrix is an old
and in some ways remarkably wholesome image—often
strong, almost maternal, protective in a complex way.
But these films are both more common and more in the
mainstream than they've been before, and like a lot of
films focusing on dominance, they may involve little or
no exchange of bodily fluids. Nor do they simply turn
the dominance of men around, because these hearty
women talk to men and command their attention in far
more succinct and startling ways than I've ever seen men

do to women in pornography. Theirs is not the dominance of gentle persuasion or seduction, but the demanding power of personality.

Some of the most tender and romantic images I've seen in porn involve men together without women in sight. Women like these films because the men are so attractive, and yes, they often have big pricks, too. (I know a lot of women who lament over the polished, sexy handsomeness of gay men, what tidy packages they can be, and none of it for them.) I suspect that some female interest in gay films has to do with the pleasure of discovering this country little heard from: The sexual relationships of gay men are hidden from women, they represent the one sexual world that women can't enter, and to me, at least, they represent a sexual world without any possible threat. I can see and be aroused by the intensity of male sexuality this way without any fear, without reference to my own life or anything that might be expected of me.

A recent film by Candida Royale, who was a porn star for years, seems to me a good emblem of what heterosexual pornography can look like in the hands of a woman. *Revelations* has a firm plot, a driving narrative, good acting, arousing but soft sex without any of the tiresome icons of conventional porn. Most of all, *Revelations* takes place in a political context; its world is a future dystopia, and its plot an exploration of the belief that censorship equals Fascism, and pleasure equals anarchy. In a way *Revelations* expresses the unconscious attraction of pornography as a form of expression: It represents sex *as* Revolution.

In talking about pornography, one can't ignore the problems of economic exploitation, labor issues, person-to-person hierarchies of power—not by any means. What I find telling is that the most vocal feminist opponents to pornography don't want to listen to *all* the women who are making these films—only to the women who are unhappy making these films. They sure don't want to listen to Candida Royale. They won't support the desire of some women in porn to create unions and control the means of production, they don't condemn the brutality inflicted by police and governmental regulation of such work, but strive instead to isolate these women and silence the ones who want to talk about why they enjoy the work. In fact, the stigmatizing that goes on around porn increases any pain women feel inside the industry, and decreases their ability to assert their own ideas for change.

When I read people's accounts of their initial sexual experiences, I am always struck by the litany of ignorance. What would we be like if people had ready access at a young age not only to reproductive information, but information about sexual pleasure and the enormous varieties of sexual experience? I hear cries of how awful it is for women's sexual identity to be shaped by traditional pornography—as though women's sexuality is not now and hasn't always been shaped by the dominant desires of other people, of men. What if women controlled this resource? Are degradation and prudishness our only choices?

Fatalism saddens me. I'm glad women are making pornographic films, writing pornographic books, starting pornographic magazines; I'm happier still when the boundaries in which women create expand. I don't believe there are limits to what women can imagine or enjoy. I don't want limits, imposed from within or without, on what women can see, or watch, or do. Even if I don't get it, even if I don't like it.

Our relative discomfort with any single piece of pornography will be directly related to whether we feel ourselves to be the object or the subject of the work—and to how comfortable we feel being object or subject of anything. Do we feel like actors, or the acted-upon? Which is more comfortable? Since pornography springs directly from an unfiltered and unedited (and still almost completely unanalyzed) imagination, eliminating porn wouldn't actually accomplish much, anyway. "[We] would still be left with the content of our fantasies," writes Richard Goldstein, who wants "excess and extremity" because that's what he doesn't have in his real life. "Those who long for realism in pornography—ordinary acts with plausible partners—ought to be condemned to dream that way." Porn is excessive in its emotional as well as its physical expression. Rarely does any sex act contain the intensity and the dramatized states of surrender, fear, anxiety, desire, and satisfaction that porn shows. We the lumpenproletariat disappear into it as into a dream.

Things change, grow more complex and strange and metaphorical, as I move from the front of the adult store to the back. Here is the leather underwear, dildos of all sizes, inflatable female dolls, shrink-wrapped fetish magazines. Here are movies with taboo themes—older films with incest plots, newer ones featuring interracial sex, and grainy loops of nothing more than spanking, spanking, spanking. Here are the films of giant breasts, or all-anal sex, food fights, obese actresses, and much masturbation. This is niche marketing at its best.

In the far back, near the arcade booths, are the restraints, the gags and bridles, the whips and handcuffs, and blindfolds. Here are dildos of truly heroic proportions. The films here in the very back are largely European and specific in theme. Back here I can't help but look at other customers; I find myself curious about which movies each of *them* will rent.

It was only last year when I stopped making friends go with me to the adult store. If I believe this should be mine for the choosing, then I want to get it myself. So I went yesterday, on a Wednesday in the middle of the morning, and found a crowd of men. There was even a couple, the young woman with permed hair and a startled look. She kept her hands jammed in the pockets of her raincoat, and wouldn't return my smile. There was an old man on crutches huddled over a counter, and a herd of clerks, playing bad, loud rock music. I was looking for a few specific titles, and a clerk directed me to the customers' computer, on a table in the amateur section. It's like the ones at the library, divided by title, category, and star.

The big-bellied, jovial clerk came over after a few minutes.

"That working for you?" he sang out. "I tell you, I don't know how the hell that works."

I tell him I'm looking for a movie popular several years ago, called *Talk Dirty to Me*.

"Hey, Jack," he yells. "We got *Talk Dirty to Me*?" In a few minutes four clerks huddle around me and the computer, watching me type in the title, offering little suggestions. From across the store I can still hear the helpful clerk. "Hey, Al," he's shouting. "Lady over there wants *Talk Dirty to Me*. We got that?"

"Pornography is the shadow side of myth, a racial memory expressed in obsessive imagery," wrote William Irwin Thompson. "Pornography, in a way, is indeed as the moralist claims, 'garbage'; it is the rotting compost-heap of old mythologies left over from all the cultures of human evolution." And maybe the new pornography to come will need a new name because it will be a new myth, a symbol of evolution into a sexual civilization, an "explanation" of sexuality as any myth is a human-size explanation of something much greater than humans.

8

A story is told about George Bernard Shaw. He is said to have met a woman and, in the course of conversation, asked her if she would sleep with him for a thousand pounds. She demurred as to how she might. Shaw then asked her if she would sleep with him for ten pounds. The lady was shocked. "What do you think I am?" she exclaimed. He replied, "Madam, we've established what you are; now we're negotiating the price."

This story is usually told with amusement—at the woman's predicament, at Shaw's quick wit. Like a lot of stories about Shaw, this one is probably apocryphal.

What if we tell it as a way of establishing not what the lady might be, but Shaw—or any man who finds amusement in the insult? "Sex is the only human activity in which the professional has lower status than the amateur," wrote Murray Davis. If the lady with whom Shaw sports is a whore, it is his particular relationship to her that makes her one. To be a whore is a shameful thing to most of us, but buying a whore's services is not. We may chide the john, but we also understand him, excuse him. There's no excuse for a whore. Even now, there's no worse insult for a woman than to call her a whore, a slut, an easy lay. And however inarticulately or unconsciously, a lot of people think whores are born, not made. Whorishness is an absolute state; it can't be cured.

And what is a whore? One working woman tells me she has no problem with the word as long as she controls it. "If someone called me a whore, I'd go, 'Yeah?' And I know women who will run around and call themselves whores, but if somebody *else* says it, oh—there's a charge there." Daphne, a twenty-year-old prostitute in London, told me privately that she finds it easier to admit she's a prostitute than to admit how much she likes sex. Because the sex she does enjoy, as well as the sex she doesn't, is "just work," she's not responsible for her own response. After all, both men and women can do prostitute work, but only women can be *whores*. Women who are good at sex, or say they like fucking and a variety of partners, are generally labeled whores whether they are paid or not; whores, in turn, who say they like their work are far more strongly censured than those who claim to despise it. At least the latter can be saved.

Various social analysts have tried to find the causes of prostitution; historical theories include the blurring of class lines, female sexual dysfunction, a hostile Oedipal complex, a lack of self-esteem. At times the perverse nature of lesbianism has been blamed for prostitution, as has, more reasonably, poverty and a lack of education. Then there's lack of moral training, a failure of religion. Female chastity as a virtue is an obvious cause, but it's never acknowledged. Instead, in perfect symmetry, the awakening of a woman's sexual urges is also considered a cause of prostitution. In the end, prostitution is "caused" by women themselves, by their nature. "She is a woman with half the woman gone," wrote the physician William Acton in 1857 in an influential tract on the subject. He blamed the "sinful nature" of women, along with the associative traits of "idleness, vanity, and love of pleasure." Prostitutes speak directly to the barely controlled sexuality of men. Prostitution depends on "demand and supply," wrote Acton, but most of all, it "is itself a cause of its own existence."

In other words, prostitutes create customers. In every modern war, prostitutes have been accused of corrupting and degrading (and giving diseases to) innocent soldiers. "Women give many more gonorrhoeas than they receive," wrote William Acton. "In fact they originate the disease." The great male myth of prostitution is circular: Female sexuality is dangerous, seductive, barely in check; "good" women avoid sex; men go to "bad" women for sex; these "bad" women are sexually experienced and therefore seductive and dangerous; these "bad" women have started the whole thing. Medieval lawyers hesitated even to punish the prostitute, because she acted only according to her nature. Her nature is to become what men want her to be; whores stigmatize themselves as sex partners to fit the stigmatized act of sex. ". . . Paid or not, she is equally called a whore," wrote Simone de Beauvoir in *The Second Sex,* "but if paid, an overshrewd one; when she wants her money, the man will pretend he did not think she was *that* kind of girl, and so on."

I was sitting in a hotel bar with a friend not long ago, at about ten o'clock on a Tuesday night. A delivery man walked in with three flower boxes, the long, slim kind for a single rose. He handed them to one of two men standing at the bar, both in their late forties, balding, one with a mustache and one wearing glasses—prosperous nebbishes. A few minutes later, three good-looking well-dressed young women strolled in—a cool brunette in a red blazer, a short-haired voluptuous blonde, a wan, long-haired blonde. The brunette approached the men at the bar, and I watched the introductions all around, the low, close conversation, the presentation of the flowers, the women's exclamations and quick kisses of thanks.

They shared a brief round of drinks and together left for a large car waiting at the curb.

"Prostitution is much, much, much, much—I can't *tell* you how much bigger and how much more underground prostitution is than anybody knows about or seems to have been willing to talk about." Samantha Miller is thirty-seven years old, a cheerful woman with a master's degree in counseling. Samantha used to run the National VD Hotline. Now she runs COYOTE, the oldest prostitutes' union in the United States. (COYOTE stands for Call Off Your Old Tired Ethics.) I had asked her about the streetwalker, the downtrodden woman so frequently seen in fiction and film, so little heard from.

"What you see, what is portrayed in the media, is about ten percent of what's really going on," Samantha told me. "And that really down-and-out, do-anything-for money kind is about five percent of the ten percent. That's what most people think of when they think of prostitution. But these women don't identify as prostitutes, or only very rarely. They just did this because they had to feed their baby, or whatever."

There are few statistics on prostitution, and COYOTE is one of the only organizations that has attempted to define the scope of the work. COYOTE's statistics indicate most prostitutes work privately and independently, far outside the view of the public. One problem COYOTE has identified time and again is the universal

racism at work in stereotypes of prostitution. Black prostitutes are arrested and convicted far out of proportion to
their numbers in the profession; about eighty-five percent of the prostitutes who do jail time are women of
color. But racism works both ways; black and Hispanic
women are far more likely to be harassed as though they
were prostitutes in the first place, as are foreign and
working-class women, as black men are far more likely
to be presumed to be pimps than white men, though
again, what statistics are available show this to be a false
presumption. But the most enduring stereotype of the
prostitute that Samantha Miller and her coworkers face
is the belief that they don't really want to be prostitutes
when they do.

The film *Pretty Woman* is probably the most widely
seen modern vision of prostitutes' lives. Prostitutes dismiss it with a snort, offended by its many pernicious and
wrongheaded ideas. One line of dialogue stands out in
particular. Richard Gere, defending himself in an argument, says to Julia Roberts, "I never treated you like a
prostitute." She demurs; it's true. And instead I want her
to scream, "How do you 'treat' prostitutes?" What does
that *mean?* What demand would he make on her if he
were to treat her like a prostitute? What is it in the
nature of being a prostitute that allows another standard
to be made? The real point of *Pretty Woman* isn't, as it
sometimes seems, that Julia Roberts's character is spunky
or naive or romantic, or even that she has really long
legs, but that *she isn't really a prostitute.* She hasn't got the

hard-core whore's soul. When I rail on, as I sometimes do, about how awful *Pretty Woman* is, people will say, "It's just a Cinderella story." And I wonder why they haven't figured out yet what a misogynystic story "Cinderella" is.

" 'Doing sex work is damaging,' people say. 'Giving all those blowjobs is damaging, it's degrading.' I think society's attitude toward blowjobs is what's degrading. Not the actual act," says Samantha Miller. "My belief, and this is really a hard one for people to take, is that given economic equality for women—all things equal—there would still be women who would choose to do sex work, to call themselves prostitutes, to sell sex for money, however you want to say it."

Prostitution is hard, perhaps impossible, to define. It is as shifting and malleable as sex itself. The ancient Latin name for a prostitute was *meretrix*—literally, "she who earns." Over the course of human history definitions have relied not only on the exchange of cash or goods for sex, but the number of men with whom a woman has sex, the percentage of time a woman spends having sex, even the degree of pleasure and lack thereof taken by the woman, this last to distinguish the professional from the merely shameless. World history has given us a great many variations on what we might consider prostitution, including travel companions for nomadic hunters, "temporary" marriages, "hostesses" for tribal guests, promiscuity during religious festivals, "hired" sex not for money but for increased spiritual harmony.

In some cultures, a whore is officially any promiscuous, unmarried woman—but there isn't necessarily anything evil attached to the name. What we may call prostitution might not be seen that way elsewhere or at another time; what another culture or time called prostitution might not seem so to us. According to the Bible, adultery is a form of prostitution. The one thing that is consistent in western history is that any "loose" woman, any "adventuress," is dangerous and must be controlled.

Prostitutes in history have often been of a lower status socially but with much greater social freedom than other women. (Status, that is, as defined by men.) "For a woman to enter male society, even at the level of an unequal, she had to lose her status as a proper woman," writes Vern Bullough, a longtime researcher in the history of prostitution. For all that the whore is always held by men to be below a lady, she has often been above the servant class. Women could achieve considerably higher social status as a prostitute than the class into which they were born. In some cases, upper-class whores were the most widely read of women. They had access to books, ideas, conversation, and an intimacy with men's powerful spheres denied to all "honorable" women. One could argue that her free roaming in the *minds* of men is as much a mark of the whore's shame as her allowing men freedom to roam in her body.

One of the more curious symptoms of the Victorian

obsession with sex was the widely held feeling that it was less degrading for a man to have sex with a prostitute than with his wife. It was, above all, the mixing of sexual passion with emotion and love that brought a woman down—or, rather, the mixing of love with anything remotely sensual. A good woman should be "above" that, enraptured spiritually by romance, and it was her spiritual purity that bound a good man to her. Men were better off going to prostitutes than debauching their wives with their unfortunate appetites. (Yes, I know this contradicts all that Victorian porn on lustful vampiric women, and it would seem that any "soul-of-woman-is-pure" philosophy has to be at odds with any "whores-are-born-that-way" philosophy, but such is the nature of human denial.)

Dichotomy and ambivalence always haunts the whore, who is so often expected to fill dual roles. The male double standard of female sexual purity creates female prostitution more than any other force. If your wife and daughter must be pure, then there must be other women who are not. The extremes of censorship seen in Victorian-era culture were believed necessary to keep good women pure and children innocent. One result was an explosion of pornography. Another was a brutalization of whores, whose status in a society obsessed with female chastity drops even as the demand increases.

The working reality of prostitution is far outside the stereotypes most people have, except for this one: Most prostitutes are in the business for the money, which is often quite good and sometimes shockingly so. Otherwise, nothing is as might be expected. COYOTE's statistics seem to indicate that most women begin doing sex work in their twenties and thirties rather than their teens, as many people assume. (Criminalization of prostitution and the stigma attached certainly makes it much harder to identify and protect teens who are in sex work and divert them into education and other kinds of help.) Many women in the business say that about half of working women are lesbians or bisexual. Everyone has a pet theory for this, or else no theory at all. Perhaps heterosexual sex is a detached experience for many lesbians, and concern with emotional relationships undistracting; perhaps the community of women within which prostitutes can work is emotionally attractive. A number of gay prostitutes talk about their clear-eyed understanding at a young age of how they could use sex with men without getting lost in it.

There are drugs in prostitution, more drugs in street prostitution than in "out-call" prostitution. But there are drugs everywhere and addicts in every profession, and people doing all kinds of things to get drugs, even selling stocks. The degree of drug use associated with prostitution—which is not necessarily drug use *by* prostitutes— has more to do with its shadowy illegal position in society than any characteristic of selling sex for money. A successful prostitute with regular clients is no more likely to be a helpless addict than a successful lawyer or physician; it's possible to be a successful drug addict, but not over the long haul.

There is also violence, fraud, and theft in prostitution, most of it directed at the working women; much of it is never investigated or prosecuted because a prostitute is seen to be a victim by her nature. She has, more than any other woman, *asked for it*.

I keep talking about the prostitute as a woman. This is both because the image of "prostitute" with which I was raised was always a woman, and because when I think of prostitution, I inevitably think of myself in that role, compare my responses to what I see and hear. But there are a lot of men working out there, and they're not being hired by women. Samantha Miller told me that just as there is a great deal more prostitution going on than most people suspect, there is a great deal more prostitution between men going on. Most of these "call guys," as it were, seem to be white, young, good-looking, healthy, fairly well-educated, and gay. "Seventy-five percent of the men that they see are married," says Samantha. "There's this huge thing going on all over the world; men are having sex with men all over the place and not talking about it. That's where heterosexual transmission of AIDS is. I wish all married men would see male prostitutes, because I know they're doing safe sex. But when men are doing it with each other, they're not."

Prostitutes are sometimes beautiful women, sometimes not; they are young and old; thin and heavy; buxom and flat-chested. They are comfortable with their bodies. I asked Jackie Daniels, a nom de plume for a longtime prostitute who happens to be well known by another name in another field, about the high-maintenance chores of the profession.

"When I first started, I had this idea that I had to be perfect," she answered. Jackie is an attractively tousled, almost maternally curvaceous woman in her late thirties. "I thought I had to have my legs completely waxed and my pussy shaved just so, and if I had a broken fingernail, I wouldn't make appointments. But there's just some men who love women, and they just want to see all kinds of women. They just love women. It doesn't matter what size, shape, smell, color, anything, they just love women. Then there are men who have a certain type they want—they want busty, or they want petite, or they want young. I have this one guy who I just adore, and he and I are just about the same age, and he wants someone older. He wants to fuck his mother."

Even now, when she's semiretired and in a relationship with one wealthy man, Jackie finds it hard to give up the idea of prostitution. The possibilities—the easy money, the no-consequences open-natured exchange— are always there, inviting. She knows it could happen right now, tonight, easy as pie, and she knows she's good at the job. She knows that the doorman and elevator operator and garageman at her penthouse apartment over the marina know what she does for a living, and seem to approve. "I want to show this apartment to people and go, 'See? I am *really* good in bed! Look at this apartment! Look at what my pussy got me!'"

Alex is a twenty-five-year-old prostitute. She grew up in the Bronx in a Puerto Rican neighborhood, the eldest daughter of a working-class family. She is a beautiful woman with pale skin, dark hair, a slender, athletic body, and a serene manner. Alex is bisexual. Alex left home at fourteen of her own accord, came to California, began doing telephone sex at nineteen, and became a prostitute at twenty-three. She has a bachelor's degree in community studies and funded her college tuition largely through sex work.

"I'd been thinking about doing this kind of work forever—at least, since I was fourteen years old," she told me. I interviewed Alex in the near-empty back bedroom of a friend's apartment in San Francisco. One of the first things she wanted me to know was that she'd given a lot of thought to prostitution before she started. "I was aware of having this sexual power that people wanted, and that I could use it to my advantage to get things I wanted. I was so sick of being poor all my life, and I wasn't looking forward to a whole life of being poor like my parents and grandparents had been."

Alex works largely out of the contact sheets that are sold cheaply through coin boxes or simply given away free in any urban area. Alex advertises as a "model or escort." Men call her, and before she'll meet them she asks them to talk about themselves a little, about their personal lives and work. "I need some form of human connection," she says, adding that she has "never, ever, not at all" had an abusive or even frightening client.

For a time Alex worked for a small "house," but the madam was busted. She would be scheduled for a three-day stretch, make a lot of money, and then take an extended period of time off work. She liked the schedule, the companionship of other women, and the ease of not having to screen her own clients.

"Would you agree to a single relationship?" I asked. "Being 'kept'?"

"Hell, no. I've never wanted *anyone* to own me. I would never be someone's little wifey. Sure, I'll be your whore for an hour, and when I leave, I go back to my own life. I'm not stuck with you for the rest of my life! I'd *much* rather be a whore than a wife."

When I ask Alex to tell me what she likes and doesn't like about the sex itself, she quickly makes a list: "I love doing couples together. S/M, totally. I will not let a client fuck me in the butt. I do that with friends, and it's one of the few things I save for friends only. Number one, it's too dangerous, and number two, it's just too intimate. And one of my favorite things sexually is being fisted, getting fist-fucked, and a couple of clients ask to do that. I have one regular client who *I* do it to, rectally, and that's fine, I love it. He has the whole setup in his house, a sling. But I wouldn't let a client do that for me, it's too personal and too close to who I really am. I've had clients who want to watch me masturbate, but when they want me to come, too, it's really tedious, because I generally don't. I guess I could fake it if I had to. I would love to do women alone, but so far there've been only a few who called, and they chickened out. Most of the women who do call are in a couple. I tried advertising in a gay paper, but mostly what I got was gay men curious about trying something with a woman.

"When I first started doing this, I was seeing a woman. I'd been involved with her for two and a half years, we were living together, and she was really upset. It was hard for her to understand that this was about business for me and not pleasure, and it wasn't like fucking other people. We split up for other reasons in the end. There's a guy I'm seeing now, and I told him right at the outset and he has a really hard time with it. If I'm going to be involved with someone, they've got to know. I'm not in the closet about anything.

"I think it's totally ridiculous that it's illegal. Totally ridiculous that it be regulated *at all*. Adults have bodies and some of us have money, and if we want to negotiate to use what we've got—I just don't understand why anything between consenting adults should be illegal. What business is it of the government? It's somebody pushing their morals on me, based on their belief system, which is totally different from mine. Totally ridiculous.

"I really believe there are some people who truly, truly love the work, a hundred percent of the time, and there's nothing they'd rather do. And then there's some people like me—sometimes I like it, sometimes I don't. I can tolerate it because the money's good, and I'm not going to make that kind of money anywhere else. And then I think there's people who just could not handle it at all.

"I like the fact that it's taboo, frankly. I've always liked things that were taboo. I feel sort of rebellious. Sometimes the sex is actually fun and I get off on it. A lot of the time it's kind of boring. Sometimes there's an attraction, a kind of chemistry. I like *people,* making connections with people. I have been so fiercely independent, all my life I've just gone my own way, and I love the fact that I can see who I want to see, not see who I don't want to see, work whenever I like, choose my hours, have total control over how much I charge.

"I think people are really hungry for touch, men come to me who are just *dying* to be touched. Paying any kind of attention to their body is so nice. Sometimes I see it as an extension of a massage, or getting a haircut or a manicure, just having another person take care of you and pamper you. Sometimes I love it and I have a great time and feel like I've done something nice for another. I've been paid well for it and there's respect on both sides. Sometimes it's like the best kind of work I've ever done. Sometimes!" She laughs.

"I don't feel like it's my life's calling. It's a means to an end. There's all kinds of things I want to do, entrepreneurial projects that take a lot of start-up money, and I'm sorry, but I'm not going to come up with that kind of money any other way. To me, feminism is about choices for women, period. I don't make it a point to hang with women who are against me. I wouldn't ask for that kind of abuse. I would love to see more options for women, I'd love to find another way to make two hundred dollars an hour, fine. You want to create those options in the world, great. But don't take away this option."

"What about the conservative feminist idea that sex workers are so oppressed, they don't even know they're oppressed, can't see it?" I ask.

"Get a life! I went to school with upper-middle-class self-identified feminist women who would argue with me in class about how prostitution contributed to the oppression of all women and how by participating in sex work I was furthering the oppression of women. Here I was, the only working-class kid in this whole classroom of upper-middle-class kids, and they were all going to tell me how horrible sex work was and how it was against feminism, and blah-blah. And it was, like, 'Fuck you! Mommy and Daddy are paying for *everything*. I have *nothing*. Don't you *dare* tell me what I can and can't do.'"

One of the sets of stereotypes that hovers around prostitution is the set relating to clients. Depending on the basic emotions you bring to the subject in the first place, you might tend to see the john as a slovenly loser, a cold manipulator, a sorry old fellow. Many women, I suspect, assume johns as a group are cruel and hostile toward all women. No one really knows—no one's done that research, either. I know of one book about johns, called *Lovers, Friends, Slaves: The Nine Male Sexual Types,* written by Martha Stein in 1974, a book talked about and passed around by prostitutes.

Martha Stein was a social worker who admits she knew little of sex, and nothing of cunnilingus, until she saw two whores perform it on each other. She became friends with a prostitute through her work, and eventually began observing exchanges through one-way mirrors and peepholes, sometimes actually hiding in the bedroom closet. She frequently tape-recorded the sessions, and kept track of the clients' statistics—age, body type, religion, amount of money spent, common topics discussed, sexual fantasies, and details of their sexual behavior and orgasms. Over four years, Stein claims to have watched 1,242 men with dozens of different women. Her methodology is suspect at best, although not original. Spying is an ancient way for novice prostitutes to be trained, and spyholes for rent to voyeurs are nothing new. Still, I can't help but enjoy such an exquisite betrayal of the contract.

Stein found surprises in her observed population of mostly upper-class professional white men. Ten percent "exhibited homosexual impulses"; four percent cross-dressed during sex; forty-three percent wanted to perform cunnilingus. (A number of others said they were interested but too shy.) One-third wanted anal stimulus or penetration. One-fourth had some kind of sexual dysfunction such as impotence. Almost every one wanted fellatio. Some men sought in the whore a kind of "hostess," a lubricant for business entertainment. Others wanted an adventure, and saw prostitutes as being open to "exotic" or "kinky" sex. Some men wanted largely to talk about their personal lives, listen, and give advice. Others preferred cuddling and sometimes cried.

Stein was surprised to find all her stereotypes defused. She found happy, attractive, healthy, prosperous prostitutes, many of whom worked part-time as whores and in their other lives were students or housewives. She also found happy, healthy clients. All the women claimed to have good personal sex lives, and any pimping was merely a matter of one whore referring a client to another whore or vice versa. She eventually came to admire and support the profession, seeing in it a twin to her own.

Stein also found that many of the clients had the same stereotypes of prostitutes as she did and were genuinely puzzled by the women's normality, so much so that sometimes the women would make up stories about sordid and abusive pasts just to satisfy them.

The step between being casually sexually active and getting paid for sex is both quite narrow and very wide. At certain moments there is a bare whisper of difference. Yet the pay, not the sex, is the source of shame for many women, who are insulted at the offer of money, gifts, or support by a lover. "I'll fuck you," they reply in essence, "but don't you dare try to pay me for it!" Taken at face value, this is rather absurd, and so there has to be more at stake, a deeper fear than insult—though the punishments meted out to women who are labeled whores are harsh and often irrevocable. Perhaps women fear that if they ever take money tied to sex, they will be seen as always available, always able to be bought. But prostitutes turn customers down all the time and may feel more in control of their relationships when they hold these purse strings. Women fear being labeled whores if the label is defined by men, because in male terms, the prostitute is outside the pale of male protection.

What happens if we—if I, as a woman, and therefore a potential whore every minute of my life—see prostitution in another way, if I move through the looking-glass to the other side?

"Part of my idea about getting into the business to begin with was to *train men,* to teach the men, get my hands on some men and teach them how we want them to *be,"* says Jackie Daniels. "To work with men around their sexuality, you have to go underground. And prostitution is a very clean relationship."

"My fantasy of it, before I got involved, was that there was this unlimited number of men and they would all want to see me once. And I was just amazed that men wanted to come back. I have people I've been seeing for years. I've had several boyfriends since, but I still have the same clients. It's very much like a therapist-patient or doctor-patient relationship. You get to know the person, details about their life, but there's the same sort of distancing. You sit all day and you listen to people's emotional problems, and you talk to them and help them process it and do all this emotional work with people. You don't then go have emotional problems at home. We will probably always need doctors, we will always need counselors, therapists, psychic healers, and advisers in the same way that we will always need prostitutes. These are sex experts, sexual healers."

"There are times when I spend an hour with somebody and nothing sexual goes on at all. There've been times when I wanted to say 'You know, if you would make an appointment like this with your wife, rent a hotel room, and lie down on the bed and talk with your wife, you wouldn't be having to lie down naked on a bed and talk with me like this.' I'm a sex therapist, that's my training."

Alex told me, "When these people come to you, they're coming to you not only for sexual release—which often is the easiest part—but with emotional needs as well. Some are lonely. It's almost as though they want a mommy for half an hour. It's weird because often I'm half their age, and here they are like little babies suckling at my breast, getting nurtured. They've had a hard day and they need somebody to rub their head and tell them they're okay. And a lot of the time they're people who in real life you *don't* care about, and you have to put all your own emotions on the shelf for that period of time."

Nina Hartley, a well-known porn actress, partly cred-
its *Our Bodies, Ourselves* as influencing her to consider
work as a stripper and in pornography. Much of that
famous book's message is female sexual self-determination and the value of the female body. Before she did
porn, Hartley worked as a nurse.

I also worked as a nurse for several years, and in
studying prostitution, listening to the women involved,
I'm repeatedly struck by how similar the jobs can be. As
with prostitution, some women are just not suited to
nursing. In both jobs you can have some, but not total,
control over your clients, and in both cases some clients
will be repulsive, obnoxious, needy, and unattractive,
while others will be charming and fun. Both jobs have
elements of unpredictability and stress, moments of great
satisfaction. The rewards are often surprising, not necessarily what one expected, and frequently the rewards are
private ones that can't really be shared or explained.
Both require a cheerful tolerance of the human body's
many quirks.

I don't think I'd be a very good prostitute for the same
reason I wasn't a particularly great nurse. I don't love
adrenaline, and both professions require an ability to
shift gears at a moment's notice, change moods and
manners, depending on the situation. I'm too much the
misanthrope to make the kind of psychic room a successful prostitute makes for her clients. Looking back, I can
see ways in which prostitution might be the better job.
There's very little paperwork, for one thing.

———

Jackie Daniels has never been arrested. "There was a shift in me, personally, where I realized I was doing sex work and that it was *fun*. I was making people happy, I was contributing to their lives, and I didn't see anything wrong at all with what I was doing. I was deeply confused about why this would be illegal. Then I realized some people just have this very small mentality. 'Well, it's *illegal*.' 'Because I'm the mommy, that's why!' There's no good reason. 'Because I said so.' Because God said."

The age of consent in Victorian England was twelve. One reason for the traffic in virgins was the prevalence of venereal disease. The Contagious Diseases Act of the mid-1800s set up a system whereby working-class women seen talking to soldiers on the sidewalk—or simply reported as having been seen doing so by a single citizen—could be arrested, imprisoned, subject to forced medical exams, and sentenced to hard labor for refusing to comply. If diseased, women could be kept forcibly hospitalized for up to nine months. Men were not examined or isolated even after contact with a prostitute found to have a venereal disease; they simply went to the next whore or the next town and infected another one, who would in turn be punished for "spreading" disease.

This sounds like the brutal ignorance of history. But today, in England and in various parts of the United States, women thought to be prostitutes can be prohibited from talking to men on the street. Anyone who thinks the "legalization" of prostitution—that is, government regulation by ordinance—is a good idea either harbors hostility toward prostitutes or hasn't taken a good look at Nevada, where this is the case. In the parts of Nevada where prostitution is regulated, prostitutes aren't allowed to live in the same town where they work. They aren't allowed to go into casinos or bars at all or be in the company of men in public—any men. They are tested weekly for venereal diseases, including AIDS, though their clients are not. A recent law requires clients to wear condoms. Condoms are, in fact, evidence of prostitution; both in England and the United States possession of a quantity of condoms is considered enough reason to arrest a woman. In England it's been the sole evidence cited in court when a woman is found guilty.

In 1985 "kerb-crawling" (soliciting women on the street) was made a crime for men in England. The law was purported to be an effort to equalize prosecution and protect women—just as prostitution stings are purported to be here. Laws against "kerb-crawling" and solicitation make any street exchange between any man and any woman potentially criminal. Women who work on the street hate the law, since it makes clients nervous. They feel less rather than more protected, more in danger. They have to make a deal as fast as possible and get out of sight, with no chance to consider uncomfortable signals. Under this law, women are much more likely to get in a man's car and go with him than bring him to their own working space.

The "red light" district, called by a thousand names, has been around almost as long as prostitution. This history, that of the regulation of prostitution, is a history of police tyranny, political duplicity, official abuse, and brutal punishments. Lots of people, including police and judges, don't believe prostitutes can be raped and are reluctant to pursue any such claim made by them. Prostitutes have long told stories of being raped and even forcibly pimped by cops.

The scorn heaped upon prostitutes greatly increases the violence against them. Easily the most dangerous and frustrating aspect of prostitution involves dealing with police. Once labeled a "common prostitute," as sometimes happens in the United States as well as elsewhere, a woman can be arrested on sight; women tell of being arrested while stepping outside in their bathrobe for the morning paper, or asking directions. Priscilla Alexander, who was codirector of COYOTE before Samantha Miller, points out that an arrest and fine for prostitution easily can result in a lost job and a huge debt, and these are the very things that sometimes push women unwillingly into prostitution. These things also enforce a woman's dependence on another person, for bail money and protection. Either way, laws against prostitution are laws against powerless women designed to keep them powerless; whether the irony is conscious in legislators' minds, laws against prostitution also encourage prostitution. "Forced prostitution cannot be addressed until voluntary prostitution is legitimate," wrote Alexander in a summary of COYOTE's findings on prostitutes' lives. "It is difficult to see how anyone benefits from the present system."

Men benefit from this system. Donna Niles, an ex-prostitute, points out that men can sell pictures of women's bodies to pleasure men, but women can't sell their own bodies for the same reason. Man-made laws ensure that money made from women's bodies will stay in male hands. Samantha Miller also agrees that there may be a semiconscious complicity in keeping prostitution illegal: "What's going on right here, today, is men don't want to take responsibility for their own sexuality, their own wants, desires, needs. So they set up this prostitute population as the scapegoat for all the bad things about their sexuality. It sets up a pool of women to be raped, because they have no rights—raped, battered, abused, because they're sexual."

One prostitute describes trying to get used to the insults, cat calls, and presumptuous grabbing at her on the street, the screams and threats from men passing by. "Maybe," she says, "it was because I looked men in their faces." Women learn at an early age not to do this. When we take self-defense classes, we have to start from scratch, learning how to look at and talk back to men. Prostitutes must do this in order to be identified *as* a prostitute, and to size the customer up. In both cases the direct look carries a veiled threat, a message—"I am in control of my body."

People who believe sex work is by definition bad, because it must by definition be exploitive, can rationalize extremely punishing behavior to save sex workers from themselves. One of the strip clubs not far from my house is routinely picketed by people who copy down the license plate numbers of customers, find their home address and telephone numbers through the Department of Motor Vehicles, and then make harassing calls to their homes and their neighbors. The same tactic is used by the antiabortion protesters of Operation Rescue.

One of my own big surprises when I began talking to prostitutes about their work was realizing that it was essentially illegal for them to talk to me. A level of trust is imperative, because a woman need only tell another woman which hotel to avoid, that the man in the red blazer is really a cop, or how to buy condoms wholesale to risk being arrested for "pandering"—pimping. And it's not an idle risk; pandering carries a much more severe penalty than simple solicitation. I asked one young woman what she would tell me about protecting myself from violence if I was just getting started, and she smiled and said, "Sorry. Can't do that. It's illegal." If a prostitute tells her friend not to get in the blue Toyota with the redheaded guy because he's dangerous, she has committed a greater crime than if she'd just gotten in the car and given the guy a blowjob, no matter how risky.

When members of COYOTE and other prostitutes'
rights organizations meet to exchange information, they
are technically breaking the law simply by being together, discussing their lives. They have, by congregat-
ing, "conspired to pander." This speaks volumes about
the hatred our society harbors not toward prostitutes, but
toward all sexual women. Their deaths are of less concern than their obedience.

The magazine *Whorezine* is published by COYOTE.
Whorezine runs a manifesto at the beginning of each
issue. It reads, in part: "This is <u>not</u> an introductory <u>offer</u>
because we <u>won't</u> hold your *hand* and we <u>don't</u> provide a
glossary. <u>This is unclear</u>, because we won't tell you when
we're winking or when we're JOKING or when we're
fucking with your mind and we don't explain the subtle
details. **This is not a toy.**" *Whorezine* and several similar
magazines are the house organs of career prostitution.
They publish everything from reports on dangerous clients, hotel etiquette, tips for when you're arrested, which
hotels to avoid, news about AIDS, where to get specialized clothing, and lawyer referrals to a history of temple
harlots. They are thick with the slang of the trade, in-
sider gossip, and the kind of jokes you don't get if you
haven't been there. Here's talk of looky-lous and turn-
over, zones and donut-eaters, mixed in with advice not
to reduce rates in a recession and to stay on top of *Bar-
rons* and *The Wall Street Journal*.

The term "sex worker" is becoming common enough now to merit a definition. A sex worker might work on a pay-telephone fantasy line, dance topless, strip, perform in simulated or real sex shows, sell sexual services to individuals, be a sexual surrogate, or work as an explicit sex demonstrator, as do a group of people in San Francisco who call themselves the Safe Sex Sluts, demonstrating erotic safe sex techniques in ways that leave nothing to the imagination. All are sex workers, and more and more often, such women and men see themselves in an alliance. They are peers and coworkers in a business called the sex industry, and their coalitions muddy the stereotypes and increase the power the workers have.

Say "sex work" to almost anyone outside the industry, and that person will hear the word "sex"; "work" is a distant and seemingly unimportant echo. To look at sex work as *work* first can turn every assumption on its head. Sex work, like all employment, has labor issues, class issues. When prostitutes compare prostitution to other jobs, like secretarial work, compare them by pointing out how badly paid, boring, subservient, and predictable secretarial work can be, by describing how frequently secretaries suffer sexual harassment, they are effectively shouted down. It is acceptable for a woman to work, and it is generally acceptable, under certain circumstances, for a woman to have sex, but even the most liberal people are troubled by the idea that a woman might work at sex. We believe, in fact, that you can do all kinds of nasty things for money, all kinds of despicable things: poison the environment, build bombs, destroy tenements, raze forests for money. Just about anything but sex.

When prostitutes point out that every job, but especially the kind of lower-paid full-time job most women must take, requires compromise and dependence, they are ignored. When they say that with sex work you get the most money for the least work, with the most minimal sacrifice of your private self, they are condemned.

A number of national and international groups are working to obtain equality and protection for prostitution: the International Committee for Prostitutes' Rights (ICPR), which has a charter of proposed rights for prostitutes of both sexes in all countries, and associated groups like COYOTE, twenty years old now, and PONY, Prostitutes of New York, and the National Task Force on Prostitution; and the International Collective of Prostitutes (ICP), with numerous national branches, which is affiliated with the International Wages for Housework Campaign, promoting economic equality for women.

Almost all these groups advocate decriminalization of prostitution rather than any legislated controls or regulation, including government-controlled brothels and zones such as are found in Germany. Decriminalization of prostitution—meaning no laws of any kind prohibiting the exchange of sex between adults for money or goods—paves the way for real unions, unions that can make contracts, engage in collective bargaining, in train-

ing and education, unions that can go on strike.
Decriminalization puts the power of prostitution in
prostitutes' hands. All these labor organizations are concerned with and actively work against forced prostitution and any sexual exploitation of young, poor, or addicted women and men. This particular liberation
movement has several sectors of agreement and disagreement, but it sees itself as feminist at heart. It *must*
be feminist, it seems to me, can't be anything but feminist, to support the right of women to control the use of
their bodies. Work for prostitutes' rights is at one with
work against poverty, lack of education, addiction, sexual inequality, and every other condition that limits the
freedom of men and women both to choose for themselves.

Sex and sex shows are versions of identity, ways of seeing and being seen, part of the long human history of
performance. Being seen is an important and perhaps
integral part of sexual intimacy, it's what we fear the
most and what we want the most from sex. Often in sex
we fake "showing" ourselves, as a smoke screen to hide
our real selves. Sex performances are a metaphor for sex
between any two people who are emotionally entangled
and trying to reveal themselves; sex shows make sex look
easy.

When I first went to a sex show, I took Don and
Jeannie both; no way was I going alone. The air was cold

and fog-damp on the sidewalk, under the flickering lights; the foyer seemed warm and welcoming. I paid the staggering cover charge, counting out several twenty-dollar bills one by one; when I asked for a receipt, the tuxedoed bouncer near the door threw back his head and laughed, and then gave me one.

We walked down a dark, mirrored hallway with doors on both sides. At the end was a high-ceilinged, shadowed room like a cave. A hundred men murmured and elbowed each other there, jostling for a view; many of them were conservatively dressed Japanese. When a few caught sight of us, I felt Jeannie suddenly shivering beside me; she grabbed my arm and whispered, "Don't leave me alone." We turned from the men to the little bar in one corner, looking for a shot of courage. But everyone wants a shot of courage here, and the theater disapproves of false bravado, and serves only soft drinks. When I turned back to look more closely at the customers, I could see how they shuffled in place, restive and sober. In the distance, over their heads and under warm yellow lights, I saw a stage, where a softly shaped blond woman soaped herself gently under a slow shower.

Don disappeared in the mob. Jeannie and I went back down the hall for the peep show. I had begun to stare back at the men staring at me, and always they turned away. We crowded together into one booth, arms around each other to fit, and pressed close to the glass. Through the window I could see a rectangular, carpeted room and rows of other booths lining the sides. In the windows floated the vague and ghostly faces of men, waiting. I heard a door open, close, the shuffling of feet, a muffled yell, and then tinny music. A woman dressed in black leather entered the room. She had long, fine, honey-colored hair, big white teeth, a sardonic grin. Her long, pale legs were covered past the knee in black leather boots. She danced and bucked energetically around the room, cracked a short whip in one hand, and as she passed I could see the rings pierced through her nipples and the slim silver chain dangling between her labia.

Money began to fall through various slots at the bottom of the windows, one bill after the other, and she tossed them over her head as she passed. The paper money floated lazily in the breeze of her movements, like autumn leaves, drifting to the ground.

Eventually she returned to us. Jeannie looked at me, her breath quick, intoxicated. The dancer caught our two surprised, female faces, and spread her legs above our heads. Her vulva was shiny with sweat.

"How do you like *that?*" she hollered, and I heard a muffled shout in Japanese from the booth beside us.

Japan, which has outlawed the depiction of pubic hair, even on news photos of corpses, is awash with nudity and live sex shows. As Nicholas Bornoff points out, looking up skirts is both a real and metaphorical preoccupation in a country with no elbow room, no leisure time, no privacy, intense segregation of the sexes, and a history replete with sex, violence, and extraordinary inventiveness. Understanding the nuances and motives of

Japanese sexual behavior is a daunting task even for a seasoned westerner, and for many Japanese. The apparent contradictions are, I suspect, more like layers than anything else, fitting quite neatly together if one only understands the code. And contradiction is certainly part of the code. Japan interests me to the extent that it is different from everything I know, alarms me with its sudden similarities.

Japanese men, who disdain women in ways impossible for a western woman to tolerate, revere female genitalia, femaleness itself, with a reverential passion that most American men would find embarrassing at best. Japanese men are fixated on mother images, passive women, whores, and virgins. They have little, if any, public embarrassment about things sexual. Their historical erotica is perhaps the most beautiful of all time; part of their current erotica, the *manga* comics, has a hero called Rape Man. These visitors around me are, if anything, getting less of a show here than they can find at home. Live sex shows in Japan sometimes include sex or an attempt at sex between an audience member and the actress. But one of the central events is often a kind of communal gynecology. The women allow the men to examine their genitals briefly, carefully, with magnifying glasses, flashlights, sometimes dildos, and sometimes their latex-covered fingers. Yet whether it is the foreignness of the place, the plethora of large white women, the absence of alcohol, or a combination of these things, they seem subdued and nervous. They huddle, the way Jeannie and I do, and maybe for the same reasons.

Later, we waited in the crowd for the next shower show to end. Men everywhere, men all around us; along the balconies, stony-faced men in booths, men in chairs against the wall, and lined up by the steps down to the tables. As we sidled our way down the steps, the men parted for us, stepped aside, stopped talking. I felt less audience than performer for a moment; I felt more like a participant in this hitherto unknown group act.

The three of us took an empty black-leather booth, higher than the tables and facing the black stage with its silver showerheads. We waited like schoolchildren, hands clasped. The blond woman I'd seen bathing earlier leaned over the booth. She was cherubic, her creamy skin damp and a ringlet of hair still wet, and her smile was soft and a little goofy. I couldn't stop staring at her feet, her bare feet solidly planted and soft and pink, leaving damp footprints on the tile floor. She set a vinyl handbag filled with sex toys on the table in front of me and asked, "Hi, I'm Georgia. Would you like a show?"

The negotiations fell to me, and I laid a few bills on the table, and then a few more, and more, until Georgia suddenly swept it all up and nodded and called to her partner. "Penny."

Penny was a slim, boyish brunette standing a few feet back. At her name she drained the Pepsi in her hand and set the can aside, and climbed up on the table. Her face was plain and intelligent and relaxed. She lay back on a white towel and stretched her white arms above her head to touch the wall, her face inches from Jeannie's, and then slowly she pulled her legs up and rolled her bottom out, and her shaved genitals appeared in the center of the table like a dish. And Georgia caressed her with her tongue while we watched, and when I looked again at Jeannie I could see her pupils were dilated so that her brown eyes were big and dark.

Catharine MacKinnon believes that these structures around us, around Georgia and Penny and Jeannie and me, are necessarily misogynistic, and that any woman's involvement in these structures will hurt the woman before it changes the structure. MacKinnon is a lawyer. I wonder why she chose to enter a profession marked by its support for patriarchal institutions, and its lack of reason when it comes to the many concerns of women. She argues the fine points of constitutional interpretation within a strictly defined social construct written by men, and I think she hopes that her presence will gradually force those social constructs to evolve, loosen. She has said it is uncomfortable, sometimes frightening, often lonely to be in her position, a woman in a man's world. I know that my presence at this table has to change the boundaries within which these things exist. Women guiding the sexual drive of men change them, gentle the institutions men have made to cope with their feelings toward women. The near silence of the men around me makes me think that Jeannie and I, like Georgia and

Penny, have taken charge somehow. Women literally emasculate male institutions, change them into something more androgynous, by nothing more than their presence.

I could hear the audience applauding the dancer in the room next door, and people moving in and out of the tables near us, but these things receded, dreamy and still. In sex there are new rules, sometimes no rules; the body takes charge. We are no longer in the quotidian sphere. Georgia's curly hair drifted across Penny's breasts, and my own hunger seemed to explode within. In front of me all this sweet, clean skin, and the rising bouquet of arousal, and in slow motion, a beringed hand slipping to stroke between two legs in the dim and coppery light. Then Georgia rose up from Penny for a moment and I caught Don's eye, and he was laughing at my punch-drunk face. I looked at Jeannie and she was staring at the women right beside her, almost in her lap; I looked back at Georgia and she'd turned in the midst of the act to watch the pair of naked women embracing on the table next to us, watched by three Japanese men in suits. And I turned to look at the men gathered around the tables a few feet below us and I could see them watching me, watching them.

The sexual fantasy not of going to a whore, but of being one, is quite common. There is a whore in each of us, the whore who conquers our desire by selling it, conquers our fear of abandonment by controlling the risks of all her relations. The urge to romanticize the prostitute and her life is just like the urge to imagine her as infinitely sordid or as an inevitable victim—more about us than the whore. The whore scares us, the happy whore most of all, because she doesn't need conventional rules to survive and thrive. She makes up her own.

"I don't look like this when I go to clients," Alex tells me toward the end of our interview, curled up cross-legged on the bare mattress in jeans and a soft flannel shirt. Her dark hair is shaggy and loose, and she wears no makeup. "When I go to clients I'm a totally different person. I do run an ad sometimes that specifically says 'tomboy,' and I get guys who really like that, and don't want me to wear makeup. Still, I've got to get into the gym and work out and be in shape, and if I gain a little weight it's 'oh, no.' I have to shave all the time, which I'd rather not do. When I work, I'm usually in full-done drag, high heels and makeup and hair done up and a little dress that shows my cleavage.

"I'm dressed in this way I never normally dress, I'm playing the whore, the slut, the nympho, whatever, and I can have fun with that, but they don't realize it's just a role. I like role-playing with friends, too, sometimes, but they know who the real me is. I think most guys *love* the whole garter-belts-and-stockings thing, they want you all done up, looking slutty and sucking their dick on all fours."

Prostitution inevitably comes back to desire. When I

interviewed Jackie Daniels, and she talked about how some men just love women, that prostitutes needn't be beautiful, she added, "You could be a sex worker. Easily." And I was flattered, in an odd way. Could I, really? And on the other hand, when I talked to Alex, sitting cross-legged on a bare double mattress in an empty apartment, I realized how attractive I found her and thought: I could pay her for sex. Two hundred dollars, one hour, what the hell, it's only money, and as soon as I imagine it my lust expands outward, and as soon as I feel the desire, I feel embarrassed about my body, anxiety about my performance, fear of rejection. The fact that I know so clearly that for her it would be just work is both a relief and a sorrow. All our fears and fantasies about whores center around the fact that they *know* us in a certain way, a professional way that is disconcerting. I wonder how many of these same confused feelings, these human feelings, are shared by every young businessman, every balding, potbellied CEO who buys Alex's time. And how she calms their fears.

The genital dance of sex work demystifies the spiritual image of sex, and, at the same time, *remystifies*. Sex work has the potential to tease the true anxiety men feel about women, the anxiety they hide in brutality or simply bravado, tease it up to the surface to be transformed into something else—desire, affection, rest, wonder.

The original "harlots" were sacred women who worked in temples, a widespread practice in the ancient world. Temple prostitutes had sex with visitors in exchange for donations to the temple and as a way of both gaining and giving spiritual merit. If we respect myth and the living power of cultural history in any way, we have to bemoan the loss of the sacred harlot; we have to mourn her translation into the pitiful whore of modern myths. The degrading of prostitutes is a direct comment on the degradation of the concept of the Goddess and the ancient celebration of the power of women.

We want sex and romance both, but not necessarily together. Most of us still think somewhere in our secret hearts that sex is nasty, and we hesitate to link it irrevocably with intimacy, love, and cherishing. But because of our training and because we long for love and intimacy, we hesitate to accept free sexual relations *without* intimacy and love. So prostitutes, who have cheerfully made the separation in their own minds, evoke a lot of hostility, much of it illogical and inconsistent. How dare they codify so bluntly that sex can be a product? And how dare they attract us to that idea so much?

The whore-with-a-heart-of-gold, longing for love. The whore-who-deserves-it, the serial killer's favorite target. When I asked Alex about this fantasy, this confused image, she said, "It was clear to me when I did finally start doing sex work, after thinking about it for many years, that all the fears and ideas I had about it weren't true. Sometimes it does feel like I'm doing something spiritual and healing and sacred, and I do like knowing the history, that there was a tradition of temple prostitutes. At another time I could have been totally respected for this. And I like aligning myself historically with women who were rebels.

"It's still true that the worst thing you can say to insult a woman is to call her a whore. 'You fucking whore.' It's hard to grow up hearing that all your life and not internalize it. I know I have and it pisses me off, because this is a great line of work and it sucks that I have to carry around everybody else's shame about it."

9

Dreams are a normal, even mundane part of everyone's life. Dreams are taken for granted, though even a brief examination of a single one reveals details terrifying and sublime. Fantasies are waking dreams, and at times I find it harder to talk about my fantasies than my actual sexual experience. What I *do* sexually is the product of many factors, not all of them sexually motivated. But what I *imagine* doing is pure—pure in the sense that the images come wholly from within, from the soil of the subconscious. The land of fantasy is the land of the not-done and the wished-for.

Sexual fantasy can be cloven into two layers. Each fantasy has a subtext, a ground upon which conscious details can be laid. This is the fundament of desire that rises at a very early age, the basic elements of sexual response that won't go away and can't be changed. If my sexual ground is seduction and courtly romance, all my fantasies will follow that road one way or the other, whatever details are added. If my ground is submission with a hint of leather, every story will contain that. Atop this ground is the texture—the endlessly varying details of plot, context, outcome, and point of view. So I might end up with courtly romances with a hint of leather, seduction scenes built on dominance—round and round the merry-go-round I go. To some extent we can control and manipulate sexual fantasies; most especially we can try to control ourselves in the fantasy so that the "I" in the fantasy behaves and feels as required for satisfaction. The fantasy world is guilt-free and distraction-free and odor-free (unless you want odors) and sweat-free (unless you like sweat) and discomfort-free (except as you like discomfort). All you have to know is what you want.

Who knows when our fantasies first get seeded? Secret glances, misunderstood phrases, odd encounters that have the flavor of the unspoken or the forbidden, gradually dreamed into sexual images, the occult of the wandering ego. The archetypes of fantasy are those of one's psychological environment. Perhaps for one person they follow themes of intimacy and separation; for another, power and surrender. These are the symbolic relationships we explore in all our meetings, and they withstand tremendous attention.

The point of fantasy, if there is any point besides the fantasy itself, is not merely exaggeration or freedom from social constructs, but a kind of comfort with the dissonance of sexual desire. (And life.) Most powerful fantasies of all kinds, and particularly sexual fantasies, have an element of dissonance, surprising or shocking combinations, confusions of all boundaries from gender on out, blurring and blending, breaking the rules. This is something the Japanese understand very well; Ian Buruma notes that brothels and hostess bars in Japan feature stewardesses, nurses, bank clerks, cheerleaders, "American" disco dancers, Jane in the jungle waiting for Tarzan, Catholic nuns, Indian maidens, and more, all ensconced in settings ranging from science-fiction futures to medieval castles to faux Shinto shrines.

Americans have Nancy Friday and her collections of sexual fantasies. Her female correspondents relish the chance to break rules.

". . . I wake him up and ask him to accompany me to the bathroom, where I proceed to teach him how to shave all the hair off his legs . . ."

". . . I have saved my best one till last. It involves picking up a stranded priest and nun at a bus stop. As we move down the highway, my beautiful blond girlfriend takes out her pistol and makes them handcuff each other . . ." And so on, and on.

There are many recurring images in these collections

of prime masturbatory material: the two-women-and-one-man fantasy, the two-men-and-one-woman fantasy, the woman-watching-two-men fantasy, the one-woman-and-a-dog fantasy. "Another fantasy has to do with bratwurst . . ." The books taken as a whole seem to represent a kind of oneupmanship of imagination, a beating-the-bush game. As a window on the American imagination—self-selected as they are—Friday's fantasies are chock full of the American porn dream: endless sex, repetitive acts of taboo-breaking, huge erections, enormous orgasms, power over and submission under authority figures—in other words, all the American pioneer elements of youth and control, robust health and infinite desirability. They are cocky, knowing, explosively pubescent. It is as though the motto of the American sexual imagination were that old Avis chestnut: We Try Harder.

Just as there are many things we want to dream about but don't actually want to experience in life, there are things we do in sex with great enthusiasm which would make boring fantasies. (They still make good memories, though.) One remembers good sex in the broken way of dreams. Any effective fantasy has to capture that quality of suspension—of sex taking place in a separate, special environment outside the ordinary realm. Or in an ordinary realm made strange by the sudden presence of sex.

I am particularly fond of one described by Norma Jean Almodovar, an ex-prostitute in Los Angeles who organizes for COYOTE. She had a client who was crazy about Julia Child, and willing to pay her hundreds of dollars to shop for a good whole chicken, put on an apron and, in Julia's voice and manner, "cook" it for him. " 'Notice its pale pink flesh, tender but firm to the touch,' " Norma would say as she pretended to prepare the chicken and he wiggled in delight on a chair nearby. " 'Oh, look at that butter! Doesn't that look good! Let's stick our impeccably clean finger in there and get a taste of that sweet butter. Mmmm, isn't that yummy! I just love to lick the juices off my fingers, don't you?" Inevitably he would reach orgasm as she started to "baste" the cooking chicken. "I always wondered what he did with the chickens after each session." *Bon appétit!*

Most fantasies have exaggerated or forbidden elements; some are genuinely scary or painful—and worth dreaming of still. But fantasies aren't about our ordinary lives. Fulfilling the plot of a fantasy in real life is almost certain to be disappointing because it means losing this control, control over what we can never control, and in exchange, returning to a world that is often mundane, uncomfortable, and ambivalent. A world that condemns the world of the fantasy in the first place. I suspect the man who goes to a prostitute to fulfill his fantasy of having sex with a prostitute is really fulfilling a wish—a psychic dare—and not the complex subconscious narrative ground of fantasy that makes prostitutes so desirable to him. If I fulfilled my *fantasy* of being a prostitute by taking on a client, I don't think the fantasy would be satisfied at all. It wouldn't be the same—couldn't be, at least in part because the "me" that is the prostitute is not exactly me.

I sometimes find it disturbing to read about people making their fantasies come true for real. I won't soon forget a long and terribly uncomfortable story by a woman who dressed in a little-girl nightie and had her "daddy" (another woman) awaken her, seduce her, spank her until she collapsed in childish weeping, and then comfort her and put her back to bed. The extraordinary courage of the writer melds with the rarity of anyone going about conquering her private fears this way. This is primal scream therapy, true-life recovery, and real sex all at once. For the most part, I suspect such efforts don't work as well, because the psychic impetus has to be so strong.

Just as we can be both subject and object of pornography, move in and out of its power that way, within fantasy we can be mover or moved, giver or receiver— we can be top or bottom, man or woman. More specifically, we can be *imagined man* and *imagined woman*. Women become boys and men become mothers, fucking boys, or girls, fucking girls, or goats, or brothers, or fathers fucking mothers or schoolteachers or angels, or dogs. Men have no penises but giant vaginal mouths, women thrust and intrude upon men. Blurring is inevitable. In our sexual fantasies we transmutate like superheroes of the boudoir, sprouting pricks, wings, breasts, tentacles, growing in stature and magical staying power.

All Americans share the fantasy of physical beauty and strength. Those with bodies beyond normal often fill our fantasies; they are dream creatures, incubus and succubus, heroines and heroes, archetypes of the possible. We would like to be them; in fantasy, we *are* them.

In the middle of the last Olympics I noticed a sudden change in the population of my fantasies. Everyone in them, male and female both, sprouted muscles. So did I, in my dreams: big, shiny muscles bulging out of tank tops and nylon running shorts, genitals outlined behind silver spandex suits. All those bodies I'd been watching were idealized physical machines, fit and enduring, self-aware. I'd been lifting weights a little and watching the wiry, sinewy old men and muscular women in my funky YMCA weight room, which always smells a bit of old sweat and chalk. I'd been learning to grunt from the lower belly with each lift, then coming home to watch the skiers with their potent thighs and short haircuts and quick, cheerful smiles; it all blended together, health and sex, hygiene and sweat, and the extreme limits of duration. What a simple creature I am, really.

Nancy Friday quotes a thirty-two-year-old woman who remembers reading the story of Prometheus at the age of eight. Prometheus remains her most intense sexual fantasy. "Sometimes I *am* Prometheus, sometimes I am the eagle, and sometimes I am a combination, or an observer. The god-giant-titan Prometheus, immortal, beautiful, primitive, instinctual, animal, is chained to the lonely cliff as punishment for caring for the fragile, barely surviving human race." Prometheus watches the eagles arrive, and I imagine Friday's unnamed informant moaning with pleasure at their appearance, "growing slowly larger as they home in on their rightful meal, that which is destined to be theirs every day, that delicious living immortal meat torn from the perfect breast. . . . When they have rested a little from their flight, they rip into the chest, exposing the vitals to the burning sun. The reddish, dark, vital liver awaits them. Blood runs from the opening down his chest. Slowly, coolly, the eagles set about the business of gorging themselves. . . ." This dream has rather more in common with fantasies of big pricks and tied-up nuns and medieval harems than it might seem. All this agony and meat, the dark, vital organs and the blood—that's texture; the fantasy's eternal oscillation, its insatiability, is the ground. The fantasy repeats, and repeats; the body is whole, and rended, and whole again; the hero is bound, helpless, punished, and repaired. The orgasm leaves us shaking, spent, but somehow complete.

For years I examined all my fantasies, analyzed them for content and import. The YMCA showers-after-hours. Kidnapped-for-love. White-slave-in-the-harem. Romance-under-the-elms, in the pool hall, on the beach. At first I just felt guilty about them. (Of course, I also felt guilty about sex and about masturbation itself, most of us do, but this was a specific concern about the fantasies.) I was guilty because so many of them were filled with images of forced seduction, sexual surrender and overpowering. I was sometimes user, and sometimes used. I called them "rape fantasies," even though rape in any sexual fantasy, including mine, rarely looks like and never feels like rape in the real world. Funny how long I knew that "rape" was the wrong word to describe them, but continued to use it anyway, castigating myself. I thought then that *any* fantasy involving subjugation was inappropriate, unfeminist, rotten at the core. My first, protofeminist, solution to the guilt was to assume that I was incorporating real-life oppression into my fantasy life, and that with the hoary solution of consciousness-raising, I could make them go away.

So I exhaustively catalogued and examined them. I neurotically asked where they came from, what they *meant*. The result of all that wasn't to make the fantasies go away or even to pull the fantasies' teeth, but to make the fantasies more complex, more detailed. The analysis was getting in the way of the heat, and so the heat increased. Fantasies of power are largely shame-driven, and if they mean anything in particular, they mean being free—of guilt and responsibility. But I was ashamed of the shame.

My second attempt to reconcile them, once my consciousness seemed pretty damned raised and the fantasies stuck around, was to say the fantasies were a reaction to being a strong woman in a world that punished strong women, and they were an extension of my need to be taken care of sometimes. Perhaps they would go away when I learned to ask for nurturing. (They didn't, and I still felt guilty.)

My third and final solution—that these are *my* fantasies and they're fun and not particularly anyone else's business—arrived only after a lot of talking and listening to and reading about similar confusion in other women, women I admired, who'd traveled much the same psychological road without successfully expunging anything. I read enough and talked enough to know that more people, both men and women, gay and straight and bisexual, prefer fantasies of being dominated to fantasies of being in charge.

Gradually I began to wonder why every other element of my life felt acceptable within sexual fantasy except the element of oppression and power. Every time I fall asleep, my dreams fill with the details of the day, with a name or a bit of news, a place I'd been, a person I'd seen, with waves if I've been to the beach and fruit if I've baked pies. And every single day of my life I see power, control, oppression, suppression, repression, sexism, anger, hunger, thwarted desire, loss of control, wrestling over control. Should sexual fantasies somehow be bound so tightly none of our daily experience intrudes? What kind of psychic fence must I build to keep often-contradictory feelings about the cultural dance I do outside my sexual imagination? I know now that it's impossible, that only by gagging and binding my own imagination could I stop imagining a gag now and then. Women suffer twin guilts: Not so long ago, we were punished for feeling or imagining unbridled desire; now we punish ourselves for imagining submission. Is only some bloodless moderation to be allowed? And how am I to account for the millions of men who close their eyes and dream of being gagged and bound themselves?

"O wondered why there was so much sweetness mingled with her terror. Or why she found her terror so delicious." Read *The Story of O* as an example of how pornography tries to teach women to submit to men and love their abuse. Read *The Story of O,* written by a woman, as a revolutionary document of sexual surrender. (Or just read it as a masterpiece of bondage porn.) O is the cipher, the orifice; she shows her lovers, and her readers, the empty door of herself, her own emptiness, her gradual surrender and release, her submission to internal forces. The book is a tragedy, an intersection of unbidden fantasies and the real world. I used to hide my copy in a box in the back of my closet; I didn't want anyone to know I'd read the book, let alone that my copy was fairly well thumbed. Then I realized how ironic that was—hiding O's story the way O hides her chains.

I reached a point where I could laugh about a fantasy I had, without embarrassment, laugh at its silliness, its obviousness, and its ability to arouse me no matter what—and that's when the guilt, not the fantasy, disappeared. And the result of *that* was the fantasies began to diminish. Their power over my conscious mind seemed to exist in direct proportion to my resistance. They *will* be there, and comfortably so, as long as I don't waste a lot of time trying to excise them.

So, over the last few years my own fantasies have become briefer, less detailed, and more effective. Now she hardly gets her pants off, so to speak. My fantasies are also becoming more fragmented, shifting, slipping. I had to stop analyzing them for meaning or significance in order to really have them in the first place. The analysis was a way to circle the fantasies, darting in and out, staying just out of reach, not quite engaged and yet bound to the images. I never surrendered to the fantasy because I mistrusted it. But only surrender makes the fantasy come to an end, be finished, be used up, be *psychoanalyzed* and not just analyzed. I surrender *to* them for the same reasons I surrender *in* them. Release.

With this simple willingness to go along for the ride, not pushing or pulling or manipulating, having a sexual fantasy for me now is a little like going to a movie, or an especially good amusement park. I'm not sure what will happen next. I'm not sure who *I* will be—that is, what point of view I will take, when the point of view will suddenly change. Questions of gender or sexual preference or fetish seem silly. I'm literally being entertained now, instead of analyzed, and there's no room for guilt. Since I believe my subconscious contains elements of male and female, and the whole range of preference from Kinsey 0 to Kinsey 6, and any number of rare perversions beside, I can't really claim to be surprised by what my giggling little hindbrain kicks up.

Now it might go like this: seeing a woman across a
room sprawled on a couch, going over to her, smiling,
kissing her, unbuttoning her blouse, stroking her breasts
—then flick, a change, to the sex-slave harem room,
rows of beds, men and women in various combinations
and poses, shifting positions—flick!—in a sauna, naked,
woman and man, embracing, hot and sweaty—flick!—
lying on rocks in the sun and opening my eyes to find
several people standing around me, smiling—flick!—
and so on. Sometimes I'm with women, sometimes with
men; sometimes I am a woman, sometimes a man, sometimes I'm dominant and sometimes I'm not, and sometimes no one is. Some images, which have gotten so
fragmentary they hardly qualify as fantasy, are twisted
and nasty, and some are postcard-romantic. One of our
long-neglected sexual freedoms is that of imagining ourselves not only with another, but in the other, *as* the
other. The letting up of pressure to be politically correct
—or correct in *any* way—has given my sexual mental
health breathing room, and now I can be anyone.

There is one specific element to many fantasies that
might be called a kind of dominance but isn't dominance
as we usually define it. I mean the dream of being dominated by sex itself—being forced, as it were, by the intensity of the sex to submit to and accept sex, be bound
by sex, mastered by sex. To give up resistance to appetite.
In this dream everything else disappears for real—not
for a single instant, not almost, not pretend. Our ego is
completely submerged. I can dream of being *made to*

until I admit that I *want to,* that I want to without
having to ask. And without asking I will get exactly
what I want. This is the fantasy of everyday life—that
those around us will meet our needs, will just know
what we want, will *understand.* It's the fantasy of pure
love.

Sexual dominance, sexual bondage can be metaphorical states. They can be metaphysical states, too, but what
I'm talking about here is the fact that we think dominance always implies another person having control over
us. But dominance is really about cowardice and courage, our unwillingness and inability to let go completely
for even a second, and our wish to be dominated by our
wish. To have sexuality itself say to us: *I know what you
want, baby, and I'm going to give it to you.*

III

Climax

10

The Japanese tradition of erotic art is one of extraordinary technique, humor, and maturity. Japanese erotic pictures are called "shunga," which means "spring pictures," but this bit of poetry implies nothing more than "sex pictures" to a Japanese. This art form reached its pinnacle during the Ukiyo-e period of the 1600s into the 1700s. I first saw real shunga—rather than reproductions —in the Orientalia Collection of the British Library, delicious dishes served up, as are all the treats of the British Library, in a civilized reading room by infinitely polite librarians.

One exquisitely made nineteenth-century "pillow
book," bound in blue fabric and opening like an accor-
dion, one drawing after the other, was typical. Shunga
drawings were often instructively named: "Posture of
the Hungry Steed Rushing to the Trough," "Picture of
the Erring Bird Returning to the Forest," and so on. In
every picture the genitals are clearly drawn and slightly
exaggerated in size. The figures are never completely
nude, and in many drawings are draped in lush curtains
of fabric. Here the man spreads the woman's labia and
scrutinizes her vagina with a magnifying glass. Here the
woman lies on her back and holds a crying infant while
the man penetrates her; in another both man and
woman, during intercourse, distract a toddler with toys.
Here one woman tenderly holds another woman's head
while a man licks her vagina. Here she lies on her back
in a wide-bottomed boat under an awning, her black
hair pulled into a tight knot, her kimono thrown open
around her legs. Beneath the boat is softly swirling water. Her legs are spread, her knees bent up, one arm held
languidly behind her head, the other around the man
who penetrates her. She smiles without hurry. There is
no sense of movement.

The participants' facial expressions are often vague,
unrevealing, the male and female faces much alike. They
wear slight smiles. When a third person watches, there is
no sense of the voyeur; the person watches as a servant
might watch, waiting to serve a couple at table. The

genitalia are enlarged, but not beautiful. These are genitalia in all their hairy, wrinkled glory—thick, fleshy rods and swollen red slits covered with crinkly hair.

Shunga reflects a time when women had virtually no power, and the art of the Ukiyo-e period is art of the brothel. It's possible to see general associations in shunga between female powerlessness and eroticism even while appreciating its beauty. Shunga is an incomplete but unparalleled record of the brothel's culture; its themes include fantasies about the sex lives of priests and nuns, frequent depictions of homosexuality, careful delineation of the immense variety and many uses of sex toys, illustrations of all manner of sexual groupings and relationships.

I pick up a red book with an embossed cover. Each page is almost neon-bright with colors, tiny delicate draftsmanship on fine paper. Often shunga has text, captions giving careful instruction, making small jokes, telling a story. Some have word balloons ("How big you are!") and others have little characters in the corners commenting sarcastically on the performance of the lovers. Pillow books were largely meant as instruction manuals, even discreetly slipped into the drawer of a bride's dresser by the salesman at times, but shunga was also seen in "laughing books" and as separate artworks. In pillow books it seems always to be daytime, and the loving couple (or trio) is often either outside or in a room open to a garden. An old Asian term for intercourse was "clouds and rain," the clouds being the vaginal secretions, and the rain, sperm. In shunga, sex and the natural world are wholly entwined.

Men and women both carry a sense of stillness about them in these drawings, and it ultimately adds to the arousing power of the images. These are clear-eyed lovers, unapologetic, controlled, at ease—as though they could stay like this for hours, as though they already have. It was quite common for pillow books to include pictures of couples post-amour, in loving repose. The last pages of this particular book show a languid couple, fully clothed and snuggling, with only a single hand lost in the folds of fabric. The impression is one of a clear spring morning, where all is green and blooming. The spare, empty rooms, clean walls, and neatly pruned gardens contrast with the chaos of draped fabric, the frenzy of tiny patterns and wild colors in the kimonos. The picture tells me that sex lies somewhere between these extremes.

Shunga was banned periodically from the 1700s on, and by the mid-1800s its style was more repressed and hostile. Explicit erotic art was banned in Japan altogether by the late 1800s. Elements of horror and violence replaced affection and genital explicitness in sexual art. Shunga is a dead tradition; nothing like it exists in Japan now, and modern Japanese are generally not allowed access to uncensored historical Japanese art. With westernization came prudishness, censorship, and harsh, violent pornography. In virtually all places, at all times, the depiction of pubic hair is forbidden. Japanese censors and Japanese artists are in a continual battle for interpretation of the law. A shaved pubis is also forbidden, say the censors, because the pubis *should* have pubic hair. Artists sometimes get away with cutting out the genitals in their art and leaving perfectly shaped blank spaces instead. In pornography, genitals are either hidden or digitally scrambled, the moaning actors deformed by vibrating cross-hatch patterns in a near-perfect parody of the lost art of the erotic.

The great alchemist Paracelsus was fascinated by Adam and Eve. He believed that their real punishment was to be given genitals. Genitals divided people from the androgynous God; they were a mutation, a monstrous refolding of the flesh in such a way that we eternally long for each other, and are eternally kept apart. The genitalia are certainly unique—messy, wrinkled even at birth, vulnerable in men and disguised in women, inexplicably ridiculous, inexplicably beautiful. Genitalia are visceral and wet; they are the body's insides, out, decay as well as life.

And most of all, they are just always *there,* unavoidable, on every person we pass in the street. Every swelling female chest, every bulge in a man's pants, every outlined buttock, serves to remind us of our own. Many mammals have a ridge in their genitals called the penis bone. Supposedly the Buddha and the Dalai Lamas can retract their genitals like many animals, tucking them out of harm's way—and, perhaps, out of mind. What a different world it would be if we all could.

Vaginas are all the same, penises all the same, and yet different. For all the variations in hue, scalloping, curvature, and size, genitalia rapidly lose the capacity to surprise a viewer. Yet they never lose the capacity to excite. With enough time, we can become so familiar with another person's penis or vulva as to give it a voice, the capacity to tell jokes and make demands. We call them names. Nice words for penises are hard words, hard-sounding: cock, prick, dick, stick. Insults are soft: wuss, pantywaist, wimp. But bad words for vaginas are the hard-sounding ones, the sharp-edged ones: cunt, snatch, box; compliments for women's genitalia, such as they are, sound soft and safe to the ear: pussy, muff, fur. We like to keep our boundaries clear.

We of the western tradition have no shunga, and little more than the Song of Solomon as a paean to sexual love. (Christian scholars have gone to extremes to find church metaphors in the Song of Solomon, but its meaning is simple and clear.) The Hawaiians, who were great poets, had a whole song tradition called *mele ma'i,* or genital chanting. When important babies were born to Hawaiian royalty, songs about their genitalia were composed, describing and celebrating their beauty and future capacity. The Hawaiian language has a lot of words for sexual gratification and delight, and the *mele ma'i* often included names for the genitals; Queen Liliuokalani's were *'Anapau,* that is, "frisky," vigorous, merry ones. What a sorry bunch that makes us look.

"The penis," wrote Masters and Johnson in a moment of inadvertent poetry, "constantly has been viewed but rarely seen."

For westerners the penis has, over the centuries, linguistically lent itself to little more than jokes and euphemisms; no other human body part is more naturally clownish or taken more seriously: it is the goose's neck, the live rabbit, a hot pudding, the flute, a sugar stick or lollipop, a roaring jack, arbor vitae, and love's dribbling dart—and the stick, the foe, the bald-headed hermit, the terror of virgins. (The Hawaiians called boy toddlers, who spent their days naked, "danglers.") The undignified balls are the dojiggers, talliwags, and whirlygigs, among a lot else, many of them variations of rocks, jewels, berries, and nuts. The ancient Chinese were more poetic than Europeans; they called the penis the Jade Stalk, Heavenly Dragon Pillar, the Swelling Mushroom, the Vigorous Peak. Japanese penis slang today still uses natural images like mushrooms, eels, and snakes. In some Tantric literature, the penis was classed as one of five kinds, depending on its relative vigor, size, and thickness. The Kundari Myō-ō penis is "long, vigorous, and full of passion . . . [it] can drive a woman wild," according to John Stevens, a Buddhist historian. The Gonzanze Myō-ō penis is average in size. "This kind of penis puts women at ease. It has great staying power." In *The Perfumed Garden,* many names are given: El heurmak, "the indomitable"; El âouame, "the swimmer"; El naourekhi, "the flabby one"; and more.

In 1963, Gilbert Oakley, the author of *Sane and Sensual Sex,* advised bridegrooms not to expose their genitals too abruptly lest their new wives be terrified. When the groom shows her what she's married for the first time, Oakley explained, it's better that he not be aroused, "so that his wife will not immediately get the impression of over-eagerness, lust or overpowering masculine aggressiveness." But respect, perhaps approaching awe, seemed inevitable. "A female has little to no argument in revolting against the sight of male testicles and penis. It may well be that in them she sees a potential 'weapon' of aggression but since woman's ultimate goal *is* to be attacked (in the nicest possible way) by *just* this weapon, denial of its existence appears merely hypocritical."

All men are anxious narcissists when it comes to the penis, which each compares constantly and secretly to the penises of other men. Comparison is bound to be distressing. Where did it come from, this male fear of a small penis? Did women start it? And wouldn't that be just like a woman? (What's penis envy? The desire to be red, wrinkled, and four inches long.)

Besides, it's not so much the penis that's the worry. It's the erection. The erect penis, however desirable, useful, and loved, is unreliable, a fleeting thing. "Nothing is more short-lived than the erection; like the crocus of spring, it is there for a moment, and then it is gone," wrote William Irwin Thompson. If menstruation is the symbol of cyclic time, he added, "the penis is the perfectly obvious and natural symbol of instantaneous time." This fear of what penises really mean may be the reason for the amazing reluctance in Hollywood filmmaking to show the naked male body. In a world rife with celebration of the penis, the male body is invisible.

The penis is loved, the body disguised—and the erection implied, as though it were always, rather than only briefly, there. Porn films use repetitive loops of the perishable erection penetrating a vagina to support the myth such looping creates: the big prick, ever erect, its capacity never-ending. If penises represent, more than anything, the *moment,* our myth of the penis is one of longing for the eternal—the permanent. Priapus may have been the god of fertility, but his virtue was stamina.

Howie Gordon, for ten years a porn star, told me about his first day of shooting a sex movie. He arrived on the set in the morning clammy with fear—fear of not being able to get it up. The director began without preliminaries. "She starts sucking, I get hard immediately. I'm looking around: 'Welcome to my blowjob, they're going to pay me two hundred dollars for this. *Great!*' About forty-five minutes later they're moving lights around and changing position and I'm getting this vibe from her. The director says, 'Okay, now come.' And my dick just shrivels. Panic! When it's not there, *nothing's* there! Fear, panic, fear. They decided to break for lunch, give me a break. I locked myself in the bathroom, trying to get my dick to work, and my dick will not work. I went back on the set and tried, from one o'clock until five o'clock. The girl had fallen asleep. Finally, at five o'clock I came. In my head, I heard the cheering of thousands. I took a Valium and slept for a day and a half."

When men are questioned about their penises, they turn the question away from themselves, and sometimes onto women, onto women's demands. Men worry their individual penis isn't enough, worry that perhaps no penis could ever be enough. Men think women won't be satisfied, not just because a man wants to satisfy a woman out of his altruistic heart (although this is often true), but because the measure of his adequacy is her observed satisfaction. The penis functions so beautifully on its own—the penis is sometimes uncomfortably independent—yet its worth depends on the judgment of others at all times. The penis is never, can't be, quite enough by itself. Its identity is given, not inherent.

Masters and Johnson found that almost all flaccid penises were between 8.5 and 10.5 centimeters long. The smallest one was 6 centimeters long and the largest was 14 centimeters. In erection the smaller penises increased in size the most, almost doubling in length. Is it big enough, long enough, thick enough, hard enough? Men hope for a big one, then women complain about penises that are *too* large, too thick, too long. In a piece of Victorian pornography, a woman complains about the flaws of a large prick: "a huge Beam requires much Strength to raiſe it, and more to keep it in a due Poſition, and give it it's proper Motion . . . what *f*igni*f*ies a great lubberly Machine, which moves but *f*lowly, and mu*ft* be propt like an old Hou*f*e, or *f*plinte'd like a broken leg to keep it from falling." What's a man to do?

In Richard Rhodes' 1992 sexual memoir *Making Love,* the author describes measuring his penis, and finding it to be 6.5 inches long when engorged. Rhodes was heavily criticized for describing such things, mundane and obvious things that have long been the stuff of novels. He talked about his erotic history explicitly, warts and all, but it was the warts—this measurement, a detailed description of masturbation, certain obsessions—that brought Rhodes a heap of surprisingly mean-spirited criticism. "Embarrassing" was one of the milder complaints; embarrassment and discomfort in response to a book say as much or more about the predilections and preoccupations of reviewers as about the book. I find it hard to believe the male reviewers who castigated Rhodes for measuring his penis have never done so themselves. Rhodes was, at least in part, being punished for saying out loud what is never said, for violating the male contract of phallic inviolability. "Men say their penises have minds of their own," he writes, "but men are geniuses at avoiding responsibility."

Rhodes captures, too, the unintended erections that plague men throughout their lives, unwieldy flags of arousal. Disobedient erections are almost as disruptive to a man's self-image as an episode of impotence. (But not quite.) The erection must be respected, above all. In England, sex stores have to lay their dildos flat rather than display them upright. Otherwise they are displaying "erections," and that's illegal—not, I think, because most people believe even for a moment that an upright penis will harm anyone. Such a law simply expresses the inarticulate fear that showing the erection, making erections commonplace, takes away the erection's power.

Texas defines both dildos and artificial vaginas as "obscene devices" if they are "marketed as useful primarily for the stimulation of human genital organs." (I suppose that means you can have them as decoration. Or for research.) It is illegal in Texas to sell "obscene devices," and it's also illegal for anyone to possess more than six of them, because any such possession is presumed to show an "intent to promote" them for sale. Recent vice raids in Houston and Austin made the world safer for ordinary erections by the confiscation of numerous phallic devices from adult stores, including the infamous G-spot dildo, made with a gentle curve designed to stimulate the upper part of a woman's vagina, a very sensitive area for many women. I feel safer already.

All this protective circling of the wagons around the erection is as much about not having one as anything else. The Inuit, whose folklore is one of the world's most salacious, can even laugh about castration. They tell a story about a man named Him-Whose-Penis-Stretches-Down-To-His-Knees. Him-Whose-Penis failed to take a taboo seriously, and in retaliation the gods sent a big raven to punish him. The raven grabbed the end of his organ and tore it off. Now he is known as Him-Whose-Penis-Barely-Peeps-From-Its-Cave.

The Papal Choir of the Sistine Chapel had eunuch singers until the late 1800s. Castration is actually a time-honored tradition, known to almost all cultures. Eunuchs were created for their voices, as palace guards, and in punishment. The image of the adult eunuch is instantly recognizable: a man muscular but hairless, smooth, strong, but safe. Formal castration was called "shaving," or "sweeping clean." To do so meant crushing, pressing, twisting, or cutting off the testicles, penis, or both. A second-century bronze castration clamp looks like nothing so much as a fancy nutcracker. Funny, but writing this doesn't cause me discomfort. I don't take it personally; my body can't imagine. And I must admit this: Every time I get a mammogram, every time the hard, flat plates are screwed down with my breast squashed flat between them, I think about how much I'd like to get that radiologist in for a good, long prostate check. Or maybe a scrotal-gram.

The penis preoccupies individual men, but the phallus preoccupies everyone. If every man thought his penis were good enough, there wouldn't be so many phallic symbols—not the roughened sculptures of Pompeii, and not the sleek missiles and Mustangs of today. The assumption endures that women want—and *should* want —a penis, while men want bigger ones. But what women want is a phallus—that is, male power.

Ancient phallic symbols are the ultimate father figure, God as Penis. But even mighty symbols fall. In Japanese porn, women give blowjobs to vibrators and dildos while a commanding male watches. His own erection is banned from the screen. The penis may sometimes be a phallus, but a phallus is certainly not always a penis. Masters and Johnson used dildos in their research, but they called them "penises," without a wink. A man whose lover keeps a dildo under the bed can feel at least two ways about the thing: pleased she wants what seems to be a version of himself around all the time, or disturbed that of all things, his penis can be so casually detached.

The phallus counts because *no* one has one. (At least, not one big enough. Phalluses can never be too big.) All that is worst in society is due to the penis envy of men and their penchant for building bigger and better pricks, long things that go fast and then blow up. The scorn of women doesn't help, I suppose, but it's hard to resist in the face of a few eons of male violence. A friend tells me a joke: "What's that ugly piece of flesh at the end of the penis called?" "A man." I tell the joke to every man I know, and, funny enough, none of them laugh half so hard as I do.

Penis envy isn't about pricks; sometimes I wonder if men understand this as well as women do. Penis envy is about something bigger, darker, more amorphous, more instructive than the body alone. We dress up in various symbolic ways to confuse and confound others into thinking we do have one after all, a real phallus—that is, power over others, potent and permanently erect. The penis can be cute, it can be arousing, it can be of great use, but it's not a wildly dangerous-looking thing; it's not a locomotive or submarine or rocket. It's not as dangerous looking as a vagina, the moist, dark cave out of which new people come, into which goes appetite, appetite almost ceaseless. Now that's a phallus for you, one little symbolized, and always desired.

According to the Navahos, First Man brought many kinds of good food to First Woman, until she was happy and very fat. One night after the meal, First Woman touched herself between her legs and said, "Thanks, my vagina." This made First Man angry. After all, *he* had killed the buck. Shouldn't he get the thanks? First Woman agreed he'd done the work—but, she pointed out, the only reason he'd gone to all that trouble in the first place was because he wanted her to let him use her vagina.

First Man was so mad, he took all the men across the Separation River. For a time the women were content. They sometimes teased the men across the water. "We have something you don't have," they joked. "Don't you miss it?" But after four years the women were starving. No babies were being born, even when the women had intercourse with sticks and with each other. The men had food, but were lonely and unhappy. Eventually men and women came back together, but ever since have blamed each other for their troubles. The men complained that the women's unnatural sex during the separation created monsters. Since it is men who tell the tales, their own behavior in that time has never been described.

Ancient Japanese manuals describe several types of *yoni,* a word that encompasses the whole of a woman's vagina and vulva. The Mizu-Tembō type is moist and larger inside than its tight opening suggests. The Ka-Tembō is hairy, hungry, and sweet. In the east, the vagina was called the Receptive Vase, or the Vermilion Gate, and the clitoris was the Jewel Terrace, the Dharma Jewel, the Gem. One fourteenth-century European name offered for the clitoris was the "sweetness of Venus"; another, suggested in France in 1612, was the "scorner of men."

"Vagina" is to women's genitals what "phallus" is to the penis—a symbolic and incorporating word. We say vagina to mean labia, cervix, clitoris, too, which have few and mostly unfelicitous nicknames. We in the West call the vagina "cat"—pussy, le chat, la chatte. The malevolent, self-involved, greedy cat. Except for the obvious, derisive "clit," I can find no common slang words—no common words at all—for the clitoris, the great unmentionable, the only human organ with the single purpose of pleasure. This is an oversight almost impossible to believe, and it makes me wonder at the depth of our capacity to suppress our experience—to suppress it so deeply, even the making of language is stopped. The clitoris is the seat of female sexual pleasure but the vagina has always been the seat of male concern.

Klaus Theweleit, in his book *Male Fantasies,* a study of Fascism as male terror, lists the almost-infinite ways in which a woman's vagina has been compared with water, rivers, oceans and waves, comparisons that appear at first to enlarge and honor women via the route of their wombs. Theweleit calls such veiled literary compliments "oppression through exaltation, through a lifting of boundaries . . . Here again, women have *no names."* They are, instead, natural forces, maniacally enlarged, out of control. My own vagina isn't always my particular focus where sex is concerned, but like the First Woman, I long ago understood that it will be taken to be so by most men, its value in their eyes having little to do with my perception of myself.

"The vagina is infinitely distensible from a clinical point of view," wrote Masters and Johnson in *Human Sexual Response.* The vagina literally accommodates whatever is penetrating it, according to the woman's sexual pleasure. A phallus that feels too big to a sexually excited woman will cause the vagina to extend almost immediately; penetrated by a phallus that feels just right or too small, the vagina won't distend a bit. It seeks the most perfectly arousing state. The vagina has this quality of tranquility, it seems to me; it is always seeking balance.

Vaginas bleed rhythmically, without injury, and when the vagina stops bleeding, people come out of it. In Paleolithic times there was little more mysterious or potent to men than this thing they couldn't do. "The vulva is a wound that heals itself." William Irwin Thompson believes that because of menstruation, women were the first to consciously note the connection between the human body and natural cycles, to see themselves as individuals within a larger pattern. Eons passed before people understood paternity, but before they could turn paternity into patriarchy, male resentment turned menstruation into evil. This *vagina* that only women had, that men longed for and couldn't duplicate, could break the unbreakable rules of the body. "The slit of the vulva appears like a wound made by a spear, and so the spear becomes a phallus." And the phallus, the penis, becomes a spear.

In many myths menstrual blood is evil and poisonous as well as being magically powerful. The god Thor reaches the land of eternal life by bathing in a river of the menstrual blood of the mothers of the gods. The river Styx was the menstrual blood of the earth. Men associated the color red with women and took semen white for themselves, a version of yin and yang reflected still in rosaries, costumes, and rites. Menstruation, the flow, is sometimes referred to as bearing a flower, and the flower bears fruit, and the man takes the flower away.

Resentment of menstrual power meant punishment

for menstruation. Menstrual blood is considered a kind of witchcraft, and thus quite dangerous, in many cultures—impure, unclean, diseased. Even the supposedly rational mind of western man often finds it hard to grapple with the touch of blood on his penis or hand. New mothers are still frequently isolated after birth, soiled by their fearsome power to make people come out of themselves, by the fact that after the birth, she still continues to bleed. The concept of original sin teaches us that because each baby has to pass out of an impure woman's body, the very soul is injured in the passage; only baptism can wash the filth of blood away. A few years ago there was a tampon commercial on television in Denmark. A young girl is shown swimming in the ocean, when the water around her turns red. The theme from *Jaws* plays, and *voilà,* she's dinner. Meanwhile another girl, wearing the brand-name tampon, swims by the shark without a glance.

Humans are either the only mammal with no visible estrus—no physical signs of fertility—or the only animal to have lost its ability to distinguish it. Individuals can; I know women who find their libido waxing and waning regularly throughout their menstrual cycle; I often feel the painful pinprick of mittelschmerz and know I've just ovulated. Both men and women probably respond on a subconscious level to the change in scent and texture of the woman's vaginal mucus. But the *race* can no longer tell. Sexual desire has peaks and valleys, some of which are tied to hormone production and monthly cycles, but in daily life sexuality is almost wholly divorced from fertility.

The biologist Lynn Margulis believes there were clear advantages for primitive women both in being able to disguise estrus and being able to show a mock estrus. In the first case, if the male doesn't know when the female is fertile, he has to stick around. He can't fight for her favors constantly, and he can't be certain of his parenthood. So he mates frequently and fights less. In the second case, an already pregnant female who can show mock estrus when a new male enters the scene can convince him the new baby is his, to protect rather than kill.

Evolution gave human women smooth, nearly hairless skin, swollen breasts and buttocks, and hidden estrus together. Humans look fertile and enticing around the calendar; pregnant women sometimes bleed lightly for a few months after conception. Everything about fertility is camouflaged now. It's possible to make a case, and several people have, that hidden estrus and constant sexuality are the basis of community, tribe, family, and home. Men had to protect and care for all the females all the time, and cooperation and a settled life made this easier. "All humans alive on Earth today may well have come from the trick loins of females who concealed estrus," writes Margulis.

Over the eons, our fashions have emphasized and even exaggerated these traits. Men like large breasts because they are signifiers of the ability to reproduce and nourish, to mother the race; they are signifiers, too, of sexual readiness; like so much in arousal, breasts are swellings. The hapless man who goes ga-ga over a young woman in a tight skirt and high heels, a woman whose buttocks protrude with a slight tilt as she walks waveringly down the street, is a man whose old ape mind has taken over. The male body is always ready and the female body constantly signals. We both are and are not still driven by instinct, by the dual nature of sex, by the life of the cave. Don't ask me why that same teetering, long-legged woman can make me feel a little ga-ga, too, because I don't know.

I think of the double-edged flattery of naming oceans, rivers, and lakes for women when I hear a woman referred to as a "fish." We smell of the brackish swamp, the wetlands at the edge of the amphibian and mammal worlds; we smell of history. The woman a gay man marries in order to appear straight is a "fishwife."

A 1940s marriage manual devotes considerable attention to the problem of feminine hygiene. Women are cursed with the incurable problem of *vaginal secretions,* and constant vigilance is required: "If they are allowed to adhere to the vulva for any length of time they become gummy and smelly, like sour cream, and their odour clings to anything that touches it, so tenaciously that washing with ordinary toilet soap and warm water will not remove it; hands must be scrubbed vigorously and linen boiled in order to get rid of it."

The social anthropologist Shirley Ardener has done research on a practice of the Bakweri women called "titi

ikoli." "Titi ikoli" is what women do to men who have
impugned their genitals. "These insults may take various
forms but that most typically envisaged is the accusation
that the sexual parts of women smell. A Bakweri woman
so insulted before a witness must call out *all* the other
women of the village. Converging upon the offender
dressed in vines, they demand immediate recantation
and a recompense of a pig, plus something extra for the
woman who has been directly insulted. The women then
surround him and sing songs which are often obscene by
allusion, and accompany them by vulgar gestures. An
example of another kind of song is '*Titi ikoli* is not a
thing for insults, beautiful, beautiful.' All the men beat a
hasty retreat (since they will be ashamed to stay and
watch while their wives, sisters, sisters-in-law, and old
women join the dance) except the culprit, but he will try
to hide his eyes. Finally the women share the pig between themselves." Many versions of "titi ikoli" punishment occur in tribal cultures. They include women stripping naked as a group in front of the offender, or
dancing in wild, inappropriate ways. Ardener, who calls
the cooperative effort of all women on behalf of any one
insulted this way a form of "corporate action," notes that
the punishments usually involve the deliberate violation
of sexual taboos that might otherwise be upheld strenu-
ously. Their indignities, and their offender's embarrassment, are a public statement of how such insults violate
the dignity of all women. Even infants participate. Not
only do I not live in a culture with this wondrous ritual,

I live in a world of douches and chemical sprays, in a world made mortally afraid of bodily fluids long before there was anything to fear. "Titi ikoli" says more than no to the lie of female ugliness; it celebrates sexual beauty, the natural inherent beauty of their genitals. And beautiful they are, infinitely variable and perfumed. Thighs spread and the scalloped edges part and blossom. The darkness inside beckons, alien, bigger than life.

The vagina is a mouth, "a devouring mouth," in Norman O. Brown's words. A man who risks intercourse risks castration, because no one really knows what's inside. The image of *vagina dentata,* the vagina ringed with teeth, is ancient; it's a shivery nightmare of men, a ghost story for the men's circle long after dark, when the women have retired. In Arab tales, to look into the vagina's maw was to risk blindness. The vagina is the scene of original generation, the cleaving of the world into heaven and earth, the scene we all repeat, ontogeny perpetually recapitulating phylogeny.

All of our landscapes are sexual; think of the way we name hills and valleys, how we compare our macroscapes to the familiar contours of the body, especially the body of a woman. A hill in Hawaii is called Kohelepelepe, or "wattled vagina." The land is mother. Exploring the land is a kind of penetration, says Brown —a going up, into, through the Mother, sadistic and loving at once. Small children dig holes whenever possible, soft and moist. "Excavation. The child is hollowing out a cave for himself in his mother's body." One man I know calls fucking "laying pipe." Labyrinths, spirals, mazes, tunnels—the planet is full of secrets, hidden places, hard journeys inward, downward, into darkness, through soil.

These invisible organs of the female are dark and strange, internal organs open to the world. They are made of the earth itself. Do I seem to be stretching here? Vagina dentata, cannibalistic and starved; wet vagina, irresistible. Lily, at twenty-four, has perfect white skin; she wears black spike heels, sheer black stockings, a skin-tight black knit miniskirt, a tailored, wide-shouldered, tight-waisted black jacket with tiny white pinstripes, with a severe cut. Underneath her jacket she wears only a big black bra with lots of cleavage showing. She licks her red, red lips and tosses bleached white-blond hair over her shoulders. As Lily eats, her tongue darts out to show the diamond post embedded in the middle, click-clicking against the spoon and her little white teeth. She pulls her lower lip out and down at one point to show me what's on the inside, and I see the word LUST tattooed in black.

Men fear being devoured by women; their ejaculation into the cavity castrates them, however briefly. Sex is murder to the "little man." A Muslim saying: "Three things are insatiable: the desert, the grave, and a woman's vulva." Many women are quick to disdain a limp penis, and almost as quick to disdain an erect one. All I can offer to men in explanation is that women's contempt for the penis is a small enough compensation for the unceasing threat of rape, so much more real than vulvar teeth.

Freud said boys are frightened when they see a woman's flat genitalia; they think women have been castrated. Klaus Theweleit says the real fear is of the "castrating potential" of the vagina. "For whatever it can take in, it can easily keep for itself." The vagina is the Medusa's head, writhing, snaky, poisonous. "How did all of those phallic forms find their way onto the Medusa's head?" Theweleit asks. "Not because the head was *missing* something, but because it had retained something: all of those pricks that tried to suppress female potency." Theweleit describes the rifle women of the European wars who castrated their dead enemies and hung the genitalia from their belts. He compares them to the women of Sparta who rode naked on horseback into battle, to all wild fighting women whose fierce hatred of the enemy spurs them to bloody victory. Women who seem far more horrible to men than male soldiers who do the same things to each other or to innocent women. The shrieking goddesses become the Virgin Mary when men get hold of religion, and aggressive women become either fiends or seducers. The Italian curse *puttana la madonna* means "whore mother of God."

And once again, Adam. After his fall, Adam avoided

sex for 130 years, but all the while he was tormented by wet dreams and tortured by succubi who stole his sperm to make demons.

After God's unfortunate experience with Lilith, he tried to make another woman, in front of Adam. But Adam was disgusted by the sight—the blood, bones, and guts involved. When she was done, he wouldn't touch her, and, nameless, she disappeared from the record. So men have always retained a shaky, often unconscious anxiety about women, especially women's interior mysteries, their physical connection between the world and their viscerae. Eve eats, and becomes a real woman, and then Adam can't resist. Male desire for women isn't the problem. The problem is that *women incite desire.*

Instead of ritual circumcision, girls have ritual clitoridectomies. The cultures who practice genital mutilation call it the rite of becoming a woman, but also freely admit it's an attempt to stop sexual pleasure in women. Female sexuality is so dangerous, it must be surgically removed if possible. Like unnecessary hysterectomies, liposuction, and breast implants, clitoridectomies are a violent form of male fright. None of them fix the problem of the vagina, but they do injure and weaken women, they interrupt the aggressive flow of women's desire.

Again and again in social histories the same curious double play occurs: Women are the weaker sex, inferior in every way. And yet they constantly endanger men. Men are superior, powerful, but helpless in the face of female lust. Nothing could be more disruptive to a Victorian gentleman than to have his wife seduce him. Because he must necessarily succumb, and wake up to find himself copulating with a hungry wife who wants more than children, who wants, period. And female sexual appetite was considered physically dangerous, to men as well as to women; he could be swallowed up in her vastness, he had to feed her appetite or she might eat all of him. I'm not making this up or being particularly purple, either; the confusions of the Victorian age make our own seem elementary.

In order to explain and solve the conundrum of sexual desire, the medical authorities of the day decided that women with sexual appetites could be cured with sperm. Her uterus "needed" sperm in order not to be dangerously congested after sex, and, conveniently, men needed to ejaculate into the uterus for the best of health reasons. This was yet another vote against contraception, of course, and another vote in favor of paternal control. Women, so delicate, so needful of protection, were also lionesses, raging. For a woman to dare ask for birth control, even by abstention, was to deny exactly what made her tolerable in civilized society.

When I was sixteen and still technically a virgin, I went to my family doctor for the birth control pill. He had cared for my family for decades. But in this particular circumstance, his attitude was dramatically changed. He gave me my first pelvic exam in a rough and perfunctory manner, refused to discuss my reasons for wanting the pill or my many questions about its side effects, shoved the prescription into my hand, and walked out of the room. A year and a half later, I traveled to Ireland for several months. I stopped taking the pill before I went, unable to imagine meeting anyone I would want to make love to in Ireland, not thinking sex at all. But I did meet someone and I needed the pill (condoms were illegal in Ireland), and to my surprise, I got it. After a long perusal of what constituted the Irish Yellow Pages, and several phone calls, I found a basement clinic in downtown Dublin, set my backpack down among the crowd of women and many, many children in the waiting room. A while later a young woman physician cheerfully gave me a gentle pelvic and a free packet of pills. The contrasts were so telling, between libidinous America and an older man unable to cope with a young woman's sexuality, and repressed Ireland, which had given birth to an underground women's culture of compassionate medical care.

Adam fell when Eve fed him. Sex is food, and food is sex. Hunger leads to sin, and one solution is to eat again —this time, the Body of God. The Christian Eucharist blends with the Hindu prayer: *Tat tvam asi*—This is my body, Thou art It, That Thou art. To live is to kill, to live is to eat, to eat is to live. "My mouth on her body, my tongue savoring her crevices was like plunging my face into a bowl of ripe summer fruits and inhaling their

mingled fragrances—peaches, apples, pears," wrote
Richard Rhodes. "All of her was fresh. All of her was
beautiful." Yet a certain kind of man insults another
man by calling him a pussy, or a pussy eater.

Porn often creates distance; with porn we are always
looking, especially looking at genitalia, two steps back.
Oral sex almost completely eliminates distance; in oral
sex we are too close to focus, too close to see. Oral sex is
ancient and perpetually condemned as excessive, abnormal, and wicked. Oral sex breaks too many boundaries,
disintegrates the everyday cosmos too far by using body
parts for new and disturbing things. James to Nora,
August 1909: "How I would love to surprise you sleeping now! There is a place I would like to kiss you now, a
strange place, Nora. Not on the lips, Nora. Do you know
where?"

The vagina is a mouth and the mouth a vagina. The
penis becomes food. The emotional impression of an
image of fellatio is often very soiled; she (or he) is eating,
like an animal, beastly, abandoned. He can hold her
down and smother her if he wants; she can castrate him
with a single bite. Cunnilingus, fellatio, and the doubling
of oral sex, what we call 69, as though it could be dismissed as lightly and neutrally as a number, were im-
mortalized on Hindu temples, in shunga, in the Kama
Sutra, everywhere in the ancient world. Then these obsessions went away, forbidden and rarely discussed, in
the face of psychoanalysis and mental hygiene.

The mouth and genitals, sex and words. "Language

and sexuality are what distinguish humanity from the angel," writes Thompson. "The 'higher' consciousness of language thus has to be crossed with the 'lower' consciousness of sexuality." But this doesn't mean that to rid ourselves of sex would turn us into angels. It might instead make us gibbering clones. Thompson's reading of cultural history tells him that oral sex is an act laden with symbolism and social implication; he considers this "mysteriously compelling act" to be a behavior of the educated class.

Are the parts of our bodies made only for certain uses, are we teleologically confined to a few "correct" actions? That is, what does it mean to say that our sexual organs are "only for" reproduction, or a vagina is "only for" intercourse, a penis "only for" penetrating? What does it mean to say that other uses are "abnormal," "unnatural"? As Annie Sprinkle pointed out, nature doesn't complain. Our mouths, more than most of our body parts, are Renaissance machines; they enable us to eat, to speak, to kiss, to drink, to suck, to breathe; which function is the mouth's most proper one? To reject any particular one is to imply that the creator loaded people with more than was needed.

Mysterious and compelling, this urge to bury our faces in each other, to retreat from isolation and distance into the most humble smells and tastes, the quivering of muscle and the crawling of skin, rough hair and wetness. To submit to another's belly, or another's mouth. Oral sex may be the most potent of sexual acts, completely divorced from biology, never mentioned in the presence of children, the most secret and secreted of acts. It is an act of power derived from the most vulnerable kind of intimacy.

Wayland Young, in his book *Eros Denied,* makes a good case that the least objectionable and value-free words to describe sex are what we think of as the lowest ones— fuck, prick, and cunt. If they are "bad" words now, it's because we made them so, not because they began that way. Only in the last few hundred years, since the first Puritans declared "fuck" to be an off-limits term, did the word ever come to mean anything *but* intercourse. Now its meanings are legion. (The word "Puritanism" also survived its origins and has new and complex meanings now.) Its scabrous and punitive uses followed the designation of "fuck" as a shameful word, which followed the gradual degradation of fucking itself into a shameful act.

The words I use for sex, the sex words I use for slang, have changed dramatically since I was a teenager, when "cunt" was a horrid word, "shit" could get me slapped, "chick" was political death. My own responses have changed over time, partly by practice and partly through osmosis. I use words now I didn't before. For a long time I tried to avoid the use of "fuck" except as a strong obscenity, the kind of aversion that naturally keeps a word feeling dirty.

Young dislikes saying one "has sex" because of the

obscure and evasive meaning of "have." To have something is to possess it, and a sexual relationship *is* a kind of possession. It means possessing moments in time that are unique, irreducible, unrepeatable. It means having had a share of another's surrender. But I dislike the phrase in the same way, because the sex act is so undeniably an *act*. It needs a verb. To "have" something is a passive state, static, an experience of being rather than doing. To fuck is to do. Fucking doesn't imply the gender of the participants or the number or the method or the duration or the quality, it just *is* fucking, and what happens in sex is often as active as an athletic feat; *action* in the purest sense of the word, requiring bodies and motion in sync. When sex is over, something has changed. I've heard the word used in simple descriptive ways so much now that "fuck" seems to be the most value-free of the possibilities, often more accurate and undemanding than the mush-mouthed "lovemaking" or the meaningless "sleeping together." (A friend startled me the other day by telling me she and her husband had "had carnal knowledge" that morning. I'd almost forgotten the phrase.) I suspect "fuck" will continue to lose its shock value, becoming, as it once was, an ordinary descriptive word. But always a verb of aggressive desire. When I say I want to *fuck* someone, there's no doubt what I mean.

Words for sex are either soft or hard, implying differences in motive and appetite. "Make love to me" is not the same request as "Fuck me, baby," and never will be. Does anyone ever say, "Let's have sex now?" No. We

say, "Do it to me," or "Come on," or similarly demanding things, depending on the degree of urgency involved.
The word that is missing, the word that interests me
because it feels so intense and deeply private and so
rarely used, is penetration. "Penetration" is both soft and
hard; penetration can mean vagina, mouth, or ass; it can
ask for penis, tongue, finger, dildo, hand. Cucumber.
Nipple. Heart. Soul. This word has range. And to say "I
want to be penetrated" seems a much nastier and more
alluring thing to say—to be willing to say—than any of
the other options.

Vaginal penetration is the essential marker of heterosexual relations—even when it may be the least important
element in heterosexual sex. Photo of a military wedding: the laughing bride, all in white, her skirts yanked
high, sits in the midst of a circle of two dozen young
men dressed identically in white dress uniforms. They
watch intently, laughing like the groom as he kneels in
front of the bride and takes off her garter. One woman
in a crowd of men, enacting a symbolic penetration. A
man's home is his castle, which means his wife is land
for the plowing. Noblesse oblige. Everyone knows what
happens next.

In the United States it is considered legal fraud if a
sexual problem is not disclosed prior to marriage; annul-
ments have been granted because of impotence, infertil-
ity, a fetish. Marriage grants the state a long-standing

and carefully delineated interest in the sexual relations between adults. We generally disdain the idea of public nudity, prostitution, and sex shows because we disdain making one's sexual relations public, showing them off. But every marriage is a public sexual relationship, legally sanctioned, and its emblem is the hymen.

We must have reverence for "the greatest gift a girl can give." Husbands in some societies still sew up their wives' labia before going on a trip out of town. The male fascination with virgins has created a myth, a quest for the grail of the maidenhead—which invariably, in men's stories, is "torn open" or "ripped" or "broken" with copious blood and great pain. Followed by the young girl's swooning appreciation for the man who has at last shown her the depth of sexual passion. To deflower a virgin has long been considered a special treat by certain men, especially certain classes of men—men with an edge of sadism who had leisure time and the wealth to afford the purchasing of female bodies.

The historian Reay Tannahill says that London brothels used to supply medical certificates of virginity to customers. But since lots of virgins don't have complete hymens, and broaching one often doesn't have the dramatic impact myth leads men to expect, prostitutes became skilled at faking the imagined symptoms of virginity—astringents to make the vagina seem tight and dry, blood-filled sponges inside, dramatic skills to pretend pain. "In some brothels, professional virgins were patched up several times a week, and not only in London, but in Paris, Berlin, New York, San Francisco, and New Orleans, where some houses at the turn of the century offered defloration as part of the floor show." Hymen repair before marriage is still common in Japan. Thus we come to the neat and probably inevitable intersection of the virgin and the whore. They are both women defined solely and completely by their sexual behavior, women who don't exist but for their perceived sexual behavior.

Why does the word "penetration" carry such discomfort and anxiety with its longing? Perhaps the best explanation is simply that the word is rarely spoken, but I suspect there's more involved. Even when we think we're comfortable talking about sex, even after an hour's deconstruction of fellatio with three friends, I'm not comfortable discussing the nuances of sensation, the little dreams that crop up here and there, the sudden urges of my body. There was a fad for a while among heterosexual feminists to talk about intercourse as "engulfment," trying to turn the power of the act on its head. But engulfment is as mushy a word as I can imagine for an experience that can feel so direct. Penetration is entry, submersion, binding, war.

So many of the words we use for sex are harsh words. Vaginas are slits, cracks, gashes; penises are drills, night sticks, pikes, hammers. What does it mean that so many of our words for genitalia have an element of intrusion, even violence? To have intercourse is to plow, to be plowed, skewered, stuck. These words imply a level of physical change usually associated with the digging of machines. (Another word for penis is pile driver.) The potential for violence in sex doesn't begin with images or even ideas, and it isn't limited to one gender or another: It's in our bodies, in our *shapes*. The act of sex itself has an edge of thrill completely apart from the erotic; sex flirts with death directly, inescapably, simply by letting another person so near. A wished-for touch can become a dreadful violation without warning—even without anything happening except in one participant's mind. The penis can be a weapon, but so can a hand, a tongue; more than weapons, we are laden with much that can be harmed, the receptacles of the body: vagina, anus, mouth, and skin. When I close my eyes, I take a great risk.

Like a lot of women, probably most women, I've seen the way heterosexual intercourse can be offhandedly brutal. I was taught that if a boy got excited and out of control, it was my fault, and the first time a boy got out of control, I spent days restlessly reviewing my behavior before his assault. Though friends intervened, I still felt shamed by the names he called me afterward: prick teaser. Slut. Whore. Harder to reconcile was the banal thoughtlessness and roughness of men, the hungry, single-minded behavior that took my fantasies of melting passion and a slow black fade at the crucial moment and turned them inside out. When a good friend had sex with a man for the first time at the age of twenty-one—a nice man, another friend—she said the next morning she felt like her cervix had been a nail, and he'd hammered it down; she felt broken by his amateurish and probably well-intentioned efforts at satisfying her. He didn't know better; he'd fallen for one of the oldest lines in the book. Maybe men don't know all the words women use in disdain and despair, maybe they do and don't get it, maybe they do and don't care. Wham, bam, thank you, ma'am, as boys liked to say in high school, laughing.

"Put a flag over her head and fuck her for the sake of glory." That's one I used to hear. "You don't fuck the face," with a leer. *This* is how men are still like the Greeks, this dismissal of the person in a woman, this snickering, winking acknowledgment that the act is separate from the relation. Not that women aren't capable of it. Thompson's equation—"Arrow is to wound as penis is to vulva"—can be reversed. "The force of the Goddess's vulva shoots into the penis of the hunter." But in the larger scheme of things the sensation is almost always the former.

I ask a gay friend about the huge dildos I see in porn stores and expect him to agree with me, that these are largely jokes. But he answers seriously. "There is a— *hunger* there," he says. Sometimes more is better, sometimes you *just want more*. A dildo in the ass rubs on a man's prostate, penetration of the right kind can make a woman's vaginal vault explode with fluid and shivering pleasure. Penetration isn't fucking, just as fucking doesn't have to imply penetration. Penetration is a specific, almost subtextual kind of fucking, it can be separate from or part of other sexual acts, it can be central, peripheral, or woven through. It can stand alone or inseparable from everything else sexual.

Penetration anywhere but the vagina is so peculiarly offensive to so many people there is one multiply defined term for its manifestations, oral or anal, male or female. Two men or two women engaging in sodomy in private can be arrested in Arkansas, Kansas, Missouri, Montana, and Texas. *Anyone* engaging in sodomy with anyone else, even in complete privacy, can be arrested in Alabama, Arizona, Florida, Georgia, Idaho, Louisiana, Maryland, Massachusetts, Michigan, Minnesota, Mississippi, North Carolina, Oklahoma, Rhode Island, South Carolina, Tennessee, Utah, and Virginia. If I lean down to a loved friend's crotch for a kiss, I can go to jail in those states. These aren't idle, forgotten laws; they are enforced, a fact that doesn't reflect whether or not these behaviors are common, whether or not the legislators and police and judges practice them, too. We call sodomy "Greek," but to Shakespeare it was the "Italian habit." The French call it "le vice allemand"; the medieval Christians called it "Turkish." Anything but close to home, because heaven knows, *we* would never do such things.

11

No one has ever duplicated the work of William Masters and Virginia Johnson. They weren't the first to study the physiology of sexual intercourse and orgasm, but they were the first, and the only, people to publish such a narrowly focused and detailed study of it for the lay person. No one else has tried, as far as I know, and I doubt anyone could anymore, funding being a continuing problem in the field of sexology, and funding for explicit research the hardest to find. *Human Sexual Response* sold out its first printing in three days, but most people today can't describe what the book was about, exactly, or how the research was done. For good reason. At the time Masters was quoted as saying of the book's incredibly turgid prose, "Every effort was made to make this book as pedantic and obtuse as possible and, may I say in all modesty, I think we succeeded admirably."

Masters and Johnson originally used prostitutes in their research—women "regarded as knowledgeable, cooperative, and available for study"—because they presumed "more conservative" populations wouldn't participate in their research. William Masters and Virginia Johnson, unlike Alfred Kinsey, weren't interested in social behavior. They were interested in the precise anatomy and physiology of sex—the minute structures of the genitalia, and especially, what happened to the genitalia in sexual arousal and orgasm. This required the researchers to observe people actually having sex and having orgasms, and, reasonably enough, prostitutes came to mind. And many did participate—giving "invaluable" tips on sexual response and technique.

It wasn't long before the researchers' efforts to find more conservative people paid off. Eventually 382 women, aged eighteen to seventy-eight years, and 312 men, aged twenty-one to eighty-nine, participated. They gave such blunt reasons for participating as anxiety over sexual performance, "the opportunity for anonymous relief of sexual tension," the chance to revive a marriage, and a unique opportunity to earn some extra cash. Clearly, the "conservative" population was full of surprises. Masters and Johnson claimed all their subjects felt the study was ultimately beneficial to their sex lives. Most of the women, who were studied longer and in more depth than men, listed two primary motives: money and a safe outlet for regular sex.

The heart of the study involved observations of intercourse and masturbation, the last involving a kind of high-tech, electrically powered recording dildo, allegedly nicknamed Ulysses. "The penises are plastic and were developed with the same optics as plate glass. Cold-light illumination allows observation and recording without distortion. . . . Orientation to this equipment obviously was necessary. . . ."

Human Sexual Response is a tough read, a textbook on a complex subject most of us know little about, written in the most technically aloof language possible. But now and then a little poetry seeps through the arid academic paragraphs; now and then a little irony peeks out, perhaps not always unintentionally. Vaginal lubrication before intercourse is called "mounting readiness." The erect penis exhibits its "full, tense demand."

Measuring a fully erect penis—one at the "final engorgement of late plateau phase"—had to be done quickly, the researchers noted: "measurement frequently was rushed." I have in mind a slightly balding, slender scientist with bookish glasses and a white lab coat, wearing latex gloves and kneeling with a measuring tape and clipboard beside his subject: a panting naked man who holds his hard-on and his breath impatiently, sweat on his face, toes and face clenched, until permission to finish is granted. The scientist jumps adroitly out of range, just in time, and the next subject, prick in hand, steps up to the mark.

Everything we know about the physical aspects of masturbation comes from this kind of observation of people masturbating. So. Go to your room. Close the curtains. Unplug the phone, pull back the bedclothes. Strip. Lie down and touch yourself in whatever private way you prefer, ways no one else ever, ever sees. (Because even if you masturbate in front of a lover, it will have a different style, a different flavor than this solitary moment.) When the tingle begins to fade from your skin, imagine this: Electrodes. Lights. A camera between your still-outspread knees. A man, or a woman, in a lab coat, with a clipboard, taking notes. The world returning.

The human body in orgasm looks remarkably consistent, male or female, young or old. The rectal sphincter contracts between two and five times, each contraction lasting about 0.8 seconds; the neck, arm, and leg muscles cramp in involuntary spasms; the big toe juts out and the other toes bend back from the arched sole in a reflex called the carpopedal spasm; the skin turns red, almost rashy, in the "sex flush"; breathing speeds up to hyperventilation; the heart races at 110 to 180 beats per minute; the face is distorted by grimaces and contortions. Both sexes do "full-excursion pelvic thrusting." In women the vagina and uterus contract at the same speed as the rectal sphincter, as many as ten to fifteen times; in men the penis contracts at the same speed as the rectal sphincter, shooting semen out in several spurts, one to two feet away from the body. Women also sometimes ejaculate, a clear and often copious fluid that used to be called "childish semen." Though Masters and Johnson noted it, female ejaculation is widely considered imaginary these days.

What *is* an orgasm? In physiological terms, orgasm is the pleasurable, rapid release from vasocongestive and myotonic symptoms caused by physical and psychological sexual stimulation. In other words, orgasm which feels so active, so much an *act,* is a kind of anti-act after the action of foreplay—it is a letting go, a surrender and return to the normal. The build to orgasm is an awful joy, full of pleasure and tension in almost equal measure; orgasm is a cool bath bathing the burn. There are many mythic images of getting stuck in copulation, like dogs unable to separate, heroes and heroines in permanent, unceasing intercourse. To avoid getting stuck forever in coitus, the myths say, one has to die—that is, move forward, into orgasm. An orgasm interrupted is a peculiar and fearsome itch, every part of the body leaning into the halted drive. The testicles swell, the penis throbs. Something of the same happens to women, on a larger scale.

Masters and Johnson describe an experiment in which a woman was kept highly aroused for six and a half hours, during which she "underwent repeated pelvic examinations." Five times the woman was brought (exactly how is not explained) to a preorgasmic state without being allowed to climax. By the end of the experiment, her uterus was more than twice normal size, her vaginal barrel was "grossly engorged," her labia was swollen almost three times normal size. The pelvic exams had became painful. She then rested for six hours without any sexual stimulation, and this level of painful engorgement continued, along with cramping and backache. (She was also, we are informed in an aside, "irritable, emotionally disturbed, and could not sleep.") Finally, she was allowed to masturbate to orgasm and felt "immediate relief" from all symptoms.

In these simple physical terms, there is little difference between men and women, between different men, different women, between one orgasm and the other. Masters and Johnson studied men climaxing during intercourse and from masturbating, and women climaxing from penetration, from clitoral masturbation, from rubbing their breasts, and in a few cases, purely from fantasy—and in each case the measured physical orgasm was essentially the same, varying only in the degree of tension achieved before relaxation. In other words, the worse it gets, the better it will be. That little blip is just a miniature version of the mind-blowing earthquake from last week, the only significant difference a difference of degree. But of course, in our real lives this seems meaningless; what really counts about an orgasm takes place in our heads.

The move toward orgasm is a move toward preoccupation with one's genitals. Whatever the stimulus, sooner or later the conscious self gets shoved down into the crotch, nose to nose with desire. Premature ejaculation can be seen as nothing more than a sudden, unplanned relocation. But for all the similarities in muscles and sphincters, the male and female experience of orgasm is markedly different. And who really cares about rectal sphincter spasms when it's a rip-roaring throat-splitting orgasm we want? The felt experience is what matters, and I know the felt experience of men is not much like my own, and that to understand them even a little I have to see the differences as having no aesthetic, no moral, meaning.

Men tell me of boyhood ejaculation contests in back of the barn; gay men I know casually describe the casserole they took to the last potluck jack-off party they attended. Many straight men find prostitution the most pragmatic sexual outlet. I was astonished when a friend of mine described a five-minute orgasmic sexual encounter in an alley simply because it could never be so easy for me, never so free of psychological consequence. Gay men can join themselves to an ancient system of anonymous sex, signified by the hole in the bathroom wall. Male sexuality seems different from mine fundamentally because nothing need be involved but the head and shaft of the

penis, no other part of the body need be troubled,
touched, undressed, or soiled, no relationship of any
kind need exist. Even conversation can be eliminated.
Most important, orgasm is usually guaranteed. In fact,
men often seem to like the environments in which such
sex takes place specifically for all the reasons I would
find it unimaginably difficult to climax in: the danger of
being caught, the unexpected opening salvo, the sudden
arousal, its sudden end. Such sex takes place literally
within one's ordinary life—in, out, it's over, back to
work. I can be snide and point out the castration fantasy
involved in putting your prick in a hole in the wall. But
there's a bit of jealousy there.

The male orgasm has always seemed to me to burst
almost from nowhere, to be infinitely more ready and
willing than my own—and to peak and race away into a
vanishing point where all desire, all interest in things
sexual, disappears. Richard Rhodes describes his effort to
hold back ejaculation by reciting the Gettysburg Address, trying to resist what Masters and Johnson called
the "sense of ejaculatory inevitability." But Lincoln was
no help under the pressure; Lincoln, like everything else,
kept turning into sex. "The onanistic spill or paternal
birth ectasy of 'Our fathers *brought forth upon this continent*' was particularly treacherous to navigate. Y——
became 'this continent,' her breasts mountains . . ." I
find it rather more important to keep my mind on the
complex process of buildup, rather than off; Lincoln
would distract me in an instant, would inevitably lead

into rumination and memory, drawing the frustrated energy away. Male orgasm seems easy to me. Men can leap into sex, make a big slimy mess of everything, and leap out, or go right to sleep, or get up for a little television. Women are dismissed as fish, while men shoot snotty come all about and forget to get a towel. It hardly seems fair. But life isn't fair.

When women described their orgasms to Masters and Johnson, it was as though they were describing a completely different event. What is a driving, linear sensation to men begins in women "with a sensation of suspension or stoppage." This moment of timelessness is followed immediately by pleasure ranging in intensity "from mild to shock level," accompanied by various strange and sometimes distracting feelings—"bearing down," "pelvic throbbing," this last growing until it is "one with a sense of the pulse or heartbeat."

Howie Gordon told me another anecdote about his early days in porn, and his first scene with an actress he'd never met before. "We started, took about fifteen minutes, whoosh, everything was perfect. After we came— after *I* came—I said, 'Do *you* want to come?' And she said, 'Are you *kidding?* In front of all these *people?*'"

My own orgasm is fragile, elusive, and commanding, and subject to other people's agendas, however old or worn. Ghosts inhabit my orgasm; long-gone spirits speak. My orgasms are hard won and often emotionally disruptive, fading only with reluctance, sometimes refusing to completely go away. Why, when the clitoris has more nerve endings in a much smaller space then the penis, is the female orgasm so much trickier to achieve? Why don't I go off like a rocket? I can try to explain the evolution of male orgasms as the inevitable result of hunters trying to procreate as fast as possible when fertile females are hard to find and predators wait behind every rock. But that explanation doesn't satisfy me, not one way or the other. Patience is what's needed, and sometimes patience is exactly what I haven't got.

In *Flesh in the Ring,* a 1960-era Mexican pulp novel, the hero sees a woman wrestler naked for the first time: "The erect clitoris poked from the thick lips like a miniature penis. The hard, long clitoris of the lesbian." This is old but enduring territory, this land of the demanding, hungry clitoris versus the receptive, accommodating vagina. A clitoral urge was thought to lead directly to lesbianism—to clitorally centered sex. Excision of the clitoris is an old cure for the evil, recommended by the Catholic Church not that long ago.

Thomas Laquer, a historian, says the clitoral orgasm was always understood and widely accepted without question until the 1800s, when first William Acton and then Freud came along. Almost every woman finds it far easier to have an orgasm from clitoral stimulation than with penetration—the elusive G-spot notwithstanding. Whether or not a woman had an orgasm wasn't that important an issue, really; she simply had to be willing to give up the easy route to one. Freud believed mature women moved in their sexuality from the clitoral focus of the little girl rubbing herself to sleep into the vaginal desire for penetration—because penetrate vaginas is what penises, in their turn, are supposed to do. In order to "qualify" as a heterosexual, a woman had to prefer intercourse to any other sexual touch. To be "clitoral" was to be arrested in one's development—immature, undone, oppositional. To be clitoral was to be disobedient —a spoiled girl wanting another slice of cake.

There have always been arguments over whether or not the clitoris is the "female penis," partly because women have always been depicted as miniature and unfinished versions of men. But no maker of culture ever wanted the clitoris to have independence, metaphorical or otherwise. The clitoris is, like the penis, frequently viewed but rarely seen. Sex-education material proposed for the public schools by members of the Christian Right omit any mention of it all; the anatomical drawings of genitalia in the curriculum leave the clitoris out. I didn't have a name for it until I started reading dirty books, and looking at paintings by Betty Dodson. My mother never mentioned it, that's for sure.

Like everyone else, I've always been alternately fascinated and repelled by the possibility of my parents' sexual relations, a fascination that changed but didn't go away when I became sexually active myself. (As a parent,

I find myself wondering what happens to a child who hears on the edge of sleep his mother cry out in orgasm.)

When my mother and father married, right after World War II, marriage manuals were filled with advice, with the labyrinthine constructions of sexual hygiene for a prosperous generation. They are most remarkable on the subject of the clitoris and the elaborate machinations required to accomplish the officially approved good of orgasm without succumbing to such temptations as the unnamed evil of oral sex.

"The clitoris, while important," wrote one mid-century therapist, "is not nearly as important as most of us have been taught to believe. It becomes erect during excitement and it bends down to make contact with the entering penis. With the penis penetrating, there should be sufficient lubrication to make the act enjoyable. In time the orgasm should occur." This author cautions women with strong sex feelings not to masturbate, since doing so will condition her to enjoy "clitoris friction." If she leaves her clitoris alone and has intercourse with her husband as much as possible, he assures us, with time the "normal channels" will develop.

A woman therapist suggested that the vagina's nerve endings and sensation must be awakened by way of clitoral sensation; the nerves "practice" sensation this way. Once the lesson is learned, the clitoris can be abandoned. Another therapist wrote that the failure of the clitoris to be adequately stimulated during intercourse "is one of the anomalies in the sexual physiology of the human female." This author, a man, discusses how to fix this nagging problem, admitting that in extreme cases the husband might consider masturbating his wife to climax ("even after he has reached his own orgasm") because otherwise tensions will develop in the marriage. But this counselor has a strong preference for another approach: Describing the missionary position as "the usual position for coitus," he adds, "It is important to bear in mind, however, that in this position the knees of the woman would have to be bent and her thighs drawn up. 'How far should the knees be drawn up?' The knees may be flexed only slightly with the feet resting on the bed, or they may be drawn up so that the legs of the wife will encircle the husband's body." Another is confident that intercourse in the missionary position will result in simultaneous orgasm. "This is it. This is the moment of ecstasy when a woman soars along a Milky Way among stars all her own. This is the high mountaintop of love of which the poets sing. Her whole being is a full orchestra playing the fortissimo of a glorious symphony."

This kind of orgasm was tricky to obtain, but one had to try. Married women who don't have orgasms suffer headaches, dizziness, "a general feeling of utter misery. Some women later become depressed, having weeping spells, digestive upsets and nervous prostration." They may suffer arrhythmias, clammy skin, compulsive behavior, and phobias. Without knowing why, "they wake up in the morning unrefreshed by sleep, having a grouchy disposition, finding fault with their husbands, their children and everything in general." (I know I do.)

The world in which my mother married seems so far away from the one in which I became sexually active; it seems safer, quieter, less intrusive, tinged with sadness, bad sex, fewer choices. I wonder how closely she read those books, how much she took their words to heart. Did she deny herself the obvious orgasm that beckoned? Cunnilingus is not once mentioned in any of the marriage books of her generation I've read, except in the one that lists it as a perversion. I imagine couples all over America shifting and wiggling about in silent pursuit of the elusive missionary-position simultaneous orgasm they are both told to have and instructed to obtain in the worst possible way. I imagine couples succumbing to the obvious in silent shame. I imagine my parents throwing the books in the fireplace.

So I bless Masters and Johnson, for calling the clitoris "a unique organ in the total of human anatomy," for stating that "the human female frequently is not content with one orgasmic experience." Masters and Johnson rather coyly suggested that women get "frustrated by male ineptitude" when it comes to the clitoris. In the 1970s, they tried to run a homosexual conversion therapy program. They had little luck with men, but even less with lesbians, whose complaints had much more to do with social and familial pressures than with sexual dissatisfaction. The therapeutic approach included trying to convince women that men could be trained to be just as nice, understanding, and satisfying in bed as women.

One possible effect of biophysiological sex research is a conflict between the observed sensations and the felt experiences of sex. The research can be used to override, contradict, dismiss, and devalue the subject's spoken beliefs, to lead accepted ideas of sexual behavior down the garden paths of social docility. Men have historically spoken of women's sexuality in either alarmed or patronizing tones—sometimes both at once—and quantitative research can make it even harder for men to understand the fluid, amorphous, and deeply psychological nature of female sexuality. If you are lubricated, you must be aroused; if you don't *feel* aroused, then your feelings are wrong, not the lubrication. If we rely too heavily on research, our feelings come gradually to be seen as both inaccurate and inadequate indicators of our lives.

I try to imagine a different world, a world in which the leading scientists and psychotherapists, all women, spend the better part of a century arguing over the relative maturity of the male orgasmic experience. After all, the male orgasm is undeniably simple, doesn't require a partner, and begins in early childhood. It is an instinct, easy, too obvious to be valued. And the penis is very badly placed, anatomically speaking, when it comes to making women come. Better if men simply left their penis alone, stopped attending to those immature nerve fibers, and concentrated instead on learning how to orgasm through their tongues.

I find myself thinking: Every orgasm is different. Then I must instantly amend myself, because every sexual event is different. Every point of arousal, every plateau, every intersection of desire with the desired is unique. The memory of sexual passion often feels as though it had been dreamed rather than done. As if it had happened to someone else, been told us, or, more accurately, been witnessed. You, the other, catch me when I fall. I, the other, catch you.

To take one's clothes off at the beginning of the sex act is "a form of role removal," in Murray Davis's words. (And putting on certain kinds of clothing at the beginning of sex is similar, a matter of putting on a role that isn't really yours.) By taking off our clothes in front of each other, we consciously take off our other selves, our relations to other people, the limits of our relations to each other. We become just a body, outside the normal strictures and plans of daily life. To be naked means to be seen, but below that, to be naked is to be emptied—blank. Taking off clothes is revolutionary, proletarian; stripping reduces and removes whatever status we rely on. And it makes us both more human and more like objects at the same time. In this sense all sex is masturbation—the other person's body is an object by which we have intense but wholly internal pleasure, and our orgasm is a self-created and unshared universe.

As arousal increases, we imagine things not in the quotidian sphere of concern; we say and do things that seem then to be perfectly logical, correct—even necessary—but that are not planned, not even imaginable, in any other state. In fact, reason and logic are completely absent from this state. This was Thomas Aquinas's main objection to sex. If what distinguishes humans from animals is their ability to reason, then what could be more destructive to humanity than a force that steals reason away? Afterward, the next day, the morning after, when desire has been sated, there remains the shocked memory: "Oh, God, did I say *that*? Did I do *that*?" Yes, you did.

In passion, the body abstracts itself, is abstracted. Damp labia loom enormous, the wrinkled apricot bundles of the scrotum grow in stature, a pearly drop of semen expands into a bell. The shapes turn alien and impressionistic, barely discerned in the chaos of color and line. They expand and ripple into something else, like a word said over and over for the sound of it until all meaning is lost and the syllables become foreign and new.

I catch myself talking about safe sex now and then, glibly, as though it had no psychic meaning. But for all the simplicity of latex, for all that protecting ourselves from sexually transmitted diseases is largely a matter of a few moments of forethought, there is a great price re-

quired. In the depth of sexual passion the skin of the
other has the quality of treasure; the mundane secretions
our bodies make are honey, manna, light. To be cut off
from each other's *fluids* is a terrible thing; our fluids are
meant to mingle, we long for this mingling that is both
so outrageous and so pure.

Tongues loosen during orgasm, things get said that
would never be said otherwise. The Navaho thought one
couldn't keep secrets, even the most important and magical ones, during intercourse. Certainly in a sexual relationship a moment arrives when you don't want to stop,
you don't want to stop so much that your brain disen-
gages and you would do anything to keep going—if you
could do anything but this; all else disappears, the lover,
the self, God; all other needs vanish, there are no other
appetites or hungers left, everything is conquered and
the land laid waste.

Orgasm is psychedelic; you can't describe it, but you
can still understand if you've been there before. Two
people on LSD; one says, "The rug!" and the other nods
vigorously—"Yeah! The rug!" They have a kind of perfect understanding—both see the rug with ecstatic eyes.
But they have no understanding at all, because they see
the rug with separate eyes. Of course, some of us get
more intoxicated than others, some days seem more
reckless. We can't really explain how arousal feels, what
an orgasm *is,* and the closer we get to one, the less value
words have, the less we can use language at all. Reason
doesn't just leave us when we enter orgasm; orgasm is

antithetical to reason—orgasm destroys reason and, conversely, a moment of reason can destroy an orgasm. A friend tells me that when he comes, he feels his penis enter his lover's vagina on Tuesday and emerge on Wednesday, eternally, endlessly, over in a few seconds. He is submerged in the ocean of the moment.

This is the most infantile state an adult can experience in an ordinary aspect of life, the moment when we are most outside the neurosis of self-consciousness, when we become only Mouth, Skin, Hunger, Cry, Smile. These are royal and holy seconds. The language of orgasm and the language of Nirvana use the same words. The fear that keeps us from intimacy with others is the same fear that keeps us from religious fever, and this fear is pacified in arousal—sexual arousal or devotional arousal. Arousal begins in the moment when desire overcomes fear, and from then on the course is happily, ecstatically, toward extinction. Naturally, this is a dangerous course; narrow roads usually are.

The merging of two into one in orgasm, this blending of identity, combines bliss and anxiety in a strange stew. This may be the best explanation for why the orgasms of masturbation can be more powerful and feel more physically whole than those shared. They are simply safer. Murray Davis uses the phrase "fear of ontological contamination" to describe how we can hold our inner self in check even when our body is fully engaged. But one of the great utilities of sex is to overcome this—to create a place of ontological surrender. The release is separate from the simply physical gratification and yet it is felt physically and has physical effects. It is possible during sex—and not just in orgasm—to get out of one's head in a quite literal way. You lose *you* for a while, and watch yourself go, and this as much as anything creates the almost total state of repose that follows. To lose oneself awhile can be such a relief. The odd thing about the human ego is how it both resists and longs for its own extinction; the ego is what gets us into bed in the first place, as much as our body; the ego is the selfish part of us that demands the pleasure of orgasm, that focuses self-centeredly on the body of another as a source of private pleasure, and it's the ego that, ultimately, is killed by the result. Orgasm is a version of the ego's death wish; it is the little death, a miniature reminder of the bigger one. Orgasm is an incandescent and inarticulate memory of the universe before birth.

In *The Tibetan Book of the Dead* rebirth is felt initially as the sexual urge for one's mother's womb. Fear of sexual intimacy is distinctly related to the fear of death; the journey in and out of the body is like a journey into another world. (The joke goes like this: When does the atheist pray to God?) The cries of orgasm are curses as well as prayers—we call on God and Jesus and for all I know, Allah and Mohammed and Moses as well, and we say Yes, and we say No. Another joke: Don't, stop, don't, stop, don't stop.

One of the unique human aspects of sex is our association of sex with fear, sex with power, sex with pain. And with death. We fear sex in a *psychic* way, which is often the way we desire it. (Certainly that's how the romantic ideal has told us to desire sex.) This meld of fear and desire, writes William Irwin Thompson, is what gives human sexuality its obsessive quality. "Gone is the casual ten-second coitus of the animal; present for good is the sexualization of human culture, and an association of erotic excitement with a thrilling sense of danger." Sexuality, not sex, is the new thing, the human addition. Sexual forms "unfold like the petals of shrapnel in an explosion. Sexuality explodes in every direction and will light upon any available appendage, orifice, or symbolic article. . . ." There's no safe place for the sexual human, no solid barricade behind which we can hide from sex, no defense so strong that the possibility of intimacy can't slip through. Sometimes I long for that release of the ego into the other, my lover, and I can't let go no matter how I try. But I remember more than once longing to be left intact, and being released against my will, like slipping at the top of an icy slide and knowing there's no way to stop until I come to the ground.

Where did the fear begin? Thompson might say it was the result of the radical cultural changes that followed the end of visible estrus and the resulting changes in mating and family patterns. The end of estrus completely changed the meaning of sex, which ceased being simply a vehicle for sperm to meet egg. Because we had to engage in sex all the time in order to "catch" the egg, the nature of sex changed, took on new qualities. What began as a biological drive ended, if it has ended at all, as something very different. Desire became constant, and the constancy is what we fear. *It never goes away for long.* So humans learned to ritualize sex and formalize sexual relationships, began to tell stories about sex—explanations needed to incorporate shifting and unpredictable urges into our lives. We've been doing that for a long time. When sexual acts became symbols, romance was born.

If sex is a problem for me, it's an unsolvable problem, repeating, immortal. Since I can't make sex go away, I can only hope to find out how to live with it, how to make it be not a problem. That makes facing fear even more important than facing shame; it means paying attention to my self, my desires and concerns, a lot more than to the voices and concerns of those around me.

I avoid sex sometimes, even when I long for it. It seems to me that men often move toward intimacy through sex, and women more often will move toward sex through intimacy. (That is, women are more afraid of the act of sex, and men of its consequences.) When I'm nervous, uncertain, prickly, or too tender, sleep is what I want. The union and annihilation of sleep, where everything falls away. Everything—the maddening other, worries, this idea, disappearing. In all our stories of rapturous abandonment, no one talks about terror. No one talks about how even when almost all of me surrenders to the momentum and union of sex, one small part reels away in terror—and in retreat takes everything else.

No one talks about coming back to the self a moment later, knocked breathless by the knowledge of having been so far gone.

Facing down sexual fear one night, fear of hunger, fear specifically of orgasm and its terrible demands, I suddenly understood something about prostitution: If I was being paid to perform the act that frightened me just then, I wouldn't have been afraid. I could see how easy it is to do the motions of sex rather than sex itself. No amount of money can seduce real abandonment, but even more important, the exchange of money for sex is clearly the buying of a physical act, not a psychological one. The prostitute might, and often does, mimic passion; she fills her conversation with sexual flattery and the theater of passion, she projects the messages of sexual love. But only a fool believes them, only the kind of fool who believes what he sees on television and tells himself in the mirror. Only a fool thinks that what the prostitute does is more dangerous than love.

The infant learns to say no, from the trauma of birth, the mother's tension, the coldness of the world. We are all filled with no. Said Wilhelm Reich of the newborn: "It just cries. And, finally, it gives up. It gives up and says, 'No!' . . . Here, at the very beginning, the spite develops. Here, the 'no' develops, the big 'NO' of humanity. And then you ask why the world is in a mess."

Is the "NO" we all sooner or later utter in orgasm the same negation? Is it fear, the NO of shame, the NO of "no more" or the NO of "Yes"? No! Don't kill me, don't scare me, don't make me. Don't stop.

Wilhelm Reich was a paranoid schizophrenic. But anyone who dies in prison on an FDA fraud rap could hardly be dismissed as *too* paranoid. Reich was a blast of news and an anachronism at the same time, going sideways and explosively away from Freud. Reich became Freud's assistant in Vienna in the 1920s, and quickly began making radical leaps connecting mental and physical spheres within psychoanalysis. He described the concept of "armor"—ways in which the body rigidifies because of emotional states, blocking pleasurable sensations along with painful or frightening ones. Reich began by treating the adult, then extrapolated from the individual to the group, and then to government, and the world, and in the end, to the infant. He believed that censors of all stripes were simply expressing the depth of their sexual deprivation and armoring, and that the fascist mind grew directly out of a fear of orgasms. Reich's ideal healthy person had "genital character"—the ability to be fully satisfied sexually by being fully at ease in one's body. With genital character one has the ability to surrender to and use the energies of the cosmos in one's own body, free of fear and anxiety. Trying to figure out the world's neurosis was confusing and difficult, until,

Reich said toward the end of his life, he made the obvious leap. *"You couldn't get at the mental-hygiene problem with ideas such as the oedipus complex. You couldn't get at it. It didn't make sense. What made sense was the frustration, the genital frustration of the population."*

Libido, to Freud, meant more than sexual energy, it meant *energy,* a life force, full of emotion. Reich took Freud's theory of libido and expanded it: If individual sexual repression led to individual neurosis, then socialized sexual repression led to socialized neurosis. Sexually repressed cultures were violent cultures, despairing, tyrannical. Sexual freedom would lead naturally to socialism. And so simply solving an orgasmic dysfunction— or, as Freud attempted, helping an unhappy person become "functional"—wasn't enough. Not nearly enough. Social change required the therapeutic community to oppose Fascism, address the causes of sexual violence, the harm done by socialized sex roles and social inequalities of all kinds.

Reich ultimately split from Freud over the theory of sublimation. He admired Freud but saw him as "bound up," limited. Reich was opposed to laws prohibiting or restricting sexual behavior of almost any kind, including that of adolescents. He was widely denounced by his colleagues as well as several governments, and wandered from country to country, seeking haven, finally coming to a reluctant United States in 1941. Here he developed the mother of all persecution complexes, and was in turn really and truly persecuted. When he built and sold

"orgone boxes" in which people could absorb the cura-
tive life energy of the cosmos—an energy he believed
could be measured, collected, and applied—the FDA
banned the boxes, and, almost as a reflex, his books. He
was sentenced to two years in prison in 1956 for contempt of court and violating FDA orders, and died of a
heart attack there eight months later. If only Reich had
quit while he was ahead—but he went on and on and
on, until Orgone was everything, until it was gravity,
weather, and God. He went nuts, but he was on to
something.

When Reich died, I was a few months old. I was
bottle-fed, the second of three quick children. My
mother was already pregnant again, and I sucked my
thumb to put myself to sleep. Reich believed that infants
were damaged at birth from their mother's armor, and
that only by treating infants could he hope to raise a
generation of women whose wombs weren't as rigid as
their backs and throats. I wasn't treated that young, but I
joined a Reichian therapy group of eight teenagers when
I was sixteen, still flexible in a few ways, and horribly
bound up in others.

Even now, twenty years later, if I meet one or the
other of the people with whom I did therapy, I need only
say the word "group" to explain a feeling. Reichian therapy was hard, rough-edged, potent, and dangerous; it
was physically painful and sometimes emotionally devastating. The powerful, almost obsessed therapists who led
us through the physical and psychological exercises de-

signed to break down our muscular and emotional armor may have done me a fair bit of harm as well as a
great deal of good. But they were the first and only
adults in my young life to talk to me as a sexual creature,
to acknowledge not only that I was sexual but that I
suffered from sexuality—that sex was important, legitimate, and real. To Reich "the body alone spoke truth."
My Reichian therapists were the first people in my life to
speak truth about my body to me.

IV

Resolution

12

Perversion is something individual, a turn-on or a necessity, essentially victimless. Taboo is different. Taboos have social implications, they are broader than perversions, culturally based; those who break taboos are disruptive and anarchic. Taboos arise to protect one part of an established order or another—to direct the energy of individuals and communities in certain directions, away from certain others. Since the community builds continually upon itself, shaking any part of its foundation shakes the whole. This is what the breaking of sexual taboos does. Our response to the breaking of a taboo may be rage or fear; the emotion is usually an enormous one, because much more than decorum or propriety is being flouted.

What is forbidden is desirable. (What is desirable is often forbidden, too, but that's another story.) Perversions have a frisson of seduction, a hypnosis—the pervert wants his perversion whether it's permitted or not, legal or otherwise; what counts is the perversion, not the rules. But breaking taboos can also be attractive in and of itself; the breaking sometimes is at least as attractive as the act involved, because more happens than the sex. Something big is deconstructed. "When I strap on a dildo and fuck my male partner," Carol Queen wrote last year in *Out/Look*, "we are engaging in 'heterosexual' behavior, but I can tell you it feels altogether *queer*, and I'm sure my grandmother and Jesse Helms would say the same."

What would completely unfettered sexual expression be like? How much can we call the moral, legal, and religious rituals and taboos of sex "natural"? Perhaps they are psychologically necessary to humans, a kind of natural repugnance we call morality. I know of no society that doesn't define and delimit sex somehow, create boundaries and parameters of one kind or another whether they be ritual or not. But no human society fails to define *any* major aspect of human experience. Perhaps this is human nature, defining and controlling human appetites. Perhaps the need to control *is* human appetite.

———

The Marquis de Sade is the emblematic taboo-marker, the taboo-speaker of all time. He is usually saddled with a lot more than his life and life's work deserves, because he's gotten so much bigger than life by now. Even writing about Sade has a taint to it.

Sade was "the very type of aristocrat who provoked the vengeance of the revolutionaries," in the words of Angela Carter, neatly turning upside down the belief that Sade himself was the revolutionary. In *The Sadeian Woman,* Angela Carter revises Sade in the contexts of history and feminist thought, portraying him as a crazy and crazed man who was able "to render every aspect of sexuality suspect." (Carter points out that this is clearly a feminist achievement, however accidental.) She sees Sade as a Puritan as well, perhaps the purest kind, the kind who hates rather than fears sex; Sade wrote against sex as much as he wrote against the state. He championed female equality and power even as he dissected male sadism, was drawn to sodomy when it was punishable by death, and while imprisoned saw his own world of privilege overthrown. I can't say I enjoyed reading Sade's work, but I can say it surprised me; the extremities of behavior he describes are so far beyond belief, so far into the bounds of the physically impossible that their metaphorical intent becomes clear. If Sade were a woman writing now, if Andrea Dworkin wrote *Justine,* the work might seem to be a great allegory of feminism and the vanishing point of misogynism. "His was a peculiarly modern fate, to be imprisoned without trial for crimes that existed primarily in the mind," writes Carter.

Shortly after the decision in the Supreme Court which defined obscenity by means of the application of community standards and prurient interests, a case involving books on sadomasochism was argued. The definition of obscenity as written by the court relies on the prurient response of the "average person" to the work in question. The defendant argued that since hard-core sadomasochism does not and never has been erotic to the average person, it can't be obscene.

Out of curiosity I rented a German film called *Discipline in Leather,* a sex film without sex, without even nudity. Two men are variously bound, chained, gagged, spanked, and ridden like horses by a Nordic woman. *"Nein!"* she shouts. *"Nicht so schnell!"* The men lick her boots, accept the bridle in cringing obeisance. I found this Nazi farce laughably solemn. But it's bread and butter to a lot of people who would find my own taste in movies boring or even dangerous. Every time I catch myself in that state of mind, that state of "I don't get it," "I don't understand," I have to grab hold and remember how it feels to be censored in my turn, to have anyone turn to me and say, "You can't do that, because I don't understand."

In this one realm, that of "rough sex"—including sadomasochism, bondage and discipline, and slave-master relationships—people seem to have been able to create the texture of sexual fantasy in real life. Many people who practice rough sex are happy to admit the inevitably therapeutic nature of their discipline. They talk, sometimes rather glibly and sometimes with great seriousness, of how community and family evolve in this world, how communication and a sense of belonging increase with the strokes of the lash. The degree of negotiation and the amount of talking necessary is high. In this kind of sex, sex acts themselves sometimes play a relatively minor part, as the defendant argued before the Supreme Court. If you don't respond to boot-licking sexually, how can you call it unacceptable sex? And if you do, why would you forbid it? A sense of humor is useful, because this sex, however serious, is play. Making a fantasy real requires a lot of effort, and rough sex is replete with laundry-listing, detail-oriented planning, tools, complicated games, rules, and toys. "[B&D] constantly tests your creativity and ingenuity," says a prostitute who specializes as a dominatrix. "A hardware store will never look the same to you again."

I can look at rough-trade sex only from the outside, from reading, listening, looking. But I've read and looked at it so much because S/M and its cousins are hypnotic to me—they represent a conscious creation of sex wholly unlike the evasive stumbling that sex so often resembles in this country and so often has resembled in my own past. Rough sex is deliberate; its participants architects rather than pawns of their desires.

The questions rough sex raises are just the questions

we all ask about sex and relationships and ourselves—
what goes, what doesn't. Yet for all I am drawn to that
world and take it seriously, I find it almost impossible to
describe without making its participants sound faintly
ridiculous. How can I describe or elucidate the fantasy of
infantilism, or the dialogue between sexual master and
sexual slave, without making everyone involved seem
like lunatics? But that's as much sex itself and the world
removed in which it exists than this particular brand of
sex—I can't even repeat the common phrases of heterosexual intercourse without laughing. These things, all
sexual things, take place in another space and time, outside intellect, outside judgment; they can be understood,
and reviewed, only there.

As with all things sexual, details make all the difference. One is never simply whipped, or spanked, one
must be scourged in quite specific ways. Just as I might
say, "Here, dear, not *there,*" another person might say,
"The birch cane, today, dear, not the leather strap." Because the birch cane is different, full of different sensations, different connotations, different meaning.

I was at the dentist yesterday, getting impressions
taken of my teeth. She inserted a big, cold metal brace in
my mouth and filled it with a strange, strangling gummy
substance, and all of a sudden I looked around at all the
contraptions and appliances and started to laugh, re-
membering what the prostitute said about hardware
stores. I was laughing because I knew from then on,
everything in my dentist's office was going to look

double-edged, that my dentist was going to as well, and that the whole world could, and did, in a way. Sex is terribly funny and terribly real and its manifestations are everywhere. I am who I am sexually because of who I was and all that has happened to me and all that has not. The fantasies of rough sex are just children's fantasies acted out in great big grown-up ways. The real, sadistic, and terrifying nightmares of dreaming children, the real traumas of childhood days, are made flesh today in our adult bodies, to be lived out once again.

If I wanted to get started in this world, there are lots of ways. Most cities have clubs, "dungeons," parties, gay and straight, for women only, for mixed groups. I could take my pick. In San Francisco and a few other cities, I could go to school. I have a catalogue for a kind of adult extension school of S/M and related techniques in San Francisco called QSM: "Beg! Fetch! Heel!: Training Your Human Pet," "The Civilized Art of Caning," "Advanced Fisting." The classes emphasize safety and observation rather than participation, and any exchange of bodily fluids is heavily discouraged. (In fact, sadomasochism is, medically speaking, very safe sex.) Here's a class in "Interrogation," another in "Branding for Beginners." Every game has its rules, its arbitrary code words, tableaus, rituals, and symbols. I could take "Customizing Your Whipping." There's a four-part course called "Bondage Potpourri." Or I could take "Knives," which really needs no explanation except that it includes shopping tips.

S/M is theater, but then, all sex is theater. For a moment as master or slave one lives in the body of another,
one pretends something else to be true until it is, briefly,
true. These primal dramas and symbols are innate in all
sexuality; every sexual act contains them. Says a woman
who practices masochism: "The most intense, special
moments of dominance or of submission are things that
probably could be described as staring into someone
else's eyes."

Pat Califia is a sadist who has written articulately and
at length about her prediliction, questioning the meaning of sexual behavior and the unexpected surprises inherent in sex. She writes about this, and then adds, "My
primary interest in S/M is in hurting people." Her primary interest in *sex* is hurting people. The honesty star-
tles me, and I resent it, because I would rather stay in a
more comfortable philosophical universe of therapeutic
relationships, would rather consider the troubling aspects of power-based sex with my intellectual tools. I
prefer to think of S/M as being largely about metaphors
of control and power, submission and surrender, but I
am repeatedly reminded that it's also about *pain* and *fear*.
S/M notes, evokes, and uses pain and fear along with a
lot of other physical and emotional states, but the pain is
central, nevertheless.

Califia, along with a number of other people who
identify both as masochists and sadists, suggests that she
is put together a little differently from the rest of us. She
believes the neurological tissues of the brain, the en-

dorphin-producing cells themselves, are wired into the body's sexual response in a specific way. No doubt rough sex stimulates endorphins and creates a state of catharsis. Califia wonders if her physical sexual response is chemically and neurologically wired into the body's reaction to pain and fear. In this way, the sexual delights of pain are just that and nothing more: Pain is delightful only in the context of sex, and sex is not delightful without pain. Sex *is* pain, in this sense; it can't be separated out. To deny a person with this need pain is to deny them sex altogether.

Some S/M practitioners brag a bit of their superior characters, their evolved understanding of relationships born from such intense exploration of the nature of trust. Practitioners sometimes compare the stimulus of their practice to any high-risk venture, compare a whipping to, say, free climbing, bungee jumping, or hang gliding. Conquering the fear of what one can and cannot do, can and cannot stand. Tolerating pain gives people pride in their self-control. Pain gives people permission to scream and cry. Spanking, of course, is almost less a kind of pain than a confrontation with the emotional baggage of childhood. Some kinds of pain function as psychological discipline, some kinds as punishment, some kinds simply heighten other, more socially acceptable sensations.

One of the most common liberal assumptions about sadomasochistic pleasures is that its primary purpose is that of switching roles: The powerless person longs to be in control, to be the dominatrix, and the person with power longs to submit. That might explain why the largest group of people who practice S/M are heterosexual men who want to be dominated. (Is it any wonder, given his background, that Joyce called Nora "my little mother"? He wrote: "Punish me as much as you like. I would be delighted to feel my flesh tingling under your hand. Do you know what I mean, Nora dear? I wish you would smack me or flog me even. Not in play, dear, in earnest and on my naked flesh.") The uses of rough sex are complex and often ambiguous. Both men and women who have childhood histories of physical and sexual abuses practice sadomasochism—not, as might be expected, because their experiences twisted them into easily victimized personalities or angry abusers in turn. They practice it as a form of healing, an explicable acting-out of trauma in an environment built on trust, an environment that has no room for secrets.

Rough sex, because it is constructed on negotiation, means one is constantly asking for something—a certain touch, or permission to touch a certain way. Nothing is taken for granted. That terrible shame of *asking for something* sexual becomes the central plot rather than the uncomfortable sidebar. And the accomplishment of asking for, and receiving, becomes liberation. I know a man who was once asked by a lover to spank her with a hairbrush; being a liberal kind of guy, the request made him uncomfortable, but he complied. And afterward told me he would never, ever do such a thing again. Why not? I asked. Because she liked it, he said. And I

liked it, too. I compare my friend's aversion to the cheerful confession I read recently of a therapist who has a
rubber fetish and likes to be all wrapped up, who warns
his friends not to leave their raincoats or boots lying
around when he comes over.

S/M acknowledges the existence of the complex and
layered power structures that are always there between
us. The real text of power fantasies is the release from all
the things they represent. Such dreams transcend mere
sex and enter the world of relationship and love through
a kind of psychic back door. Some people call painful sex
"cathartic sex" because it isn't really about dominance
and submission split between two real people, but about
the way we split dominance and submission inside ourselves. How in the world can domination be exciting?
But we're not in the world. We're in a place of our own
making, where we choose to imagine having no control
at all, no responsibility, no mind, where we can be devoured and love it. Where we can imagine annihilation
and survive.

Pat Califia sees S/M the same way Sade saw all of sex,
as unavoidably political. She knows that the wider world
of S/M practitioners has for some time been promoting a
more hygienic image of itself, as a "safe, sane, and consensual" sexual practice, a motto designed to make the
rest of the world relax. Since rough sex by its nature is
outside the realm of the norm, when any part of it becomes "normal," a new wall gives way. The nature of
some people's sexual desire is to be outside the wall, to

always go a little further than what is allowed, rebel a little more. Says Califia, "I think there is an indigestible core of S/M activity that people who don't do it are always going to find repellent." There will be if she has her way.

Sadomasochism is a kind of dressing up, a putting on of fantasy costume to create a fantasy world. We can also put on each other's costumes, to enter our fantasy of each other's worlds. Transvestism, or cross-dressing, seems like a deep existential expression one day and a silly game the next. Certainly what we call drag has a thousand meanings and can be stretched to include everything from Halloween and Carnival to Joyce's love of frilly underwear on his Nora.

Drag queens are history's common, foolish perverts; cross-dressing has always been a psychologically complicated business. I've never cross-dressed in a traditional sense—I've never tried to pass as a man, though the politics attract. Cross-dressing women are bitches, ball-busters, *dykes*. (When I was born in the 1950s, it was still illegal in places for women not to be wearing at least three items of "women's" clothing at a time.) For years, though, I had a strong interest in a kind of drag. The many phases of fashion and image that each of us puts on and takes off over the years between adolescence and adult maturity are all forms of drag, and what I mean by "drag" in this context is only a transition from one mode of dressing, one attempt to discover who I was, to another. For several years, off and on, I liked to see if I could look like a drag queen, as though I were a man being a woman. Sometimes it meant being the dark Vampirella with bloodred lips; sometimes it meant being the overwrought permed housewife. But it never worked. I'm a woman, not one of the girls.

My old friend Don and I were walking along Sutter Street in downtown San Francisco on a sunny cold day, when I asked him to describe the drag queens he knew.

He said, "Auntie Helen is twisted. Lola is sad, used up. Co'lean Bleach isn't sad. She's a stain-resistant codependent." Snorting laughter. He is Co'lean Bleach himself.

"But what does that *mean?*"

"It means she's a survivor. Everything is just *water* off her back."

I'm thinking out loud about what I would want to do. "Maybe I'm the cousin from Cleveland who comes to visit, and you're going to show me the city. Very trashy and very cheap. Don't know class when I see it."

"Yes. *Very* slutty. We've got to rat your hair. *Big* hair. Get some spandex."

"I look awful in spandex!"

"I *know,* I *know!*"

Just then a woman wearing an orange knit minidress with beads stitched on it walks by and Don swivels around to watch her pass. "Now," he says thoughtfully, "if that dress were a *little* bit tighter and a little shorter, Co'lean would love it."

Genitals may be the least important part of masculinity and femininity, both from the inside and the outside. There is great eroticism in that gray and ill-defined middle ground, in crossing and criss-crossing, mixing and matching, fitting new folds around unexpected extensions. A woman wearing a dildo, a man wearing lipstick and lingerie—depending on your taste, and your taste may surprise you, the combination is what works. The cross itself, the pregnant, promising image that is both and neither.

The taboo is born where fabric ends and skin begins. The difference between transvestites and transsexuals could be called the difference between being and becoming. Woman-with-cock—does that mean woman first and cock second? Or the other way around? The excitement is the same, a sexual paradox, unbounded. Dangerous, because no one knows the rules here. A man tells me the sight of two men kissing makes him squeamish. But, he adds, "I've always said I'd be happy to suck a dick if it was on a beautiful woman."

When I was in my late twenties, my mother called to tell me, almost in passing, that the young woman who had been my best friend for several years in adolescence was now a man. Terry's transformation was less a shock to me than my mother had expected it to be. Though it had never consciously occurred to me to think of Terry as a man, the moment I did I felt the eminent logic of the idea. It felt right—suddenly obvious. Terry had always had about her the quality of a man, the ineffable, indefinable masculinity I associate with men and which is different from the masculinity of women. I was more surprised that Terry stayed in our hometown after his surgery, willing to endure whatever was dished out. To this day my father calls him "It."

When we were high school students, Terry was befriended by Linda, our biology teacher. She remained a friend of Terry's long after Terry graduated, and after his surgery, they married. When I went to see Terry and Linda not long ago, they showed me around their split-level and told me about their five long-term foster children, none of whom they've been allowed to adopt because of Terry's background. Terry and I flipped through yearbooks, gossiped about old friends, listened to old music. He looks almost the same. He is almost as she was, but for the unmistakable male-pattern baldness and a few crow's-feet around his pale eyes. If anything is missing, it is tension; if anything is new, it is his peace.

No one knows the origin of the transsexual's plight. There are cases of transsexual brothers and sisters who become sisters and brothers, of husbands and wives who have switched genders and become wives and husbands. The biology and sociology literatures both tend to claim social factors are stronger than any biological ones, a somewhat silly claim given that no one knows if there *are* biological factors at work, let alone social ones. A lot of these theories of causation are suspiciously similar to

traditional ideas about how men "become gay" as children—domineering mother, weak or absent father, and
so on. They rely on the psychoanalytical standards that
began with Eve.

That most transsexuals are men who want to become
women (MTF, or male-to-female) is perhaps the most
commn stereotype about transsexualism. There is a
dearth of information in the professional literature re-
garding women who become men (FTM, female-to-
male), although according to current research, at least a
quarter of all transsexuals are FTM and the ratio is
increasing.

The second presumption—and one I confess to
have held—is that male-to-female transsexuals are ul-
trafeminine in manner and appearance, more traditionally girlish than the girls. Anne Bolin, who has
written a powerful book about her anthropological
studies of a group of male-to-female transsexuals
called *In Search of Eve,* considers this one of several
stereotypes that transsexuals themselves reinforce in
order to be accepted as transsexuals. Permission to
take hormones, to have surgery, to be *believed,* has
often depended on a person's willingness to portray
outdated and sexist roles through literally years of
scrutiny by physicians and psychologists. Perhaps the
researchers help to skew their own research even
more, by selection. The people allowed to have surgery, "approved" as transsexuals, who form the basis
for most researchers' conclusions about transsexuals,

may be selected on the basis of their traditional femininity—a maddening cycle of sex-role rigidity in which the paternal institution of medicine allows a person to become a woman only if the person becomes the kind of woman traditionally favored by paternal institutions. Transsexuals are subjected by their counselors to everything from the Minnesota Multiphasic Personality Inventory to testing on perceived social roles, career choice, and preferred styles of clothing. "Transsexual lore is rich with information on manipulation and utilization of caretaker stereotypes," writes Bolin with admirable brevity.

The third stereotype about transsexuals is that transsexuals are generally heterosexual. That is, a man who thinks he's really a woman is sexually attracted to men, and vice versa. Get it? My friend Terry was always attracted to women, as a girl, and as a man. So *she* was never gay, and *he* is straight—a psychic man longing for a woman. Each of us, transsexual or no, must contend with two separate characteristics of sex: The first is gender, and the second is preference, and these are not inextricably bound. Anne Bolin claims her own research supports no preference for heterosexuality among transsexuals at all. What it certainly supports is a predilection to lie about it—to claim heterosexual feelings when they don't exist. People who work with "gender dysphoria" can be just as homophobic as anyone else. A false claim to Donna Reed–like wardrobe and romantic preferences may help a person get permission for hormone treatment and surgery. But it doesn't help at all to dispel the stereotypes that create the climate for lying in the first place.

"When you ask me what is a woman, I think, what is an apple? I don't know."

Kate Bornstein has a careful, elegant, cultured voice, a voice molded by years of training and constant vigilance. Still, her accent shifts without warning, her inflection rises from an almost breathy whisper to something deeper and more sure. She has reddish hair worn to her shoulders, short, blunt nails on large, almost bony hands. Kate was, for many years, a man named Al. She has been a woman for more than seven years now. Kate passes as a woman, but is also public about being transsexual, which upsets some people. "I used to catch a lot of flak—'You're not socialized as a woman.' I've got my own battles, but I have some things on my side, because I was socialized with an attitude of entitlement, I was socialized with an attitude of empowerment, I'm middle class, I'm educated. There are privileges. But there's also a privilege in being a man or a woman— being gendered at all. By being nongendered, I don't have nearly as many privileges as you have.

"There are a lot of people who want to excuse my existence by saying I was born with this defect, and I had to go get surgery to correct it, and now, 'Shut up, you've corrected your defect, why won't you just be quiet?' But I made some choices here." Some of the people who say this to Kate are other transsexuals, hoping to disappear into their new gender, wishing Kate with her performance art and frequent interviews would stop calling attention to the issue. "I think anyone who has a stake in being a man or a woman has a problem with me. I've been asked to leave synagogues, I've been asked to leave AA meetings, I've been asked to leave jobs because I'm transgendered. One thing that's key to transsexuals is the lies transsexuals are told to tell. Why do you have to pass? Why do you have to get electrolysis? Why do you have to do all this *stuff?* Why can't you just be—halfway? You *can't.*"

Male-to-female transsexuals value people like me—a "GG," a genetic girl. GGs "have been women all their lives and have spent a lifetime involved in the cultural back regions of women's worlds," writes Anne Bolin. GGs know "an immense amount of information about the cultural baggage of women, their intimate ideas, beliefs, cosmology, etc., that perhaps they would only tell another woman. . . . Genetic women have a sort of *mana* (power) in the eyes of transsexuals by virtue of their lifelong history as women."

I find it odd to look upon my own life with the kind of flexibility implied by a phrase like "lifelong history as women." Femaleness seems embedded within me, it feels *inalterable*—but so, I've come to realize, does it feel to the transsexual stuck with a penis and longing for breasts, smooth skin, and a vagina. So does maleness feel embedded in a man stuck with breasts and a vagina, longing for a beard and scrotum. Both are longing for the ineluctable *mana* of the other gender. What the transsexual is doing is very simple, in a way: He or she is altering the form of gender, not gender itself. It is the inalterable nature of their internally perceived gender that gives them the strength to perform this incredibly painful and difficult transformation.

The baggage some transsexuals seek is the baggage a lot of genetic women are trying to leave behind. She must get smaller, nicer; she must lower her voice and change its pitch and inflection, learn to touch others during conversations, change her very choice of curse words, stop interrupting. Conventions last much longer than we suspect, like corpses left unburied. The traditional MTF all dressed up sometimes looks to me like my mother, circa 1958—a version of Woman from another time, a past and passing time.

"I *know* I'm playing a role, I know I'm playing a game," says Kate. "Do you?" The MTF transsexual must adjust to physical danger, to job discrimination and lower wages. Her willingness to do these things is part of what marks her as a "true" transsexual. She will never pass as a woman if she continues to expect the quiet privileges of the man.

I like being a woman, and it's easy enough for me to

understand why someone would want to be one. I cannot explain or define this except in the most dissatisfying ways, but I feel that female *mana;* it affects the way I dream and think and feel, it describes my inner cosmos. The "cultural back regions" of women are what I most value about being a woman—that community of women that no one but women can enter. I am more befuddled by female-to-male transsexuals. I have longed for the privileges of the male, but never for maleness, never at all. What would I be if I had a penis? Who would I be? How different would the self in myself become?

Last summer I met a man named Chris who is so attractive that when he walked into a room everyone there turned to watch. Chris is not traditionally handsome; he is short, stocky, bearded, somewhat weathered, but he exudes a relaxed confidence, a direct and feline grace. I would never have guessed he was transsexual.

After three years, his girlfriend, Polly, forgets sometimes as well, except insofar as his female past makes him a comfortable partner. Polly describes her first meeting with Chris as feeling as though she'd "taken a consciousness-expanding drug." That same night she realized Chris was "prime 'relationship material,'" able to talk to women in a way no man she'd ever met could talk.

"When she says she has cramps, I know what it means," Chris laughs.

"Right! We talk about our periods!" Polly laughs uproariously. "He says, 'When I had my period.' And then again, there's times when I forget Chris used to be a woman."

"She asked me once what I did during Vietnam, and I just looked at her."

Chris told me he'd been a kind of "role model" for several men in his men's support group, men who thought he "had something" they didn't, who couldn't believe it when he told them he used to be a woman. ("I was never a woman," he corrects me. "I had a woman's body and a woman's experience.")

"What do people most want to know about you?" I ask.

"People want to know: What do your parents think? What do your friends think? Do you date? But what they really want to ask is What does your penis look like?"

Transsexuals long to be recognized in ways that cohere with their hidden, internal identity. The first step in becoming a woman is to stop acting like a man. MTF transsexuals must learn the details of how women walk, dance, hold a glass, smooth their clothing, how women talk, and more often, listen, to men. Male-to-female transsexuals are *really* women in some raw, inchoate way, but they must also *become* women, join themselves to a mutable, socially constructed and changing state.

Some transsexuals change every piece of identification,

destroy photographs, edit their past lives to eradicate every marker of the hated gender. Men becoming women bind their clothes and pad their bras; women becoming men bind their breasts flat and pad their crotches.

Kate Bornstein resents the need to pass, to be "gendered" at all, but considers it a necessary evil for now. "I don't want to be beaten up. A lot of gay bashing occurs not because people worry about the kind of sex the person is having, but because the person is violating a gender code. Once I was walking down a badly lit stairway in the subway in Philadelphia. And this guy puts a knife in my stomach and says, 'Give me your money.' I just *bellowed* in this big male voice, and he jumped three feet up the stairs, and he was shaking, and shouting, 'Faggot! Faggot! Faggot!' And then he just ran."

A lot of MTFs do dress with more attention to the feminine than I, as a bulwark against the little shivers of uncertainty. To not pass is to be "read." The most expert readers, besides other transsexuals, I'm told, are drag queens and many gay men, who are often familiar with the nuances of "faking it." Children are excellent readers of gender secrets. I am an amateur reader now myself, especially of men becoming women. They are easier to read, because they're permanently laden with the effects of testosterone, with large hands and feet, height, broad shoulders, square jaws. Sometimes I look twice at a store clerk, a person I pass on the street, caught by a certain undefinable twist, something out of kilter, but I often can't tell beyond a guess. Most people, I suspect, haven't the foggiest idea about transsexuals, and encountering one, may feel only that something is off, something is wrong. Gender is a quality we establish and rely upon in the first seconds of contact; it determines our etiquette, our posture, our safety. When we're with someone of uncertain gender, we literally don't know how to behave.

Cross-dressing to pass is a lot of work. I'm glad I don't have to do it, glad that without even trying I'm immediately perceived as a woman. I don't do my nails or other such emblems of femininity routinely partly because of the time involved, partly because such things sometimes signal a social norm I resist, but mostly because these emblems literally get *in the way* of my other pursuits, of the free and easy movements I enjoy, the passage from garden to kitchen, typewriter to grocery store. Recognizable emblems of femininity are often designed to hamper movement, to be decorative rather than functional, to require a distracting amount of attention. If I had been born a biological male, and still my essentially female self, they would certainly become worth the time, I imagine. Their value as well as their meaning would change and expand. Doing my makeup would be a daily part of becoming myself.

One of the major events in a transsexual's passage is getting hormones. Hormones are so desirable that a real and dangerous black market in them exists among transsexuals. They are medicine, the drug that begins to cure the disease. After about six months on female hormones, a man's libido can almost disappear. He becomes impotent and develops breasts. A woman on testosterone becomes more energetic, her clitoris swells and lengthens, and her libido can get larger than life. "Suddenly you understand why men tend to be more interested in pornography," one new man says about going on male hormones. "You understand why there's prostitution. I have tons of energy; I masturbate three, four, five times a day." Hair patterns change, muscles develop or atrophy, the deposition of fat layers migrates across the body. Moods change, sometimes dramatically, into tranquilization, rage, euphoria.

Kate Bornstein takes estrogen every day and another hormone, Provera, seven days a month, a standard postmenopausal therapy. "The reason is to prevent cancer of the cervix," she told me. "I don't have a cervix, but I have this—well, the head of my penis is now where my cervix would be. They don't know if it will respond the same way; there's two schools of thought on this. So back east they said, yeah, continue with the Provera. Here the doctors have been telling me no, no, you don't need the Provera. But I *like* the Provera. It gives me PMS. I'm in the middle of it right now, I'm in a cranky, cranky mood, I really am. What it does is, it brings all these emotions to the surface."

Chris says now that he regularly takes male hormones, he gets angry more quickly, is physically warmer, more energetic. "When I was in my mid-thirties, I got some testosterone from a body builder. I was scared to get into a gender program, so I thought I'd try the hormones and see. I took half the dose. After a month I got really bad acne, but for the first time in my life I felt normal. I just couldn't deal with the consequences." So he stopped the drugs. "Several weeks later I went through the most bizarre incident. I'm positive it was the resurgence of estrogen, because it was like every emotionally intense thing that happened during my adolescence recurring within twenty-four hours. I was completely out of control, crying, ranting, rolling on the floor, hanging from the banister, rocking back and forth trying to stop the feelings. Absolutely horrible."

All this makes me wonder about (worry about, actually) the role of hormones in behavior and thought. Certainly hormones change the entire environment of individuals, their personalities, bodies, appetites, and cognition. One theory about the origin of transsexuals is that their fetal hormone mix was confused, enough to muddle identity but not to actually mutate genitalia. To consider identity as a side effect of a chemical is distressing enough. I may not feel much like a man right now, whatever a man may be, but a few months of testosterone might make me wonder, might literally transform my own psychic sense of self. But to whatever degree it's true, giving hormones to a transsexual merely reinforces the gender dysphoria.

Some transsexuals themselves define a transsexual by the willingness to have the surgery: castration in ex-

change for a vagina and breasts, mastectomy and hyster-
ectomy in exchange for a penis. Research shows that
suicide rates among transsexuals, six times higher than
the rest of the population to begin with, don't signifi-
cantly drop after surgery, that at least one-fourth of post-
surgical TSs regret the operation. But hormones and
living the role is not always enough. If you believe
women are people who have vaginas, you have to have a
vagina at the point at which you have socially and culturally become a woman. "Because we are men, not
having a penis is very traumatic," says an FTM transsexual, neatly transcribing the most acute and persistent
penis envy in human nature. Once he has a penis of
some kind, that envy merges into a lifelong fear of castration.

Transsexuals willingly undergo the kind of mutilation
rituals associated with great rites of passage in many
cultures. Where in another culture a person may face
circumcision, tattooing, piercing, and other rituals of endurance and pain, the transsexual has body-transforming
hormones, castration, bilateral mastectomies or breast
implants, voice lessons, rhinoplasty, jaw reductions. Most
male-to-female transsexuals have their entire beards removed by electrolysis. Some have their trachea, or
Adam's apple, surgically shaved to a more feminine
curve. And last is the reconstruction.

How do you make a vagina? You can invert the penis,
or use rectal tissue, which provides natural lubrication,
or use an intestinal segment, each of these alternatives to

be placed in a constructed abdominal cavity. Part of the scrotum becomes labia, complete with hair follicles, and a clitoral bud is taken from "sensitive" tissue. Postoperative care is extensive—the vagina must be stretched to keep it from closing, using a dilator for a period of weeks. Orgasm is common after surgery, and the surgery as a whole can be so good, it fools gynecologists. But not usually; there is often disappointment. On the other hand, only about one out of every ten FTMs go all the way through surgery, into the making of a penis. They often live in between, multihued, passing as men, but not men. Men have penises.

To make a penis is much harder than making a vagina. One surgery simply releases the enlarged clitoris from its hood, removes the vagina, and constructs a scrotal sack out of the labia, adding implants for testicles. Others create new penises out of tissue from the abdomen. A partial change leads, sometimes, to partial acceptance; says one FTM of his mother's reaction: "On Mother's Day I get flowers, and on Father's Day I get ties."

Things don't necessarily get easier after surgery. Kate Bornstein's live-in girlfriend of several years has begun her own sexual transformation—into a man. "I don't know if I'll be able to call myself a lesbian after she goes through her gender change. Virilization takes femininity away, but that's culturally defined femininity. I want to be there during her transition and through it, so when he emerges on the other side, I can see if I still love him.

I think I do. It's hard even to confront this one. But it would be very inappropriate for me to say, 'You're changing your gender, goodbye!' "

There is much more here than meets the eye. I sense in the implications of transsexualism a deep *ecology* of self, a way to see how the body, desire, identity, relationships, and society work together in a system. Transsexualism throws the sexual ecosystem out of whack, changes the balance, and like a rise in the tides or a drop in the temperature, sparks evolution.

"Promiscuous" is a naughty word. Everyone lusts after a stranger now and then, but relatively few people pursue such lusts seriously. Ancient Dionysian rites solved the lust conundrum rather neatly by ritualizing it: setting aside one night a year in which the culturally imposed boundaries of sexual relationships were released without social consequences for what followed. The Dionysian participants were thought to be possessed by the power of sex in the service of the gods, as good a rationalization for casual sex as any my own generation has thought up.

Instead, we invented an industry of phone sex. Phone sex really upsets people, not just because it facilitates masturbation so well—masturbation all over the house, all hours of the day. What better sign of the decline and fall of a society than that people can so cheaply and easily engage in sex with another person but without any kind of relationship and no consequences whatsoever?

Phone sex is an emblem of what is probably the most condemned regularly practiced sexual act—sex with a stranger. Anonymous sex, group sex, public sex—sex baldly proclaiming its existence outside formal commitments. This is a taboo in the truest sense of the word, an act that thumbs its nose at the demands of propriety, flagrantly breaks the rules. It is also, not coincidentally, a widely relished act, at least in fantasy.

Anyone who's been to a crowded, dark dance floor or a football game knows the infective and reckless effect groups can have on the individual. Teen makeout parties, '70s swinging clubs, singles' bars, all flirt with the urge to slip into the crowd, lose yourself, your name, your past and future, to act without forethought. To act without consequences.

Gay men more than any group have taken the taboo of anonymous sex and made it normal, knowing all the while that it remains taboo outside gay male realms. Men who pursue anonymous sex sometimes speak of it as a political act, literally an act of revolution—illegal, anarchic, almost supernaturally distressing to those outside the culture. "Bathhouses are my home away from home," writes a young man, neatly connecting his comfort there with the distress of those around him. Bathhouses, interstate rest stop bathrooms, public beaches, parks, department store toilet stalls, all form a network of places where succinct sex with strangers is available. Those who frequent them know an etiquette, a lingo, a way of behaving there, and most of all have a sense of the familiar. This is not strange or exotic sex if it's the kind of sex you do. The exotic is only what other people do.

A friend—a therapist—is facing felony charges and a prison term for having sex with a man in the bushes of a park. He broke a rule, big time. The fact that many thousands of men break the same rule every day—including cops, lawyers, and judges—isn't going to help him. What will my friend learn from a prison term for consensual adult sex? Will he be rehabilitated out of his desires? Will he see the error of his wrong, wrong ways? Politics is personal experience whether we like it or not, a monolith built one increment, one individual, at a time. My friend's experience is more likely to build a politics of change in him than anything like remorse. Repression always makes revolution more likely, always. If sex is woven throughout our personal experiences, as I believe it is, if sex is part of all we know of love, loss, identity, meaning, hope, and desire, then it's woven throughout all we can say of politics, communities, and power. Perhaps "the road of excess leads to the palace of wisdom," perhaps not, but a lot of people are going to go down that road either way.

In November 1987, Buzz Bense reached out from the San Francisco gay male sex scene with its long history of group sex, and organized the Jack and Jill Off, a group safe-sex experience open to men and women of any sexual preference. The Jack and Jill Off was propelled by a lot of unpredictable changes in the zeitgeist, one of which was the ongoing epidemic of AIDS, forcing people to find new ways to be erotic, to help each other, to be sexually inventive. Another was the gradual loosening of the reins of sexual preference walls, making the presence of men and women in each other's formally segregated spaces more possible. The rise in female sexual spaces was part of it, too; women had started their own bars, had their own strip shows, their own private clubs. The combined party was meant to be something more like a Bacchanalia than a makeout party.

"To be a sexual being, a wildly sexual being, is good," Bense said in a later interview. "This is a divine, ecstatic experience that we are all having here. Not *sleazy*. These are aspects of ourselves that we are *proud* of, that we treasure and are sharing with these other people." Roving sex clubs for men, women, and mixed groups continue in San Francisco today. These clubs aren't a new society, just new events representing people's continued willingness to figure out how to be sexual with each other in a way that works. Compared to a man who picks up a new woman at a bar every weekend or a supposedly monogamous partnership riddled with deception, they seem both honest and safe.

Bense hosted such parties at his own building until it was shut down after frequent clashes with the city and the police. He opened the parties with blessings and prayers. "I found that when you give people a temple to play in, they deal with each other as if we are all gods." Bense is not being fatuous; his reach is simply a long one.

The same words we use for good and loving sex, words like passion, ecstasy, oneness, are the words of religion. Carol Queen had her first group sex experience at the Jack and Jill Off and now helps organize sex club experiences for women as well as mixed groups. Besides the immediate benefits of good, safe sex with a number of people, there is the broader one of coping in a time of plague. "We are a community coming to terms with a troubling reality in a way that can wind up getting people *off.*"

When people complain about how "exploitive" or "degrading" something like a sex club is (having never been to one), they fail to acknowledge how terrible and exploitive marriage, monogamy, and the nuclear family can be for millions of people; how painful and harmful are traditional gender roles for many people; how downright dangerous heterosexual, patriarchal culture is for all women. If radical sexuality works, if sex clubs, underground magazines, anarchic sex shows, and safe-sex education do what they aim to do, then a falling away will happen. Yes, as is feared, a crumbling of boundaries: between male and female, feminine and masculine, top and bottom, gay and straight. The center will not hold. Whether or not the culture that results will be more or less exploitive than the one in which we live is an unknown. All bets are off; anything could happen.

Much of the noise and fury about sex, almost all of it, has been on the side of humiliation. A lot of dirt has been flung about to make the case that people should not be proud, should not show off, brag about, exhibit, demonstrate, or share their sexual selves except in a few restricted ways not to be discussed. What if the fury about sex became a celebration, a joy, a shout? What exactly are we afraid of, besides change? Every revolutionary figures out how important it is to break rules—to be *bad,* bad as defined by the prevailing culture. To be a sexual revolutionary these days requires little more than public discourse, because even discourse is discouraged, and creates change.

"It helps me forget," someone tells me about their uncommon sexual predilection. "It helps me get over it," says a prostitute. "It helps me cure it," says a masochist. Whatever *it* is. God knows, sex has helped me forget and get over and cure a lot of things. It? Maybe. Maybe just talking about sex this way, this much, is half a cure. A cure for what? For It, the loss, the longing, the hole inside, the little deaths of passivity and despair, the loneliness, the fear of growing older, of dying, being left behind—It, the hunger, the urge to love, to give, to live independently of how others think I should live, the persistent urge to and fear of truly letting myself go in front of another.

Richard Nixon said in 1970 that freedom of expression could be protected only by suppressing pornography. Any permissiveness toward pornography, he felt, "would contribute to an atmosphere condoning anarchy in every other field." Nixon was really talking about permissiveness toward sex itself; pornography was just an easy target. Sex is threatening. Sex undermines the conventions of our mental life; we go back to them in time, but first they disappear for a while.

What works to fix "it," in the words of all these seekers, is that which contraverts the given, creates psychic anarchy. In the sexual moments of greatest intensity there are no rules, no givens, no paradigms but the immediate—the one right in front of your eyes and hands. Practice anarchy long enough and it becomes a way of life. The most personal and the most political moments in our lives always strike us like blows, knock us to our knees with their sweet truth.

13

Most ethical systems have holes in them, spots where one conundrum or another can slip through. This is all to the good, annoying though it may be in the middle of an argument. A solid ethical system is a dangerous system. Nothing gets sifted without holes. Augustinian Christianity is like this—as a blueprint for living it has no flexibility, no give. Even though this isn't my blueprint, it concerns me because I live in a society largely, erratically, based on its principles—confused between authoritarianism, Puritanism, and rebellion. Augustinian Christianity, generally known as the Christian Right these days, also concerns me because its believers are concerned *with* me; part of their interpretation of Christianity is that nothing and no one is outside the purview of Christendom. It is literally prescriptive. If you base the value of other humans on your own absolutes of behavior, then those who behave outside those absolutes sacrifice their humanity. They are (and we've heard this word before) beasts.

One point of philosophy inherited from both Augustine and Descartes, so often forgotten, is the belief that civilization is a triumph of mind over body—in Jamake Highwater's words, a place where sexuality is "a moral concept rather than a physical experience." As a moral concept, sexuality is quantified—its attributes can be counted, defined, boxed, and sold. Everything falls inside or outside the equation.

Freud, who was no Augustinian, nevertheless believed that civilization arises in proportion to how much the all-encompassing sexual drive is directed into thought—into work. Both individuals and the culture must sublimate to exist. With sublimation people naturally and necessarily narrow the focus of their sexuality as they leave infancy, repressing the child's omnivorous and indiscriminate appetite. The pleasure principle gives way to the reality principle, desire is delayed or subverted, gratification transformed, and with that energy redirected, lasting, complex achievements are possible. Sex still exists, but romantic love becomes essential. Sex without love was dangerous in Freud's view because he thought it naturally selfish. Love creates a protective urge and it creates jealousy, which encourages monogamous, tightly bound relationships. There's only one small step from here to the belief that real love transcends or eliminates "baser" sexual feelings altogether. Sometimes I wonder how the spiraling traditional theories of sublimation ever come to a stop—if less is better, then none must be best.

What if the pleasure principle is allowed to ripen? What if the only absolute is to protect one's health without harming the health of others? To do so, I think, requires a particular belief that in fact goes against much of the morality we've inherited—this requires us to believe in human goodness, and most of us don't. "All beings are words in the language of God," wrote William Irwin Thompson. And all of their being is included in that word.

Herbert Marcuse thought sublimation isn't natural, but that it is done to us, both consciously and unconsciously, by people who are themselves choked by damaged sexuality. Sublimation is "never complete and never secure." To Marcuse, happiness comes from a return to true "perversity"—that is, eroticism, an animated embrace of the world. Even sexual activity is a form of sublimation. It is only a part of, a *version,* as it were, of sexuality. Our sexuality is so complex, so omnivorous, so perverse, that to act it out in any particular given way is necessarily incomplete. We sublimate our huge, unwieldy, uncivilized libido into a manageable identity. It

doesn't matter what we choose or that the choice is almost wholly unconscious and immutable; the choice itself will always be a part of a much greater whole.

In *Eros and Civilization,* Marcuse's solution for social
ills goes beyond Reich's post-Freudian belief in better
orgasms. What Marcuse calls "erotic reality" isn't based
in sex so much as in a life-affirming and loving acceptance of others. Children know a kind of ecstasy in their
bodies; they tolerate pleasure. Erotic reality is a return to
"the anarchic and total sexuality of early infancy," a way
of living in which we don't cut off or turn away from
others out of fear of them, or of our feelings for them,
and we don't turn away from ourselves out of fear of our
desires. The surges of erotic response that are so continual and varying in every human life are, to Marcuse, a
kind of cellular expression of the spiritual.

Scarcity of every kind is artificial to Marcuse. We
make scarcity, both economic and interpersonal. Sexual
energy is an abundance that fills more than one void.
Marcuse merrily glides from Freud into Marx, pinching
both on their cheeks with a cheerful smile. The return to
a world of polymorphous perversity both requires and
helps create an abundant society. Marcuse believed that
in an abundant civilization people could freely release
their instincts and get something other than chaos and
barbarism in return. The release of repressed instincts
would cause a "subversion of culture—but *after* culture
had done its work and created the mankind and the
world that could be free." This wouldn't be chaos but

"transformation"—"a spread rather than an explosion of libido." (We've seen the explosions of suppressed sex in both Fascism and individual violence.) An erotic reality would be one in which everyone is connected to us, where there is no *moral* distinction between friend, lover, and stranger. Erotic reality doesn't mean promiscuity, though promiscuity might occur; nor does it mean celibacy, though certainly celibacy would exist. Both, and everything in between, would be equivalent acts. An erotic vision is one of engagement in the lives and experiences of other people, embracing them as they are, and living fearlessly. Small changes. To Marcuse, civilization really begins when eros and agape blend into something new.

Aldous Huxley once said that, viewed with the eyes of history, the Puritan is "the most abnormal sexual pervert of whom we have record." Sex would seem to be the ultimate example of what is meant by the solid American tenet to "live and let live." But people who are uncomfortable with sex in their own lives find it almost impossible to leave the sex lives of others alone. Of all private matters, sex is the one that we *can't* ignore, can't quit wondering about, because *we have sex, too.* No human arena can compete with sex for the sheer amount of ill-thought emotional claptrap that surrounds it, and no human behavior seems less amenable to outside control. But attempts at control are ever with us.

First Amendment decisions on obscenity and freedom of speech rely to some extent on the difference between "thought-like" and "act-like" speech. The more abstracted a work of art is, the more impersonal it is, the less likely it is to be censored. The more emotionally arousing, disturbing, and effective the work is, the more likely it is to be censored. As expression moves away from idea and into feeling, hackles rise. By any ordinary definition of art, the more artistic a work is, the greater its risk of suppression. Pornography is censored because it arouses people—by its own definition, it works. That's why it's bad.

The single most important thing to consider whenever such words as "moral," "immoral," "obscene," and "degrading" are used is whether or not the speaker presumes these ideas to be absolute. Questioning the meaning of these words is useful. Sex outside of marriage is "immoral"? To whom, when, where, and why? Sex with someone of the same gender, of a different race, with an object, is wrong, degrading? How, when, and why? Immoral, immoral—the speaker means necessarily immoral, that morality is a fixed object, a given, a law.

The main reason I resist censoring any form of speech or expression is a selfish one. I know that sooner or later something I write or something I want to read or see or talk about is going to be forbidden. Censorship can be done only by the established order. (Only the established

order has an interest in censorship.) The establishment
cannot know what offends me, though censorship is so
often framed as being for my own good and the good of
many nameless others. Obscenity is defined partly by
community standards, but community is defined politically by a certain class of men and community standards
largely reflect historically visible male experiences. Catharine MacKinnon and Andrea Dworkin have taught me
this: Women can't make these choices for me, either,
because they are able to be just as wrong about me, in
different ways, as men. There is no such thing as a social
consensus—not on obscenity, politics, art, religion, or the
use of vouchers for private schools. Any consensus that
attempted to combine all points of view would cease to
be a consensus, and instead be a shouted-down compromise of "anything goes," or "nothing goes." A gay friend
says of some of the straight people he knows, "It's like
they're birds, and I'm a fish. They want me to fly, not
swim."

Men can't, literally can't, share my erotic needs or
appetites. No one can, but because political and legal
power is still amost exclusively in men's hands, I worry
about men. In a world where the dominant ideal of
female sexuality has been that women can't, don't,
shouldn't, mustn't and will cause damage if they do—I
can't see how community standards can do anything *but*
oppress me. The same goes for my ideals placed upon
anyone but me. I'm always struck by the people who

expect me to follow their absolute standards, but who have no desire to follow mine—self-determination and the goodness of the body.

We are still arguing about whether or not free sexual behavior is morally negative. So-called sex-positive people (like me) are simply trying to get as far as a theory of sexual moral *neutrality*. Whether one sees sex as a benign biological force free of cultural meaning or a dangerous and powerful force full of meaning, I want people to see sex as good. Not just sexuality, but sexual acts. But if they don't, I don't want it to be my problem.

There is a great canyon of *unknowableness* at work when we discuss sex. Those who are convinced their version of truth and beauty is the one right version don't consider tolerance a good. Tolerance, in fact, becomes the slippery slope, an invitation to anarchy, because tolerance permits. Those who wish to legislate and punish private sexual behavior for a greater good are convinced that the more I express another view, the more I will benefit from theirs. The more I seem to need their saving grace. I wish I had a solution, but what it comes down to, for me, is being willing to tolerate *their* strange sexual predilections, even if they don't want to tolerate mine.

We are fallen creatures. We are divided from each other and ourselves, despising joy, despising what we desire because we despise ourselves. The only way out is by incorporation. Never by exclusion. Never by fencing off, escape, separation, or destruction, because those things leave us on the run, undone. There is peace in the chaos of sex, because it is one place we can find each other in ourselves and our selves in each other.

I talk about sex, and that alone puts me out on an edge somewhere. In fact, I'm a sniveling neurotic when it counts, and there's a lot of stuff I don't like talking about. But I talk about it anyway because to *talk about it* is strange in this society, talking about it is a kind of deconstruction all by itself. Talking about it helps. A friend said I was writing my "accommodation," as though I'd found a way to make room, make sex fit. I've only been trying to accommodate myself, my abyssal self, my personal underworld. I became sexual in a generation that has explored sex more thoroughly and perhaps less well than any before, a generation that broke a lot of rules and didn't know how to make new ones or live without the old.

When I was first learning about sex, I had to learn to see my body as *the* body, a body, separate from myself. My body was a tool, and my ego the artisan. This was my first step out of shame, this removal. What I want to do now is return my *self* to my body, so the tool becomes a home—so I become my body. What the tool makes, I make; what happens to the tool—all the wear and aging that proper use gives to the tool—happens to me. As I chisel, I wonder: Which works, which is worked upon? Which is the tool, which tooled?

The translating of belief into behavior is the most radical sexual behavior of all. My personal sexual revolution will come when I do what I really want to do sexually, don't do what I don't want to do, let others do what they want to do, with a whole heart. It's not how mundane or exotic our behavior is, but how whole-hearted we are that counts. I want to be the agent of sex. I want to *own* sex, as though I had a right to it, as though sex belonged to me, to us all. Sexual freedom in my life means forgetting about sex because sex is so much a part of me as a healthy human animal that I can hardly see it at all anymore. I get there day by day, on tiny, halting steps.

ABOUT THE AUTHOR

Sallie Tisdale, the winner of several literary awards, is the author of four nonfiction books, including, most recently, *Stepping Westward.* Her work has appeared in *Harper's, The New Republic, The New Yorker,* and other magazines. She lives in the Northwest.